Henry Jacob Winser, Railway Company Northern Pacific, William C. Riley

The Official Northern Pacific Railway Guide

Henry Jacob Winser, Railway Company Northern Pacific, William C. Riley

The Official Northern Pacific Railway Guide

ISBN/EAN: 9783744677783

Printed in Europe, USA, Canada, Australia, Japan

Cover: Foto ©Andreas Hilbeck / pixelio.de

More available books at **www.hansebooks.com**

THE "DACOTAHS" FAREWELL TO THE BUFFALO.

"Waṇaġ! tamakoće ekta yáwo unkish ećadan nihakuŋ ínyaŋpikta."—(Go to the land of spirits, we shall soon follow you.)

THE OFFICIAL
Northern Pacific Railway
GUIDE

FOR THE USE OF

TOURISTS AND TRAVELERS

OVER THE LINES OF THE

Northern Pacific Railway
AND ITS BRANCHES.

CONTAINING DESCRIPTIONS OF STATES, CITIES, TOWNS AND SCENERY ALONG THE ROUTES OF THESE ALLIED SYSTEMS OF TRANSPORTATION, AND EMBRACING FACTS RELATING TO THE HISTORY, RESOURCES, POPULATION, INDUSTRIES, PRODUCTS AND NATURAL FEATURES OF THE GREAT NORTHWEST.

PROFUSELY ILLUSTRATED.

ST. PAUL:
W. C. RILEY, PUBLISHER.

DONUE & HENNEBERRY,
Ptrs, Binders and Engravers
CHICAGO.

CONTENTS.

	PAGES.
INTRODUCTION	13-18
FROM ST. PAUL TO THE PACIFIC COAST—*Main Line*	20-23

MINNESOTA:

The Twin Cities of Minnesota	25-45
Lake Minnetonka	46
The Overland Train	48-49
The Upper Mississippi Valley	46-52
Staples to Detroit	53-58
White Earth Reservation	58-60
The Red River Valley—Moorhead	62-69

NORTH DAKOTA:

North Dakota—Bonanza Wheat Farms	70-83
Fargo to Jamestown	77-89
The Coteaux—James River to the Missouri—Bismarck	91-95
Fort Abraham Lincoln—The Great Bridge—West Missouri Country	96-105
Mandan to Dickinson	99-109
In "The Bad Lands,"	109-122

MONTANA:

The State of Montana—Historical	123-130
The Yellowstone Valley	132-134
Glendive to Miles City	131-135
Explorations of the Yellowstone	135-138
Fight with Indians at Tongue River— Massacre of Custer's Command	138-143
The Brilliant Work of Gen. Miles	143-148
Fort Keogh to Pompey's Pillar	148-152
Crow Indian Reservation—Legend of Skull Butte	154-156
Montana Stock Raising—Grand Mountain Views	157-163

Contents.

	PAGES
Billings to Hunter's Springs	156–168
Livingston to Bozeman	170–175
Yellowstone National Park	172–174
A Big Barley Farm	177–178
The Three Forks of the Missouri	178–180
Helena	182–184
Across the **Main Divide—Garrison—Hell Gate** River and Canyon	185–189
Beaver Hill—**Missoula**	190–194
Flathead **Indian Reservation**	195–198
Ravelli—**Paradise Valley** and Horse Plains	198–201
Thompson's Falls—On the Clark's Fork	201–206

IDAHO:

The State of Idaho	207–208
Cabinet Landing—Lake **Pend d'Oreille**	208–211
Hope to Hauser Junction	211–214

WASHINGTON:

The Evergreen State	215–221
Spokane	221–223
Spokane Valley **and** Lake Cœur d'Alene	224
The Palouse **Country**	225–228
Cheney—Sprague—Pasco	228–231
West of the Columbia	231–234
Kennewick—Prosser—**Zillah—Sunnyside** Irrigated Lands	234–236
The Yakima Basin—North Yakima—Yakima Canyon	236–239
The Kittitas Basin—Ellensburg	239–240
Roslyn—**The** Great Stampede Tunnel—Along Green River	240–241
The Great Forests of Washington—Felling a Giant Fir	244–252
Buckley—Puyallup Valley	252–254
Tacoma	254–260
Tacoma & Seattle **Line**	260–262
On Puget Sound	262–264
Seattle	264–267
Port Townsend	267
(Victoria, **B. C.**)	267–268

Contents.

	PAGES.
Everett—Anacortes—Fairhaven—New Whatcom	268-270
From Tacoma to Portland	270-272
Olympia—Centralia—Chehalis—Kalama	272-275
Tenino—Bucoda	275-276

OREGON:
Portland 276-284
River Excursions from Portland 284-290

BRANCH LINES.

WISCONSIN.—*Lake Superior Division:*
    Ashland 291-292
    Superior 294-300

MINNESOTA:
    Duluth 300-303
    Carlton—Aitkin—Deerwood 304-305
    Brainerd 305-307
    Gull River to Staples 308
    Little Falls and Dakota Branch:
        Little Falls 51-52
        Sauk Centre—Glenwood—Morris 309-311
    Little Falls to Brainerd:
        Belle Prairie—Fort **Ripley** 311
    Northern Pacific, Fergus Falls and Black Hills Branch:
        Henning—Clitherall—Battle **Lake** 312-315
        Fergus Falls—Breckinridge 315-317

NORTH DAKOTA:
    Wahpeton—Milnor 317

MINNESOTA.—*The Manitoba Division:*
    Summary 318
    Winnipeg **Junction** 61
    Fertile—Red Lake Falls—Crookston—East Grand Forks 319-321
    Red Lake **Reservation** 320-321

Contents.

	PAGES.
NORTH DAKOTA:	
Grand Forks—Grafton—**Drayton**—Pembina............322-325	
MANITOBA:	
West Lynne—Morris.............................	325
Brandon..326-327	
Winnipeg—Portage **la Prairie**...................327-330	
NORTH DAKOTA.—*Fargo and Southwestern Branch.*	
Fargo..	77-79
Sheldon—**Lisbon**—LaMoure—Edgeley.............331-333	
Sanborn, *Cooperstown and Turtle Mountain Branch:*	
Cooperstown.....................................334-335	
James River Valley **Railroad:**	
Jamestown.......................................	89-90
Grand Rapids—Glover—Oakes....................336-338	
La Moure.......................................332-333	
Jamestown and Northern Railroad:	
Carrington—Sykeston—**New Rockford**...........339-341	
Fort Totten—Minnewaukan—**Devil's Lake—Leeds**..341-342	
MONTANA:—*Rocky* **Fork** *& Cooke City R. R.*	
Laurel (163)—Red Lodge.........................343-344	
Rocky Mountain Railroad of Montana—Yellowstone Park Line:	
Livingston (170-172)—Horr—Cinnabar.............	346
Northern **Pacific** *& Montana Branch:*	
Bozeman—Logan..................................175-178	
Butte **City**....................................347-358	
Anaconda—Deer Lodge...........................358-360	
Helena & Jefferson County and *Helena, Boulder Valley & Butte Railroads:*	
Helena (182-183)—Boulder—Elkhorn—Wickes......**361**-362	
*Helena & **Red** Mountain and Helena & Northern Railroads:*	
Rimini—Marysville..............................	363
Drummond & Phillipsburg Railroad:	
Drummond (183) — Phillipsburg — Granite Mountain..364-365	

Contents

	PAGES
Bitter Root Valley Railroad:	
Missoula (191-194)—Stevensville (Tyler)—Victor—Grantsdale.................................	366-367
DeSmet & Cœur d'Alene Branch.	
Missoula—DeSmet (191-194).....................	368

IDAHO:
Mullan — Wallace — **Murray** — Wardner — Mission — Cœur d'Alene City 368-371

WASHINGTON.—*Spokane & Palouse Railroad:*
Spokane (221-223)—Spangle —Oakesdale —Farmington —Garfield—Palouse City—Pullman................. 372-373

IDAHO:
Moscow —The Potlatch Country —The Genesee Country—Lewiston................................. 373-375

WASHINGTON—*South of Snake River:*
Whitman — Walla Walla — Waitsburg — Dayton — Pomeroy.............................. 376-379

OREGON:
Athena—Pendleton—The **Snake River**................. 379-381

WASHINGTON.—*Central Washington Railroad:*
Spokane (221) —Medical **Lake** —Davenport —Wilbur—Coulee City................................ 383-385
N. P. & Cascade Branch—Crocker (main line)—Douty —Burnett—Wilkeson and Carbonado................ 387
United Railroads of Washington:
Tacoma (254) —Elma—Montesano — Cosmopolis —Aberdeen—Hoquaim—Ocosta— Westport—Chehalis —Willapa City—South Bend.................... 388-390
Seattle, Lake Shore & Eastern Railway:
Seattle (264) — Snoqualmie Falls — Snohomish — Sumas................................... 391-397

BRITISH COLUMBIA:
New Westminster—Vancouver................... 398-400

A TRIP TO ALASKA................................ 401-442

ILLUSTRATIONS.

	PAGE.
The "Dacotahs'" Farewell to the Buffalo............... Frontispiece.	
Headquarters Northern Pacific Railroad, St. Paul..............	19
Lumbering in the Minnesota Pineries........................	24
A View in St. Paul...................................	29
The Falls of St. Anthony, from the Stone Viaduct across the Mississippi.....................................	36
Detroit Lake, Minnesota.................................	47
Threshing No. 1 Hard Wheat...............................	63
Plowing on a Bonanza Farm................................	72
Seeding on a Bonanza Farm................................	76
Harrowing on a Bonanza Farm.............................	80
Harvesting on a Bonanza Farm.............................	84
The Northern Pacific Railroad Bridge over the Missouri River.	97
Indian Camp, on the Line of the Northern Pacific Railroad....	104
Buffalo Hunting in Early Days.............................	108
Pyramid Park Scenery...................................	112
Buttes in Pyramid Park..................................	116
Driving Cattle from the Range to the Railroad................	120
Eagle Butte, near Glendive, Montana......................	128
Current Ferry over the Yellowstone........................	147
Big Horn River, Bridge and Tunnel.........................	150
Pompey's Pillar, Yellowstone Valley........................	153
Valley of the Yellowstone above Billings....................	158
Trout Fishing on the Big Boulder..........................	164
Yellowstone River and Crazy Mountains.....................	166
Gate of the Mountains, near Livingston.....................	171
Three Forks of the Missouri—Gallatin, Madison and Jefferson.	179
The Gate of the Rocky Mountains, Missouri River, near Helena	183
Beaver Hill, Hell Gate Canon, near Missoula.................	192
Mission Mountains, Flathead Country.......................	196
Thompson's Falls, Clark's Fork of the Columbia..............	200
Along the Clark's Fork..................................	203

Illustrations.

	PAGE.
Cabinet Gorge, on Clark's Fork...............................	204
Skirting the Clark's Fork..................................	209
Lake Pend d'Oreille..	210
Lake Cœur d'Alene...	213
Distant View of Mount Tacoma.............................	218
Northern Pacific Railroad Bridge over the Columbia River at Pasco...	230
Pictured Rocks on the Nachess River.......................	233
In the Yakima Canyon.....................................	238
Eastern Slopes of Cascade Mountain, near the Stampede Tunnel	242
Western Portal of Stampede Tunnel.........................	243
Lake Kichelos, near Summit of Cascade Range...............	245
A Glimpse of Green River..................................	248
Three Bridges and Tunnel of Green River...................	251
Hop Picking in the Puyallup Valley.........................	253
Loading Vessels at Tacoma.................................	255
Mt. Tacoma from Commencement Bay.......................	257
Glaciers of Mt. Tacoma....................................	259
" " "	261
Mt. Tacoma in August.....................................	263
Snoqualmie Falls..	265
Castle Rock...	269
Leaping Salmon at the Dalles..............................	271
Cape Horn..	277
Cascades of the Columbia..................................	281
Multnomah Falls..	283
Pillars of Hercules and Rooster Rock.......................	285
Mt. Hood...	287
On Docks at Ashland, Wis.................................	293
Coal Docks at Superior....................................	295
Birdseye View, Duluth and Superior........................	297
Lower James River Valley.................................	337
Palisades of the Yellowstone	345
Silver Mine and Mill at Butte..............................	351
Medical Lake...	382
Lake Chelan	386
Greek Church, Alaska.....................................	401
Sitka...	402

Illustrations.

	PAGE.
Thlinket War Canoe	407
The Thousand Islands	411
Fort Wrangell	419
Muir Glacier	421
Grave and Totem Poles	427
Juneau	432
An Alaska Steamer	488

INTRODUCTION.

Outline of the Northern Pacific Railroad's History.

THE charter and organization of the Northern Pacific Railroad Company date from 1864; but the project to build the railroad over substantially the same route now traversed by the company's main line is much older. Indeed, it is the oldest of all projects to open railway communication with the Pacific coast. A railroad from the upper Mississippi to the mouth of the Columbia river was advocated as long ago as 1835, soon after the railway system was introduced in this country. About ten years later, an enterprising New York merchant, named Asa Whitney, who had made a fortune in China, urged upon Congress, session after session, a plan for building a railroad from the head of Lake Michigan, or from Prairie du Chien, on the Mississippi river, to the mouth of the Columbia river, in Oregon. He asked a land grant of sixty miles in width along the whole line of his proposed route. Many State legislatures passed resolutions in favor of Whitney's project, and Congress gave it much serious consideration. At one time Whitney's bill was within one vote of passing the Senate.

After the Mexican war came the annexation of California, followed by the gold discoveries and the rapid growth of population in that State. Then the general opinion in Congress and the country naturally favored the building of the first transcontinental line of railroad on a route ending at the Bay of San Francisco. Accordingly, the Union and Central Pacific Companies were chartered in 1862, with a grant of public lands and a large subsidy of government bonds. Among the projectors of a line to California, was Josiah Perham, of Maine, then living in Boston, who had a charter from the State of Maine for the People's Pacific Railroad Company, and who, in vain, attempted to get Congress to adopt his company, and give it the grants subsequently given to the Union and Central companies. Failing in this effort, Mr. Perham turned to the northern road, which had been long and ably advocated as the best line to the Pacific coast by the eminent engineer, Edward F. Johnson, and by Governor Stevens, of Washington Territory, who had been in command of the Government expedition that surveyed the northern line of 1853. Stevens' surveys had shown the northern road was not only feasible, but was a better line in respect to grades and in regard to the character of the country traversed than any other.

In 1864, Congress passed a bill chartering the Northern Pacific Railroad Company, and naming as incorporators, among others, the men concerned with Perham in the old abortive People's Pacific Company. Under this charter, the company was organized in Boston, with Mr. Perham as president, and an attempt was made to raise money for the construction of the road by a popular subscription to shares of stock at $100 each. This attempt was an absolute failure, and after a year's futile effort Mr. Perham and his associates turned over the charter of the company to an organization of New England capitalists and railroad men, who proposed to make the road tributary to Boston. They elected J. Gregory Smith, of the Vermont Central Railroad, president of the Northern Pacific Company. Smith and his associates tried in vain for several years to obtain legislation from Congress guaranteeing the interest on the company's stock. The original charter did not allow the issue of bonds. Attempts in this direction were abandoned in 1869, and amendments to the charter were procured allowing the company to mortgage its road and land grant. A contract was then made with the banking house of Jay Cooke & Co., of Philadelphia, to sell the company's bonds. Mr. Cooke had negotiated the great war loans of the government, and was regarded as the most successful financier of the country. In the short period of about two years, his firm disposed of over thirty millions of dollars of Northern Pacific bonds, bearing interest at $7\tfrac{3}{10}$ per cent. With the money thus obtained, the work of construction was begun in the spring of 1870; and by the fall of 1873 the road had been completed from Duluth, at the head of Lake Superior, to Bismarck, on the Missouri river, and from Kalama, on the Columbia river, in Washington Territory, to Tacoma, on Puget Sound, the total number of miles completed being about 600.

The great financial panic of 1873 prostrated the house of Jay Cooke & Co., wholly stopped the sale of Northern Pacific bonds, and made it impossible to go on with the road. The company was insolvent, and, after a time, its directors threw it into bankruptcy, and, with the cordial assent of the bondholders, reorganized its affairs so as to free it from debt, by converting its outstanding bonds into preferred stock. When the effects of the panic and the succeeding hard times had begun to pass by, the managers of the Northern Pacific recommenced the work of building its long lines across the continent. Its construction began with the Cascade branch, from Tacoma to the newly discovered coal fields at the base of the Cascade mountains. Then a loan was negotiated for building the Missouri division, from the Missouri to the Yellowstone river; and shortly afterward another loan for the construction of the Pend d'Oreille division, from the mouth of the Columbia river to Lake Pend d'Oreille, in Idaho. In the meantime, several changes had occurred in the presidency of the road. President Smith had been succeeded, in 1874, by General Cass, and he by Charles B. Wright, of Philadelphia. Mr. Wright's resignation, in 1879, was followed by the election of Frederick Billings, under whose management the work of construction was carried on until 1881. A general first mortgage loan was negotiated to provide the means for completing and equipping the entire line. The credit of the company had by this time become so good that its bonds were readily sold above par by a syndicate of the leading bankers of New York City.

In 1881, Henry Villard, who had previously obtained control of all the transportation lines, both rail, sea and river, in Oregon and Washington, purchased for himself and friends a controlling interest in the srock of the Northern Pacific Company, and was elected its president. His purpose was to ally to the Continental Trunk Line, as feeders and extensions, the lines then under his management on the Pacific coast. Under the management of President Villard and Vice President Thomas F. Oakes, the work on both ends of the Northern Pacific was prosecuted with great vigor during the years 1881, 1882 1883, until the ends of track, advancing from both sides of the continent, met near the summit of the Rocky mountains.

The last rail on the Northern Pacific railroad was laid with impressive ceremonies on September 23d, 1883, at a point in the valley of the Hellgate river, near the mouth of Gold creek. Four trains of invited guests came over the road from the East, and one train from the Pacific coast. Among the distinguished guests were a number of members of the English and German parliaments, all the British and American ambassadors at Washington, and members of the American Congress, General U. S. Grant, the governors of all the States and Territories traversed by the line, and the former presidents of the Northern Pacific company; also a number of distinguished engineers and scientists from both sides of the Atlantic, and many representatives of leading newspapers in America and Europe. An oration was delivered by Hon. W. M. Evarts. The last spike was driven by Henry Villard, then president of the company, and the road was immediately opened for traffic.

In 1884, Villard was succeeded in the presidency by Robert Harris, long a director in the company. Under his presidency the Northern Pacific built its line up the Yakima valley from Pasco to the junction of the Columbia and Snake rivers, over the Cascade mountains to Puget Sound. It had already built from Tacoma to Portland, and the new road now had a line of its own to those cities independent of its former connection with the Oregon Railway Navigation company, running down the Columbia river, which had passed by lease into the hands of the Union Pacific. The new road was opened to travel in 1887, using a high grade switch line across the Stampede pass of the Cascade mountains, pending the completion of the great tunnel, which was finished in 1888. In that year, Thomas F. Oakes, the vice-president of the company since 1880 and its general manager at Saint Paul since 1884, was elected president. Under his presidency numerous additional branches were built in Dakota, Manitoba, Montana, Idaho and Washington.

The Northern Pacific, which was predicted as a single line from Lake Superior to Portland, Oregon, a distance of a little over 2,000 miles, has now grown into a vast system of main line and branches, aggregating in length nearly 5,000 miles.

FROM ST. PAUL TO THE PACIFIC COAST.

MINNESOTA.—The tourist leaving St. Paul for the Pacific coast travels through the State of Minnesota for the first 250 miles of the journey, and will naturally wish to have some condensed information concerning this great commonwealth. In its natural features, Minnesota possesses many elements of special beauty. It has within its borders over 7,000 lakes all well stocked with such excellent food fish as the black bass, perch, pickerel, pike and muskalonge. These lakes form beautiful features in the scenery and are favorite summer resorts for pleasure seekers and sportsmen. The State has a shore line of over 100 miles on Lake Superior, the largest body of fresh water in the world. It is traversed for the greater part of its length by the Mississippi river, which rises in Lake Itaska in the heart of the great forest in the northern part of the State, and is fed by a multitude of lakes and small streams. On the plateau, where the Mississippi rises, the Red river of the North and the Rainy river have also their sources, their waters flowing northward to Hudson bay, and the St. Louis river starts in the same region and runs into the head of Lake Superior.

In its industrial life, Minnesota possesses many features of special interest. It produces annually more wheat than any other State in the Union. It makes more flour at its great milling city of Minneapolis than is made at any other place in the entire world. It ships more wheat over its great fresh water port at Duluth than goes directly from the wheat fields to any other place in the world. Minnesota is also one of the very great lumber producing States of the Union, sending out annually from its pine forests about 1,500,000,000 feet of lumber. It has become in recent years one of the great iron mining States and was surpassed in this respect in 1890 by only two other States. With the opening of its new Mesaba mines it will soon lead them all. Its population is about 1,500,000 and is pretty evenly divided between people of American birth and ancestors, emigrants of foreign birth and their children. The strongest foreign elements come from the Scandinavian countries—Sweden, Norway and Denmark. Next in relative numbers come the Germans, Canadians and Irish, while there are considerable contingents from Poland, Finland, Bohemia and other countries.

The State of Minnesota lies between Wisconsin on the east and North Dakota and South Dakota on the west, stretching from Iowa on the south to the Canadian province of Manitoba on the north. It extends through five and one-half degrees of latitude, the 49th parallel being its boundary from the Red river of the North eastward to the Lake of the Woods, from which the line of demarkation between the State and the British possessions follows the course of Rainy Lake river and the chain of lakes eastward, beyond the western point of Lake Superior. Its western boundary is regular, its eastern very irregular. Its average breadth is about 250 miles, and its length 381. Its area, according to the Government surveys, is 83,531 square miles, or 53,459,840 acres. More than 3,000,000 acres of this is water surface, the State being especially noted for the number as well as the beauty of its inland lakes. Only 42,477,682 acres of its surface has been surveyed. The most of the unsurveyed portion lies in the northern and northeastern counties, which are largely timber and mineral lands. Its area exceeds that of all the New England States together, and is nearly as great as that of Ohio and Pennsylvania combined. The general elevation of the State above sea level is high. There are no mountains, properly so called, within its boundaries. As a rule the surface is pleasantly varied, while there are within the State sufficient elevations of a considerable height to redeem it from monotony, and give ample drainage. The highest point, so far as ascertained, is about 2,200 feet above sea level.

The climate of Minnesota possesses those characteristics which are peculiar to the northern belt of the temperate zone at a considerable distance from the seaboard. The range of the thermometer is great in all seasons, frequently exceeding 50° during the winter and spring months, and showing variations of 40° in the summer season. For six years the mean winter temperature, as given by the United States Signal service at St. Paul, was 18° 45′ in winter, 45° 50′ in spring, 70° 49′ in summer, and 44° 14′ in autumn, and this included two remarkably cold seasons. The bright sunshine of summer forces vegetation with great rapidity and luxuriance. The thermometer in winter often drops under zero, sometimes registering 30° below; but the stillness and dryness of the air make the cold far from disagreeable. An ordinary still day in Minnesota, with the thermometer ranging from zero to 10° or 12° below, is really enjoyable, and mechanics are able to work out of doors at this temperature without inconvenience. Spring does not linger in the lap of winter, but bursts forth on the approach of May; and the Indian summer, late in November, is a season of almost magical beauty and softness. The climate, indeed, is considered one of the most healthy in the world. Persons afflicted with pulmonary diseases are sent to Minnesota to recover their strength and vigor, and thousands of consumptive patients bless the dry and balmy qualities in the atmosphere, which are potent enough to rescue such sufferers from untimely death.

Lumbering in the Minnesota Pineries.

THE TWIN CITIES OF MINNESOTA.

St. Paul.—The capital of Minnesota is a handsome and wealthy city of about 175,000 inhabitants, situated at the head of navigation on the Mississippi river. It is the most important railway center in the entire Northwest, and the greatest center of general jobbing and trading. St. Paul is also extensively engaged in manufacturing, her principal industries being the making of reapers and mowers, boots and shoes, cordage, harness, stoves, steam engines, clothing and agricultural implements. It is built upon benches and hills on both sides of the Mississippi river, and is one of the most healthful and agreeable cities for residence in the world, being well drained, well paved, and being supplied with pure water from numerous spring-fed lakes. Six railways connect the city with Chicago, three with the Pacific coast, two with Manitoba, and four with the head of Lake Superior. Steamboats run on the Mississippi for both freight and passengers. The banks, insurance companies, wholesale houses and principal retail stores occupy very substantial and magnificent structures. The best residence district is noted for its beauty, and Summit avenue is regarded as one of the finest thoroughfares in America.

St. Paul was fifty years old in October, 1891. In that month of the year 1841, Father Gaultier, a Catholic missionary, dedicated a log chapel on the river bank near the foot of Jackson street, and expressed the hope that it would become the nucleus of a city. The Catholic churches of St. Paul celebrate the semi-centennial of the building of this chapel, and in the course of an eloquent discourse Archbishop Ireland spoke as follows:

"St. Paul in 1841, and St. Paul in 1891! What a change! St. Paul, linked with her sister Minneapolis—so near together that they should not be named apart—hold in their embrace 350,000 souls; two million and more dwell in the old haunts of Sioux and Chippewas between the St. Croix and Missouri rivers. This territory sends bread and meat to the nations of the world. A dozen iron ways—Rome's imperial roads were merest shadows of them—spread out from our cities as vast arteries of trade, and travel to the Pacific and Atlantic oceans, to Mexico's Gulf and Canada's remote regions. Palaces of commerce line the streets; their avenues and mansions scarce have rivals. Colleges and Universities speak forth the wisdom of ages past and the newness of scholastic prowess, of which the past never did dream. The lightning of the skies changes our night into day and whirls us in our daily journeyings whither we would go with the rapidity of the wind. And further on impatient we race; fifty years hence what a story there will be to tell!

"Fifty years hence! What will it be? God knows. I confess to a wish to be present at the centennial celebration, to see on the first of November, 1941, the city of St. Paul and the diocese of St. Paul. My soul shall crave from God on that day the privilege to roam the streets of my beloved city and listen to the Te Deum in its majestic cathedral. For you, my friends, and for myself I pray that we do our part in the time allotted to us, so that the celebrants in the festivities of 1941 may speak as tenderly and as gratefully of us as we do of the priest and the people of 1841.

"Priest and people of 1841 have nearly all left the scenes of life. So shall we leave them, and so, too, they that are coming to take our places. What then is life for man? Life for the individual, if nought there be but earth, is the spray cast up by the breeze above the flowing waters, to be again absorbed by them, and anniversaries and recollections of past years awaken in us but sadness and despair, as they betoken our own annihilation. What then is life? It is immortality. Through all the ruins of earth and over all the graves of men, the whisperings of hope are heard; man's conscience and the revealing voice of God confirm them and make certain for us the knowledge that we shall live forever, and that our works done on earth shall obtain retribution from God. Life has its most solemn meaning, and there is a reason for our well-being. The good done by those who have preceded us remains for them, whether it is yet remembered in the world, or all vestige of it has been swept away. The good done by us shall remain for us. Let us work well; we work for eternity."

St. Paul is built upon a succession of four distinct terraces, which rise in gradation from the river. The first is the low bottom which forms the levee. This was formerly subject to overflow, but it has been raised above high-water mark, and is now a very valuable property, occupied by warehouses, railroad tracks, the Union Depot and business offices. On the second and third terraces the principal part of the city is established. The second terrace, which is about ninety feet above the level of the river, is also devoted to business, and is thickly studded with fine blocks of buildings. Some of these are so commandingly situated on the high bluffs which overhang the Mississippi as to be visible a long distance up and down the stream, giving the city an imposing architectural appearance as it is approached by rail or river. The third terrace, very little higher than the second, widens out into a broad plateau, upon which stands much of the residence portion of the city. These upper terraces are on a foundation of blue limestone rock, from twelve to twenty feet in thickness, forming an excellent building material. Beneath this stratum is a bed of friable white quartzose sandstone of unknown depth, which is easily tunneled, and through which all the sewers have been excavated. The fourth, or highest terrace, is a semicircular range of hills, inclosing the main portion of St. Paul as in an amphitheatre. The pictureesque sweep of these heights, conforming to the curve of the river, with their growth of native forests, and the stately residences which are scattered over their slopes, is a characteristic charm of St. Paul. Fine avenues have been laid out over many of the hills, leading away to the prairie lands beyond, or to some of the beautiful lakes in the neighborhood, and the residence part of the city is rapidly extending in every direction.

The best views of St. Paul are obtained from the Indian mounds on Dayton's Bluff; from Merriam hill. near the State capitol; from the lookout on Summit avenue, and from the bluffs in West St. Paul. Tourists should not fail to drive on Summit avenue, which is one of the most beautiful residence streets in the world. They should also cross the new Smith avenue bridge, one of the highest viaducts in the world, from which a superb view of the city and of the river may be enjoyed; and should return through West St. Paul by way of the Robert street bridge.

A View in St. Paul, the Capital of Minnesota.

There are many beautiful drives in the city and its suburbs, and a large number of resorts in the neighborhood, which may be reached by river and rail. The drive to *Lake Como*, four miles distant, is over a fine, hard gravel road, and the jaunt thither on a cool summer evening is delightful. There is a handsome boulevard drive around the lake, passing through Como park, a beautiful pleasure ground of 400 acres. Electric cars run to the park from the center of the city.

The most conspicuous building in the city is the new county court house, built of stone at a cost of about one million dollars. It is the most imposing public structure in the entire Northwest. Other noteworthy buildings are the new $1,000,000 State capitol, now under construction, the new United States Postoffice and custom house, approaching completion and to cost $1,200,000, the *Pioneer Press* newspaper building, thirteen stories high, the *Globe* newspaper building, the Endicott Arcade, the Union depot, the Ryan hotel, the German-American National bank, the New York Life Insurance building, the Germania Life Insurance building, the Bank of Minnesota, the great apartment houses known as The Albion, The Colonnade, and the Barto, the Minnesota Club house, numerous handsome churches, the Northern Pacific building, and the Chamber of Commerce building. The principal hotels are the Ryan, Merchants', Metropolitan, Windsor and the Aberdeen. The new Metropolitan opera house is the largest and best built theatre in the Northwest.

St. Paul is an important educational center, having four well-established colleges: Macalester, a Presbyterian institution; Hamline University, under the control of the Methodists; St. Thomas', a Catholic school; and the new Hill University for the training of Catholic priests, liberally endowed by J. J. Hill.

St. Paul's Lake Resorts.—White Bear Lake is the most popular summer resort in the immediate vicinity of St. Paul. It is reached by the St. Paul & Duluth railroad in about half-an-hour, and by electric cars from East Seventh street in about 45 minutes.

It is about nine miles in circumference. Its picturesque shores are lined with summer hotels, excursion and picnic resorts, and beautiful villas, and a large wooded island, recently connected with the mainland by a causeway and bridge, has been laid out by the wealthy residents of St. Paul into plats of summer residences. The lake affords excellent fishing, boating and bathing. Bald Eagle lake, a mile beyond, noted for its scenery and good opportunities for fishing, is quite popular for picnic parties. Lake Elmo, on the Chicago, St. Paul, Minneapolis & Omaha railroad, twelve miles eastward of St. Paul, is also a much frequented summer resort, offering great attractions for boating, bathing and fishing.

On the shores of Lake Phalen, in the eastern part of the city, the municipality has recently established a park. Lake Como and its park have already been mentioned. Other attractive lakes near St. Paul are Gervais, Vadnais, McCaren's and Josephine, all lying within an easy drive from the hotels.

Fort Snelling.—This military post, the headquarters of the Department of Dakota, was established in 1819, with the view of protecting the few settlers who, at so early a date, were brave enough to penetrate the great wilderness west of the Mississippi. The fort is massively built on the northern bank of the Minnesota river, just at its junction with the Father of Waters. The situation of the fort is strikingly picturesque, its white walls reared upon the brink of a jutting bluff with an almost vertical face, its base being washed by the flood one hundred feet below. Fort Snelling was finished in 1822. Its form was circular, and its high walls were broken at intervals by embrasures for cannon to sweep the approaches. It has since undergone some alterations; but the original structure still remains. This fort has had an eventful history, having witnessed many scenes of savage warfare. It is still one of the most important posts in the West. Fort Snelling is about half way between St. Paul and Minneapolis, being connected with the main road by a long iron bridge which airily spans the Mississippi.

The Falls of Minnehaha.—This beautiful waterfall, made immortal by Longfellow in his poem "Hiawatha," is to be seen on the road toward Minneapolis, two miles beyond Fort Snelling. It is formed by an abrupt break in the bed of Little Minnehaha creek, one of the outlets of Lake Minnetonka. This stream babbles along through miles of verdant meadows in the most quiet and commonplace way, to make an unexpected leap at last into a deep gorge, and find itself famous and beautiful. In a recent issue of *Harper's Magazine* the Falls of Minnehaha are aptly characterized by Ernest Ingersoll in this wise:

"The outlet of Lake Minnetonka is a sparkling little brook that encircles the city, steals through the wheat fields, races under a dark culvert where the phœbe birds breed, and then, with most gleeful abandon, leaps off a precipice sixty feet straight down into a maple-shadowed, brier-choked cañon, and prattles on as though nothing had happened but a bit of childish gymnastics.

"It is very charming, this rough and rock-hemmed little gorge through the woods and fern-brakes, and this fraudulent little beauty of a cascade; and it laughs without a prick of conscience, laughs in the most feminine and silvery tones, from a rainbow-tinted and smiling face, when you remind it that it is a bewitching little thief of credit, —for the true Minnehaha is over on the brimming river, a slave to the mills. But, right or wrong, little stream, thou art a princess among all the cascades of the world. Thy beauty grows upon us and lingers in our minds like that of a lovely child, whether we wade into the brown water at thy feet, scaring the happy fishes clustered there, and gaze upward at the snowy festoons that with a soft, hissing murmur of delight chase each other down the swift slope, or creep to thy glassy margin above and try to count the wavelets crowding to glide so glibly over the round, transparent brink; or walk behind thy veil and view the green valley as thou seest it, through the silvery and iridescent haze of thy mist drapery. Thou hast no need of a poet's pen to sing thy praise; but had not the poet helped thy fraud, enchanting Minnehaha, not half this daily crowd would come to see thee and to drink beer on thy banks, and murmur maudlin nonsense about Hiawatha and his mystical maiden. Nevertheless, thou art the loveliest of cascades, and an enchantress whose sins can be forgiven because of thy beauty."

Minnehaha Falls can be conveniently reached from their St. Paul or Minneapolis—from the latter by electric cars and from the former by rail from the Union depot, or by electric cars to either Ft. Snelling or Groveland and thence by small steamboat on the Mississippi. If the tourist has the time to spare for a carriage drive, the route from St. Paul past Snelling will be found a delightful one. The Minnesota Soldiers' Home, for veterans of the Civil War, is in the immediate vicinity of the falls and is a model institution of its kind.

The **Inter-urban District**.—St. Paul and Minneapolis are connected by three lines of railroad owned by the

Chicago, Milwaukee and St. Paul, the Great Northern and St. Paul & Northern Pacific companies and by an electric line running cars every few minutes. Numerous suburban villages have sprung up along the lines of these roads, and the whole territory between the well-built portions of the two cities is fast building up with residences and manufacturing concerns. The corporate limits of the two municipalities touch each other, and the distance between the thickly built districts is only about five miles. St. Paul and Minneapolis are plainly destined to become a single commercial centre. The distance from the western limits of Minneapolis to the eastern limits of St. Paul is not as great as that from the extreme northern portion of Chicago to its southern boundary. By the time the present population of these two cities shall have doubled, the whole territory between them will be covered with buildings.

The principal suburban towns in the Inter-urban district are now *Merriam Park* and *Union Park; Minnesota Transfer*, with its elevators, stock yards and twenty miles of track—one of the most important transfer points in America; *Macalester Park*, with its college; *Hamline*, with its university; *St. Anthony Park; Como*, with its beautiful lake; and the suburb surrounding the big Northern Pacific shops.

Minneapolis.—The beautiful and prosperous city of Minneapolis adjoins St. Paul on the west and like St. Paul is built on both sides of the Mississippi river. Originally it consisted of two villages,—St. Anthony on the east side of the river, close by the falls of the same name, which was settled as a milling point soon after the foundation of St. Paul, and Minneapolis, on the west side, the growth of which was long delayed by the fact that the ground was held by the Government as a part of the Fort Snelling Reservation until after the village on the east side had obtained considerable size. Soon after the opening of this part of the reservation the development of the west side went forward with great rapidity and the two places were consolidated into one city with the pretty invented name of Minneapolis, which is half Greek and half Sioux in its origin and may be translated to mean the smoky or cloudy city. Its inventors no doubt intended it, however as a contraction of Minnesota's metropolis.

Minneapolis has a population of more than 200,000 and is the heaviest wheat-buying city in the country and the largest flour-milling city. It is also the seat of an enormous lumber manufacturing industry, the logs for which are run down the Mississippi and its tributaries and stored in great booms. The industrial spirit is paramount in the city and thriving manufactories of woolens, paper, farm machinery and a multitude of other articles are carried on. In fact the place is often nicknamed the Western Boston, from its pushing New England spirit and its success in a great variety of industrial enterprises. A large part of the population is of New England birth or ancestry. The leading foreign elements are Scandinavian and French-Canadian.

The topography of the city is greatly in its favor. Situated on a broad plateau, high above the upper level of the river at the falls, there is no danger from overflow; and yet the level of the place is so near that of the surrounding country, that the grades to and from the city admit the construction of rail and wagon roads with comparative ease, while the subsoil affords a foundation upon which the most massive buildings may be safely erected. The relation of Minneapolis to the surrounding country is every-

The Falls of St. Anthony, from the Stone Viaduct Across the Mississippi.

thing that could be desired. The city lies on the eastern border of the great wheat belt of the Golden Northwest, and on the southern border of the pine and hard-wood timber region of Minnesota. Here the wealth of raw material naturally finds its way to be conveniently converted into flour and lumber by the use of the grand waterpower, estimated at the capacity of 120,000-horse, within the city, and the product of the mills is afterward forwarded to the markets of the world.

The Falls of St. Anthony, upon which the prosperity of Minneapolis is mainly founded, have a perpendicular height of eighteen feet, and the Mississippi has a rapid descent of eighty-two feet within the limits of the city. The view of the rapids above the cataract is very fine; but the picturesqueness of the water-fall has been sacrificed to purposes of utility. To prevent the wearing away of the ledge of rocks, a broad, smooth wooden apron has been constructed entirely across the river, sloping from the edge of the fall to a point far beyond its base, and, on reaching this, the water slips over, calmly and unvexed. The best view of the scene is from the new steel bridge on Hennepin avenue which spans the flood in graceful length, and with picturesque effect, at about the center of the city. From this vantage-point an outlook is obtained upon the railroad tracks that stretch along below the bluffs, and also upon the river, with its channel above the falls almost choked with booms of logs that are to be cut into lumber by the extensive mills which line the shores. The water-power—40,000 H. P.—is used for driving the machinery of the foundries, woolen mills and many other branches of mechanical industry of which Minneapolis is the seat.

Minneapolis is regularly laid out, broad avenues running from east to west, crossed by streets from north to south. The thoroughfares are usually eighty feet in width, with wide sidewalks, shaded by rows of forest trees. There are many imposing business blocks, and the residence portion of the city is attractive, with its fine, spacious houses, and well-kept lawns and grounds. On the outskirts of the city are thousands of pleasant cottages, which are the comfortable homes of industrious mechanics who find employment in the mills and manufactories.

The business center of the city of Minneapolis is about ten miles distant from that of the city of St. Paul. The two places are frequently called the twin cities of Minnesota, and also the dual metropolis of the Northwest.

The most notable buildings are the Chamber of Commerce, the Exposition building, the Public Library, the new Court House and City Hall, the Guaranty Loan building, the New York Life Insurance building, the *Tribune* building, the Corn Exchange, the Lumber Exchange, the State University, many handsome churches, the High School building, the West Hotel, the Syndicate block, the Union depot, and the flouring mills of the Washburn and Pillsbury companies. Many of the business blocks are built of stone, and present lofty and handsome architectural fronts. The importance of the lumber trade may be judged by the fact that the saw-mills cut annually nearly 500,000,000 feet of lumber, besides large quantities of shingles and lath. The annual output of flour is about 14,000,000 barrels. Minneapolis has become in recent years the most important wheat market in the United States. The receipts of wheat are over 75,000,000 bushels per annum, a larger amount than is received in either Chicago or New York.

The best points from which to enjoy comprehensive views of the city are the tower of the Exposition building and the roof of the tall Guaranty Loan building. To see the best residence district tourists are advised to take a carriage drive through its western districts as far as the boulevard which skirts Lake Harriet and other small lakes. These lakes form a very beautiful suburban feature and their shores are generally improved with handsome homes and grounds. The leading hotels are the West and the Nicollet, the former a very spacious, handsome and well-built structure, hardly surpassed in any respect by any hotel in Chicago or New York.

The Mammoth Flour Mills.—It is aptly said that the history of the flour mills of Minneapolis is like the story of Aladdin. In 1860 the product was 30,000 barrels, and in 1897 over 13,000,000 barrels. The maximum daily capacity of all the Minneapolis mills is about 60,000 barrels. An idea of the gigantic proportions which this branch of this industry has assumed may be obtained by remembering that the number of barrels of flour manufactured by one of the largest mills in the course of twenty-four hours is greater than that produced by an average-sized mill in the course of a year. The capacity of the largest mill, the Pillsbury "A," is 5,200 barrels per diem; that of the Washburn "A," 3,000 barrels; and six other mills range from 1,200 to 2,000 barrels per day. The capital invested in the flour milling industry is enormous, and the amount is constantly increasing. This is the result of the changes in the mode of manufacturing flour, which have been almost radical within the past twenty years. The use of the old mill-stone has given place to the system of gradual reduction by iron rollers. The new process has not only raised the grade of flour from the dark and inferior quality formerly produced, to the standard of the best Hungarian fancy brands, but has increased the quantity obtained from the grain, as well as the capacity of the mills; thus better flour is now made at less expense than that which the inferior quality previously cost to manufacture. The flour of the Minnesota mills finds a ready market in all the Eastern cities, and also in Great Britain, France, Germany, Holland, Spain and Italy. Single orders are frequently taken for from 10,000 to 15,000 barrels, and the millers find it necessary, in securing the best trade, to control a great manufacturing capacity. Otherwise they would not be able to fill large orders promptly, nor obtain that uniformity in quality without which both the foreign and American market would soon be lost. Moreover, there is economy both in the construction and operation of a large mill over a small one. For example, the cost of one mill with a capacity of 4,000 barrels daily, is much less than that of sixteen mills of 250 barrels capacity, or of eight mills of 500 barrels capacity, or even of four mills of 1,000 barrels capacity. The relative cost of operating a large mill is still less, and the chance of a uniform grade of flour is increased in the same ratio as the capacity of the mill. So medium-sized mills, a few years ago considered the safest and most profitable, have been superseded by those of great capacity.

In order that some idea of a large Minneapolis flour mill may be obtained, the following facts relating to the Pillsbury "A" mill are given. This establishment is 180 feet in length by 115 in width, the building material being Trenton limestone, rock-faced, and laid in courses to the height of seven stories. Inside, on the basement floor, is a stone wall, 125 feet in length, and 15 in height, which holds the water from the canal after its passage from the falls before it descends to the wheels. Within this canal are the wheel-pits, dug out of the solid rock, fifty-three feet in depth. Inside these pits are flumes of boiler iron, twelve feet in diameter, in which two fifty-five inch wheels, each weighing, with the shafting, thirteen tons, are placed. The hydraulic power of a column of water twelve feet in diameter, with a fall of fifty-three feet, is enormous. Only the strongest and toughest metal could withstand the strain. Seventeen thousand cubic feet of water rushes down each flume every minute, and the combined force of the wheels is estimated at 2,400 horse-power, equivalent to that of twelve steam engines, each of 200 horse-power. This power is geared and harnessed to the machinery requisite to grind 25,000 bushels of wheat in every twenty-four hours. On the first floor there are the main shafts of the driving apparatus, with pulleys twelve feet in diameter, weighing 13,000 pounds, over which runs belting of double thickness, forty-eight inches wide, at the rate of 4,260 feet in a minute. From the shafts also run thirty-inch belts perpendicularly to the attic floor, over eight-foot pulleys, at the rate of 2,664 feet per minute, furnishing the power which drives the bolting and elevating machinery. There are other pulleys and belting attached to the shafts for operating the rollers and purifiers, the electric light and other machinery. On this floor, also, is the wheat bin for stowing grain. This holds 35,000 bushels, and extends through to the ceiling of the floor above, where it is connected with the weighing hopper. On the second floor the wheat is ground; the third floor is mainly devoted to packing; the fourth, fifth, sixth and seventh floors are filled with bolting chests, middlings-purifiers, bran-dusters and other machinery. Before going to the rollers to be ground into flour, the wheat is cleansed by passing through eight different sets of machinery. It is purged in this manner of wire, nails, cockle, small and imperfect kernels, and becomes actually polished before it is converted into flour. On the packing floor the flour is discharged constantly from twenty-four spouts, and accumulates so fast that a car is either loaded with flour or bran every twenty-five minutes throughout the day. Any lack of transportation facilities at once clogs the mill. To every bushel of wheat there are thirteen pounds of bran or shorts; but for this "offal" there is a steady demand on the part of stock-raisers in the East. There are railroad tracks on either side of the mill, and the loading and unloading methods are complete. The establishment is provided with fire apparatus, electric lights, passenger elevator, machine shop, and every appliance for its convenient working. In fact, it is one of the model flouring mills of Minneapolis, and the visitor who examines its features in detail will be well repaid.

The process of manufacturing flour in a typical Minneapolis mill is clearly described by Ernest Ingersoll, in *Harper's Magazine:*

"When the wheat comes in it is unloaded from the cars by the aid of steam shovels into a hopper bin, whence it is elevated to the fifth floor and fed into a receiving bin, the bottom of which extends down to the fourth floor. Out of this it empties itself into conveyors, consisting of small buckets traveling upon an endless belt, and is taken to storage bins on the first and second floors. Here it rests until wanted for milling. When this time comes the wheat travels by conveyors to the top floor, whence it is fed down into the grain separators in the story beneath, which sift out the chaff, straw, and other foreign matter. This done, it descends another story upon patented grading screens, which sort out the larger sized grains from the smaller, the latter falling through the meshes of the screen, after which the selected portion drops into the cockles on the floor beneath, and, these escaped, falls still further, into the brush machines. All this time the wheat remains wheat—the kernel is entire. Its next move, however, begins its destruction; for now the ending stones are encountered, which break the germinal point off each grain. This matter accomplished, the wheat is shot away up to the attic again and, traversing the whole length of the mill, falls into an aspirator on the seventh floor; having passed which it slides down to the second floor, and is sent through the corrugated rollers. These rollers have shallow grooves cut spirally upon them, with rounded ridges between. The opposing rollers are grooved in an opposite direction, and it is impossible for a grain of wheat to get through without being cracked in two, though the rollers are not sufficiently near together to do much more than that. It comes out of this ordeal looking as though mice had chewed it, and, pouring into special conveyors, speedily finds itself up on the seventh floor again, where the flour dust which has been produced by this rough handling is bolted out in reels, and all that is left—no longer *wheat*—is divided into 'middlings' and 'tailings.' The tailings consist of the hard seed-case and the refuse part, and go into market as 'feed' and 'bran,' while the middlings are reserved for further perfection into flour: they are the starchy, good centres of the grains.

"The first operation toward this end is the grading of the middlings, for which purpose they pass upon silken sieves arranged in narrow horizontal troughs, and given a gentle shaking motion by machinery. There is a succession of these bolting cloths, so that the middlings pass through ten gradings. Next they go to a series of purifiers, which resemble fanning machines, and thence to corrugated rollers, each successive set of which are more closely apposed, where the meal is ground finer and finer. There are five of these corrugations in all, and between each occurs a process of bolting to get rid of the waste, and a journey from bottom to top of the mill and back again. Nevertheless, in spite of all this bolting, there remains a large quantity of dust, which must be removed in order to make the flour of the best quality. And hereby hangs a tale of considerable interest to Minneapolis men:

"In the old mill which not long ago occupied the site of this new one there stood upon one side the usual rows of buhrs, in this case twenty in number. Through the conveyor boxes connected with them was drawn a strong current of air that took up all the fine particles of flour dust, and wafted it with the strength of a tempest into two dust-rooms, where it was allowed to settle. The daily deposit was about three thousand pounds, which was removed every morning. In addition to these small chambers, there were several purifiers on the upper floors, that discharged their dust right out into the room. The atmosphere of the whole mill thus became surcharged with exceedingly minute and fuzzy particles, which are very inflammable, and, when mixed in certain proportions with the air, highly explosive. This mixture had apparently been brought by the millers to just about the right point, when fate supplied a torch. A piece of wire fell between the buhr stones, or into some rollers, and began a lightning express journey through the machinery, in the course of which it became red hot, when it found an exit, and plunged out into the air. It was a most startling instance of the conversion of heat into motion. A lighted match in a keg of powder is the only analogy to illustrate the result. One room down stairs burst into flames, and the watchman had only time to pull the electric fire alarm near his hand, when he and the mill together disappeared from the face of the earth. A terrific explosion, generated throughout that great factory in an instant, rent all parts of the immense structure as suddenly as a child knocks over a tower of cards, leaving nothing but blazing ruins to show where, a twinkling before, had stood the largest flour mill in the country. Nor was this all. The land was dug from under the foundations, and the massive machinery buried out of sight. Two other mills and an elevator near by were demolished, so that not one stone remained above another; while of three other mills cracked and tottering walls and charred interiors were the only mementoes of the day's flourishing business.

"The good that came out of this seemingly wholly harmful episode, which scratched an end mark to one era of the city's prosperity, was the introduction into the new mills of a system of dust-saving that renders such a calamity improbable, if not impossible, in future. Now, instead of being thrown abroad into a large room, the dust is discharged by suction pans into close fire-proof receivers, where it accumulates in great quantities, and is sold as a low grade of flour. This dust having been removed, what remains is the best quality of flour. It is barreled by the aid of a machine permitting the precise weight of 196 pounds to be determined, packed and branded with great speed.

"Bakers, however, use what is know as 'wheat' or 'straight' flour, which is the product of the five reductions, all the subsequent processes through which the middlings pass in making fine flour being omitted. 'Fancy' flour differs from the ordinary superfine in that the middlings are ground through smooth rollers."

Lake Minnetonka.— Fifteen miles west of Minneapolis lies Lake Minnetonka, the most popular summer resort of Minnesota. It is a beautiful sheet of water, about twenty miles long, of very irregular form, having a varying width of from half a mile to three miles. Its shores are bold and prettily wooded with oak groves, affording admirable sites for summer residences. A large number of visitors come every summer to Minnetonka from the Southern States, attracted by the cool and agreeable climate, the excellent hotels and facilities for boating and out-door life. The principal hotel is the Lake Park Hotel, which has room for about 500 guests, the St. Louis for about 300, and numerous other summer hotels and private cottages have summer boarders. A fleet of nearly a score of steamboats, large and small, ply upon the lake, and hourly trains are run during the season to and from St. Paul and Minneapolis.

Hundreds of pretty cottages fringe the shores, each with its lawns, boat house and carriage house. A drive fifty miles long makes the entire circuit of the lake. There are two pretty villages on the lake, Wayzata and Excelsior, each having a number of small hotels and boarding houses.

The Upper Mississippi Valley.— The Northern Pacific crosses the Mississippi river twice within the limits of Minneapolis, first on a magnificent steel bridge, near the University of Minnesota and in sight of many of the large flouring mills, and then in the upper part of the city, on a steel bridge, from which the principal saw-mills and

Detroit Lake Minnesota.

the great log booms may be seen. The road after leaving the city follows the east bank of the Mississippi for ninety-seven miles, to Little Falls. The river was formerly navigated by steamboats on this part of its course, but now there are two railroads on the east bank and one on the west bank and the boats have been driven off, so that the only commercial function of the river is for running logs from the pineries down to the Minneapolis and other mills. The valley presents many pleasing features of scenery. Occasional glimpses are caught from the car windows of placid stretches of the river, which everywhere flows between low, wooded banks. Many neat villages are passed. The country is well-cultivated and the farms have a prosperous look. A chief crop is Indian corn, which flourishes in spite of the high northern latitude, because of the warm, sandy soil and the protection afforded by the numerous belts of woodland from cold winds.

The Overland Train.—Although an every-day occurrence, it is always an interesting and impressive sight to watch a Northern Pacific through train wind like a huge serpent slowly out of the shadows of the Union depot at St. Paul, as it starts on its long journey of two thousand miles to the Pacific coast. It is more impressive, perhaps, to one who has made the trip; for while it is rounding the curve in the yards he will think of it scudding across the level prairies between the Red river and the Missouri, following its tortuous path through the Bad Lands, climbing the eastern slope of the Rockies and hurrying on to the still harder climb over the Cascades, then bowling easily toward the ocean, as if conscious that its struggles were over for a time. He will hear the dismal creak of the wheels as the train crawls like a mere worm around some huge mountain and maybe catch the rebounding echo of the engines' labored breath that breaks in upon the awful stillness of the gorge.

The mail, express and baggage cars, the tourist cars, the smoker, the day coaches, the dining car and the sleeping cars altogether make a handsome train. The comfortable tourist cars are usually filled with immigrants, but frequently with fairly well-to-do families from the East, to whom these cars offer conveniences not to be had elsewhere. Local male passengers generally occupy the smoker, and the luxurious day coaches carry both local and through passengers. The "diner," another popular feature of the N. P., serves breakfast at 7 to 9:30; lunch at 12 to 1:30, and dinner at 5:30 to 7:30 o'clock, at a price of one dollar for breakfast and dinner; luncheon is served a la carte, with an attractive menu at each. It answers also as a sort of club room between meals, where gentlemen may enjoy the liquid contents of a well-stocked sideboard, with good cigars and plenty of room, and wide, deep windows through which to view the varying scenery. The conductor of this car goes through to Portland with his cooks and waiters, as does each of the Pullman conductors. This means that they travel eight to twelve thousand miles a month and that two thirds to three-fourths of their year is spent on wheels moving over six big States. The conductor in charge of the train, his brakemen, baggageman, engineer and fireman are changed many times between St. Paul and Portland, each crew having a run of from two hundred to three hundred miles. The ten or fifteen minutes' wait while the engine is taken to the roundhouse and another brought out, is usually taken advantage of, in the daytime, by both ladies and gentlemen to indulge in a walk up and down the long platform and to fill their lungs with prairie ozone or inspiring mountain air.

Anoka (29 miles from St. Paul).—This town, the county seat of the county of the same name, is situated twenty miles from Minneapolis, at the mouth of Rum river, one of the most important logging streams in the Northwest. Anoka has 6,000 inhabitants, and is a flourishing manufacturing town being principally engaged in the sawing of lumber and the grinding of wheat. Rum river, crossed by the railroad at Anoka, is the outlet of Mille Lac, the second largest lake in Minnesota.

Elk River (41 miles from St. Paul; population, 1,500) is the county seat of Sherburne county, and is located on the Mississippi at the mouth of the Elk river, a logging stream heading in the great pineries. The town has a water power, and manufactures flour and lumber.

St. Cloud (76 miles from St. Paul; population, 8,000) is one of the most important manufacturing and commercial towns and railroad centers in Northern Minnesota. It is the county seat of Stearns county, one of the most prosperous agricultural counties in the State, and has many fine public and private buildings. One of the State Normal schools is located here, and the city is also the seat of a Catholic bishop. The city is built upon a high plateau, about fifty feet above the Mississippi and most of its business blocks are built of yellow brick.

Here are a number of valuable granite quarries situated at distances varying from one to four miles from the city, on both sides of the Mississippi river, which furnish excellent material for building, paving, etc. At one of these quarries on the eastern side of the Mississippi, the State of Minnesota is erecting a reformatory, employing the convicts is stone cutting. Jasper is also quarried near St. Cloud. The Mississippi is dammed just below the city and furnishes a valuable water-power which is used for various manufacturing enterprises. East St. Cloud is a suburb in Benton county, on the east bank of the river, and is connected with the city by a steel bridge.

Sauk Rapids (77 miles from St. Paul; population, 1,200).—This village, the county seat of Benton county, lies on the east bank of the Mississippi river, at the falls of Sauk Rapids, from which its name is derived. The Mississippi river at this point is 600 feet wide, and has a fall of eighteen feet in one mile. There are extensive beds of granite in the immediate vicinity, the stone, it is said, being equal to the celebrated Quincy granite of New England, varying only in color. A fine water-power is furnished by the rapids which begin where the Sauk river enters from the west, at the upper end of the village. The rapids continue over a bed of granite a distance of half a mile, and, viewed from either bank, present a picture of great beauty.

Royalton (95 miles north of St. Paul; population, 800).—It is situated two miles east of the Mississippi river, in the midst of a prairie dotted with groves of hard-wood trees. The Platte river affords a water-power. The town is a centre for farming and lumbering trade.

Little Falls (105 miles northwest of St. Paul; population, 3,000).—This town was named from a fall in the Mississippi river. It has one of the best water-powers in the United States, constructed in 1887-88, at an expense of $250,000. The dam rests upon a solid rock bed, and is firmly supported by a rocky island in the centre of the river. The water-power is utilized by flouring-mills and factories, and the town is evidently destined to become an important centre of manufacturing industry. It is built on both sides of the Mississippi river, on a sandy plateau. It is the county seat of Morrison county, and the junction of the Little Falls & Dakota branch and the Brainerd branch of the Northern Pacific R. R. with the main line. Two handsome and commodious modern hotels accommodate sportsmen, summer visitors, and travelers. There is good shooting for deer in the big woods west of the Mississippi, and for ducks along the river and on the numerous lakes and ponds in the region. One of the largest sawmills in the State is located here. Brick making is an important industry. The court house is a handsome and conspicuous structure.

The scenery near Little Falls is diversified and interesting. Finely wooded bluffs cropping up between rich prairies make the neighborhood favorable for hunting. Five miles east is a pleasant inland lake named Rice lake, from the large quantity of wild rice growing around its shores. This is a resort for wild ducks, and in season large numbers are bagged. The woods abound with partridge, and the prairies with grouse, or prairie chickens, while deer are found in great numbers within easy distance.

A Wilderness Region.—The through trains on the Northern Pacific formerly ran by way of Brainerd, following the Mississippi to that town before turning westward, but a cut off line was built a few years ago from Little Falls to Staples, which shortened the distance 25 miles. The road crosses to the west side of the Mississippi at Little Falls and for about 30 miles runs through a forest of hard-wood trees, mingled with pines, where cutting oak ties and cord-wood are the principal industries. The soil is good, however, and farms are gradually cleared up. Fish-trap and Alexander lakes, at Lincoln station, are recommended as excellent fishing ground to sportsmen who enjoy camping out and roughing it. These lakes have bold, picturesque banks.

Staples (142 miles from St. Paul; population 1,000) is an important railway junction and division terminus town, inhabited chiefly by railroad empioyes. Here the Northern Pacific line from Lake Superior joins the main line. Trains run to and from Brainerd, Duluth, Superior and Ashland in connection with the trains to and from the Pacific Coast. The town is well-built and prosperous. Before the building of the cut-off line it was a mere saw-mill hamlet.

Verndale (153 miles from St. Paul; population, 1,000). —This town is pleasantly situated in Wadena county, in the Wing river valley, (one of the most fertile and beautiful valleys of the Northwest), of which it is the commercial centre. This valley is twenty miles in length, by five or six in breadth, and consists of a number of small prairies or openings, so admirably arranged by nature that almost every settler has timber and prairie. The village is about one mile east of the river in a beautiful opening, or small prairie, sheltered on the north and west by a dense growth of pines, while about two miles south and east can be seen the dark line of the Big Woods, which stretch away for many miles.

Wadena (160 miles from St. Paul; population, 1,400).— This town is the county seat of Wadena county and is the diverging point for the Northern Pacific, Fergus and Black Hills railroad, which runs westward to Milnor, North Dakota, 120 miles through Fergus Falls, Breckenridge and Wahpeton. The country adjacent to the town is a slightly rolling prairie, dotted at intervals with picturesque groves and strips of timber. Oak, poplar, birch and ash are the most common growths. A few miles north of the town begins the timber line, beyond which lie some of the famous logging camps of Minnesota, where are found large tracts of white and yellow pine.

New York Mills (172 miles from St. Paul; population 500).—This is the largest Finnish settlement in the United States. There are over 500 Finns in the town, and nearly 3,000 in the surrounding country. A weekly paper is published in the Finnish language, and religious services are held in that language in two churches, one in the town and one about six miles distant in the country. The Finns have only commenced emigrating in considerable numbers during the past twenty years. They prefer Northern Minnesota to any region in the West because of its close resemblance in climate, scenery, soil, forests, lakes, etc., to Finland. The Finns in and around New York Mills are engaged in lumbering, farming, and the mechanical trades. The Finns are an educated people and all read and write their own language. Finnish is an Asiatic language in its origin, belonging to the Turanian family, and is kindred to the Hungarian and Turkish. The Finns have a great national epic poem, called the Kalevala, which embodies the mythology and poetry of their remote ancestors.

Perham (183 miles from St. Paul; population, 1,200).—This town is situated in the northeastern part of Otter Tail county, on an open prairie of five by ten miles square. The population of the town and tributary country is about half German, one-quarter American, and the other quarter composed of Poles and Scandinavians. There is a flouring mill in the place and several minor manufacturing concerns. The scenery about Perham is attractive. In coming from the East, for some distance nothing can be seen but pine forests, which suddenly open into a beautiful rolling prairie, through which the famous Red river of the North passes. To the right, only a short distance away, lie two beautiful lakes, called *Big* and *Little Pine*

Lakes. The latter is about two miles wide and four miles long, while the former is nearly three times as large. The view from the passing train is very pleasing.

Many Lovely Lakes.—After leaving Perham there are lakes without number, which, to travelers from Eastern cities, would be considered marvels of beauty. All of these lie in sight of this thriving town. They are now becoming popular, and many tourists, spend the summer on their banks. Among these resorts is *Otter Tail Lake*, four miles wide and eleven miles long. It is situated eight miles south of the town. *Marion Lake*, three miles distant, in the same direction, is perhaps three-quarters of a mile in diameter, and nearly circular in form. No better hunting ground can be found in the Northwest than that surrounding Perham. The lakes are full of fish of every description, including pickerel, pike, muskallonge, black and rock bass, catfish, sunfish and whitefish. In spring and autumn ducks and geese are killed in great numbers. During the season the prairie and groves are alive with quail, grouse, swan, brant, woodcock, prairie chicken, partridge, snipe, curlew and rabbits. In early winter the deer, elk and moose are an easy prey to the sportsman.

There is a small Indian village about two miles from the town. These Indians are Chippeways who belong to the White Earth reservation, but prefer to remain in their old home. They are self-supporting, the men working in the pineries and the harvest fields, and the women gathering berries for sale.

Frazee (194 miles from St. Paul, population, 300).— This town has one of the largest flouring mills west of Minneapolis, the product of which is shipped to all parts of the world. There is also a large saw mill, which is supplied with timber driven down the Otter Tail river from ten to twenty miles. Otter Tail river, running through the town, is full of all kinds of fish, and so are the numerous lakes that find an outlet through this river.

Detroit (204 miles from St. Paul; population, 2,000) is the county seat of Becker county, and is situated at a beautiful timber opening, the surface of which is gently undulating, the soil being of a sandy nature. Half a mile east of the village runs the Pelican river, which stream is the western boundary line of what is known as the " Big Woods" of Minnesota. To the west there is but little timber, and on the north the country is about equally divided between timber and prairie land.

South of Detroit lies what is known as the Pelican Lake country, one of the finest, as well as the most fertile and beautiful sections of Minnesota. The surrounding region is very productive, and each year the farmers are blessed with abundant crops, for which a good and ready market is always found. The advantages of Detroit are many. Its abundance of excellent oak, maple, elm, birch, basswood, tamarack and ash timber, suitable for the manufacture of all articles made from wood, invites industrial enterprise. The new county court house, erected at a cost of $25,000, is one of the handsomest buildings of its class in Northern Minnesota.

Prominent among the features of this section are its advantages as a summer resort. *Detroit Lake*, one of the most beautiful sheets of water in Minnesota, lies only half a mile from the business portion of the village. Each year it becomes more popular with the people of the neighboring towns, and also with those who are accustomed to flee from the hot and dusty cities, and from the treeless prairies, during the summer months. The lake, which is about a mile and a half wide, and seven miles long, in form somewhat resembles a horeshoe, with a sand-bar reaching from shore to shore, about midway between the two ends of the lake, which is converted into a most delightful driveway. Here is a high bank towering above the clear waters of the lake, and there the broad and pebbly beach, with an occasional "opening," where a sturdy frontiersman is carving out a farm. To the east, Detroit mountain, whose heights are covered by a dense growth of timber, towers far above the surrounding country, lending its rugged charms to the scene. The lake is stocked with all kinds of "gamey" fish, which are attraction to the sportsman, the variety including pickerel, black and Oswego bass, wall-eyed pike, perch, and also California salmon, which were planted in the lake some time ago by the State Fish Commissioner.

The Detroit Lake and St. Louis Boat Club has a commodious club house, and a number of cottages on the lake. The club is limited to 100 members.

Detroit Lake is only one of many which abound in the immediate vicinity, the following being also within the township, and varying from one to four miles in length; viz., *Floyd Lake, Lake Flora, Lake Rice, Oak Lake, Edgerton Lake, Long Lake* and *Lake St. Clair.* Here, too, are mineral springs, iron and sulpher, the health-giving qualities of which have been known to the Indians for many generations. The Detroit Lake Pleasure Grounds are the most popular place of amusement in Northern Minnesota; steam yachts, as well as sail and row boats, are furnished on these grounds to visitors at a small cost. A steamboat makes the tour of the lake.

The Hotel Minnesota, built in 1884, answers the double purpose of a first-class hotel for the town, and of a summer resort, being kept open the year round. It is four stories in height, with wide piazzas and well-furnished rooms. In its architectural and general management, it is entitled to rank with the best class of summer resort hotels in the State. The advantages of Detroit for summer tourists and residents are numerous. The place is situated on a high plateau, near the headwaters of both the Mississippi and the Red River of the North. This plateau has a constant sweep of the cool breeze blowing over the great Northwest forests. Excellent drives through woodland and farming country, with numerous lakes, are here; and, for both fishing and hunting, the place has few rivals. Although the country immediately surrounding the town is well settled, a short ride brings the sportsman to the primeval forests where elk, moose and bear are killed in large numbers every year. The lake abounds in water fowl and fish.

The White Earth Reservation.—Twenty-five miles north of this village is the White Earth Reservation of the Chippeway Indians. These Indians, who call themselves Ojibways, have always been the friend of the white man. They were a kindly disposed race, and contact with white men had dragged them down into a depth of degradation never known to their fathers. The deadly fire water flowed throughout their country, and disease, poverty and death held a carnival in every Indian village. Their friends secured for them this beautiful reservation, as fair a country as the sun ever shone upon. This action might have been prevented by the pioneers of the Northern Pacific Railroad; but in this case, as in every other, where the rights of the red man were concerned, the railroad company was his friend. A few years after Bishop Whipple had commenced his mission here, the treasurer of the company, the Bishop, Lord Charles Hervey and others paid the Indians a visit. The Bishop consecrated their hospital, and held confirmation. After the services, the Indians made a feast for the Bishop and his friends. When all had eaten, the chief, Wah-bon-a-quot arose, and addressing the Bishop, said: "We are glad to see our friends. Do they know the history of the Ojibways? If not, I will tell them." In a few graphic words he described the Indians as they were before the white man came. The woods and prairies were full of game, the lakes and forests with fish, and the wild rice brought its harvest. "Hunger never came to our wigwam," said he. "Would your friends like to see us as we were before the white man came?" Suddenly there appeared a tall, athletic Indian, with painted face, and dressed in a robe of skins ornamented with porcupine quills; and by his side a pleasant-faced woman in wild dress. "There," said the chief, with eyes gleaming with pride, "there see Ojibways as they were before the white man came." Turning to his guests, he continued: "Shall I tell you what the white man did for us?" Then dropping his voice, he added, "The white man told us we were poor; we had no books, no fine horses, no fine canoes, no tools. 'Give us your land, and you shall become like the white man.' I can not tell the story: you must see it." Then stepped out a poor, ragged wretch, with tattered blanket, and face covered with mud; by his side a more dreadful specimen of womanhood. The chief raised his hands: "Are you an Objibway?" The Indian nodded. Sadly the chief said: "Oh, Manitou, how came this?" The Indian raised a black bottle, and spoke one word, "Ishkotah wabo" (fire water). "This is the gift of the white man." It went like an electric thrill through every heart, and brought tears to many eyes. The chief said: "A pale-faced man came to see us,

I am sorry to say he has seen me and my fellows drunk. He told a wonderful story of the Son of the Great Spirit coming to save men. He told us his fathers were wild men; that this religion had made them great, and what it had done for them it would do for others. We did not hear; ours ears were deaf; our hearts were heavy. He came again and again, always telling one story of Jesus, the poor man's friend. We knew each summer, that, when the sun was high in the heavens, the Bishop would come. He gave us a red minister. At last we heard. Shall I tell you what this religion has done for my people? You must see." There stepped out a young Indian in a black frock coat; by his side a woman neatly clad in a black alpaca dress. "There," said the chief, "there is only one religion which can take a man in the mire by the hand and bid him look and call God his Father."

There are 1,500 civilized Indians at White Earth. They have two churches—Episcopal church and Roman Catholic. Visitors are always received with kindness, and no excursion on the line of the Northern Pacific Railroad will be more pleasant than a visit to White Earth.

Lake Park (217 miles from St. Paul; population, 800).—This is an active business town in the western part of Becker county, situated in the midst of a rolling prairie country, interspersed with lakes and groves of hard-wood timber. The population is chiefly Scandinavian. The large farms of Thomas H. Canfield are in the neighborhood. Mr. Canfield has five sections, most of which is under cultivation, affording employment to a large force of men and teams. The principal production is wheat; but the raising of blooded stock is also extensively engaged in. Lake Park is situated on Flora lake. The town has a summer hotel, accommodating a hundred people.

Winnipeg Junction (225 miles from St. Paul; population, 200) is a new place created by the building of the Duluth & Manitoba road in 1887, which runs northward through the Red river valley to Crookston, Minn., Grand Forks, Grafton and Pembina, North Dakota, and Winnipeg, Manitoba, 257 miles.

Hawley (228 miles from St. Paul; population, 350).— The town, named in honor of Gen. Joseph R. Hawley, of Connecticut, lies in the depression east of the hills which skirt the Red river. Its population is largely Scandinavian. From the town, the distance is but a few minutes' walk to the Buffalo river, where there are two flouring mills. *Silver Lake*, three miles south, a beautiful body of water covering 300 acres, is an excellent fishing resort. Good hunting and fishing are also to be had in the surrounding country, geese, ducks and grouse being quite plentiful, while deer and bear are found in the timber regions southward.

Muskoda (232 miles from St. Paul; population, 125).— Muskoda is an Indian word, said to signify "the buffalo river." The Buffalo river runs adjacent to the town, and is a beautiful, swiftly flowing stream, fifty feet wide, with high timbered bluffs on either side. It is well adapted to milling purposes, and abounds in black bass, pike and pickerel. *Lake Maria*, two and a half miles southeast of Muskoda, and a half-mile south of the Northern Pacific track, is a curiosity in itself, inasmuch as it is not known to contain a living thing, although every other lake in the region is full of fish. This lake covers 300 acres, and is twelve to fifteen feet deep. A beautiful forest surrounds it, and its shores are a gravelly beach. *Horseshoe Lake*, two and a half miles north of the Northern Pacific railroad, covers 200 acres, and is well stocked with fish. The soil of the surrounding country is rich, and well adapted to the production of cereals and grasses, the region being noted for wheat and stock raising. There are a number of springs here, from which pure water flows the year round. This neighborhood has an abundance of small game; geese, ducks, prairie chickens, snipe and rabbits being among the varieties. In former years the country was a favorite hunting ground of the Indians.

The Red River Valley.—We now enter the valley of the Red river of the North, which is often called the "Bread Basket of America," by reason of its enormous production of wheat. The land is nearly level and stretches away to the horizon on all sides with no elevations to break the range of vision. The prominent objects are stacks of wheat sheaves after harvest, the farm buildings, the grain elevators at the railway stations and the moving trains. Every object seems to be magnified in size. This is accounted for by the absence of really large objects with which the eye can make comparisons. In the time of growing crops the whole landscape is a vast sea of grain. The Red River valley is about 250 miles long and has an average breadth of about fifty miles. It lies about equally in Minnesota and North Dakota and extends further north to Manitoba, terminating at Lake Winnipeg, into which the Red river flows. The soil is everywhere a black, rich loam, having a depth of from three to six feet.

The farmers and other residents of the fertile valley plain of the Red river of the North are well aware that they live on the area once occupied by a great lake; for its beaches, having the form of smoothly rounded ridges of gravel and sand a few feet high, with a width of several rods, are observable extending horizontally long distances upon each of the slopes which rise east and west of this

Threshing No. 1 Hard Wheat.

broad, flat valley. Hundreds of farmers have located their buildings on these beach ridges as the most dry and sightly spots on their land, affording opportunity for perfectly drained cellars even in the most wet spring seasons, and also yielding to wells dug through this sand and gravel, better water than is usually obtainable in wells on the adjacent clay areas. While each of these farmers, in fact everyone living in the Red River valley, recognizes that it is an old lake bed, few probably are aware that it has become for this reason a district of special interest to geologists, who have traced and mapped its upper shore along a distance of about 800 miles.

Numerous explorers of this region, from Long and Keating in 1823, to Gen. G. K. Warren in 1868 and Prof. N. H. Winchell in 1872, recognized the lacustrine features of the valley; and the last named geologist first gave what is now generally accepted as the true explanation of the lake's existence; namely, that it was produced in the closing stage of the glacial period by the dam of the continental ice-sheet at the time of its final melting away. As the border of the ice-sheet retreated northward along the Red River valley, drainage from that area could not flow as now, freely to the north through Lake Winnipeg and into the ocean at Hudson bay, but was turned by the ice-barrier to the south across the lowest place on the watershed dividing this basin from that of the Mississippi. This lowest point is found at Brown's Valley on the western boundary of Minnesota, where an ancient water course about 125 feet deep and a mile or so in width extends from Lake Traverse, at the head of the Bois des Sioux, a tributary of the Red river, to Big Stone lake, through which the head stream of the Minnesota river passes in its course to the Mississippi and the Gulf of Mexico.

Detailed exploration of the shore lines and area of this lake was begun for the Minnesota geological survey in the years 1879 to 1881 by Warren Upham, under the direction of Professor Winchell, the State geologist. In subsequent years Mr. Upham was employed also in tracing the lake shores through North Dakota for the United States geological survey, and through Southern Manitoba to the distance of a hundred miles north from the international boundary to the Riding mountain, for the geological survey of Canada. For the last named survey, also, Mr. J. B. Tyrrell has extended the exploration of the shore lines more or less completely for 200 miles farther north, along the Riding and Duck mountains, and Porcupine and Pasquia hills, west of Lakes Manitoba and Winnipegosis, to the Saskatchewan river.

This glacial lake was named by Upham in 1879 in honor of Louis Agassiz, the first prominent advocate of the theory of the formation of the drift by the land ice; and the outflowing river, whose channel is now occupied by Lakes Traverse and Big Stone and Brown's Valley, was also named by Upham in 1883 the River Warren, in commemoration of General Warren's admirable work in the U. S. engineering corps, in publishing maps and reports of the Minnesota and Mississippi river surveys. Two special reports of Mr. Upham's exploration of Lake Agassiz have been already published, the first in 1887 by the geological survey of the United States, and the second in 1890, by that of Canada. From these we gather the following notes and descriptions of the old lake area.

Several successive levels are recorded by distinct and approximately parallel beaches, due to the gradual lowering of the outlet by the erosion of the channel at Brown's Valley, and these are named principally from stations on the Breckenridge and Wahpeton line of the Great Northern railway in their descending order; the Herman, Norcross, Tintah, Campbell and McCauleyville beaches, because they pass through or near these stations and towns. The highest, or Herman Beach, is traced in Minnesota from the northern end of Lake Traverse eastward to Herman, and thence northward, passing a few miles east of Barnesville, through Muscoda, on the Northern Pacific railroad, and around the west and north sides of Maple lake, which lies about twenty miles southeast of Crookston, beyond which it goes eastward to the south side of Red and Rainy lakes. In North Dakota the Herman shore lies about four miles west of Wheatland on the Northern Pacific railroad, and the same distance west of Larimore on the Pacific line of the Great Northern railway. On the international boundary, in passing from North Dakota into Manitoba, this shore coincides with the escarpment or front of the Pembina Mountain plateau; and beyond passes northwest to Brandon, on the Assiniboine, and thence northeast to the Riding mountain.

Levelling along this highest beach shows that Lake Agassiz, in its earliest and highest stage, was nearly 200 feet deep above Moorhead and Fargo; a little more than 300 feet deep above Grand Forks and Crookston; about 450 feet above Pembina, St. Vincent and Emerson, and about 500 and 600 feet, respectively, above Lakes Manitoba and Winnipeg. The length of Lake Agassiz is estimated to have been nearly 700 miles, and its area not less than 110,000 square miles, exceeding the combined areas of the five great lakes tributary to the St. Lawrence.

When the ice-border was so far melted back as to give outlets northeastward lower than the River Warren, other beaches marking these lower levels of the glacial lake were formed; and finally, by the full departure of the ice, Lake Agassiz was drained away to its present representative, Lake Winnipeg. The entire duration of Lake Agassiz, estimated from the amount of its wave action in erosion and in the accumulation of beach gravel and sand, is estimated by Upham to have been only about 1,000 years, and the time of its existence is thought to have been somewhere from 6,000 to 10,000 years ago.

Glyndon (241 miles from St. Paul; population, 450).—Glyndon is in Clay county and is the crossing point of one of the lines of the Great Northern railroad. The Barnes and Tenney farm, 4,000 acres in extent, is one of the features of the locality, affording a specimen of the rich and productive agricultural lands which surround the town.

Moorhead (250 miles from St. Paul; population, 4,000).—This well-built town, in lat. 46° 51' N., long. 96° 50' W., and 840 feet above the level of the sea, is the last place on the line of the Northern Pacific railroad in the State of Minnesota, distant 251 miles from Duluth, on Lake Superior, and was named in honor of W. G. Moorhead, of Pennsylvania, formerly a director of the Northern Pacific road. It is the county seat of Clay county, advantageously situated on the east side of the Red river of the North, immediately opposite the city of Fargo, North Dak., with which it is in communication by means of bridges which span the stream. Moorhead is the crossing point of two trunk railroads, the Northern Pacific and the Great Northern, and the diverging point of the Moorhead & Northern, from Moorhead to Fisher's Landing, Minn. It is the seat of one of the State Normal schools and of a Norwegian college. The court house is a conspicuous building and the Grand Pacific hotel is the largest hotel building in Northwestern Minnesota.

The Red River of the North.—After leaving the Moorhead station the train crosses the Red river, which is pretty sure to disappoint the tourist by its small size. Most of the year it resembles a sluggish canal, but in the spring when the snow melts it becomes a **raging** torrent. Although little used by commerce in these days of railways it played a great role in the development of the Northwest in early times. The first steamboat that navigated its waters was built largely in St. Paul and hauled in sections on wagons across the forests and prairies. This boat and others which were built later ran from Fort Abercrombie, above Fargo, to Winnipeg, carrying supplies to the Hudson Bay company's trading posts and bringing back furs. The goods were taken up the Mississippi to St. Cloud and thence hauled to the Red river in ox carts and the return cargo of furs took the same slow route. The Red river of the North is named to distinguish it from the Red river of Louisiana. It has two branches which meet at Wahpeton, the Bois de Sioux rising in Lake Traverse, and the Otter Tail rising in numerous lakes in Northern Minnesota (lat. 46°); flows due north a distance of more than 200 miles, entering Lake Winnipeg in the northern part of the Province of Manitoba. The Red river marks the boundary between Minnesota and Dakota. Its elevation above the sea level at Moorhead and Fargo is 807 feet. The whole valley is well watered by nature, there being a large numer of small rivers tributary to the Red, on either side, which perform the double office of supplying water and draining the land. The most important of these streams on the Minnesota side are, the Buffalo, Wild Rice, Marsh, Sand Hill, Red lake, Middle, Tamarac, Two Rivers and Red Grass. From the west there are several rivers of considerable size, the principal being the Sheyenne, Goose, Turtle, Forest,

Park, Tongue and Pembina. All of these have branches, which penetrate the level prairie in every direction, affording an abundance of excellent pure water. The rivers are, for the most part, skirted with a good growth of oak, elm, soft maple, basswood, ash and box elder, which is ample for fuel purposes. Extensive pine lands are about the headwaters of most of the rivers on the Minnesota side.

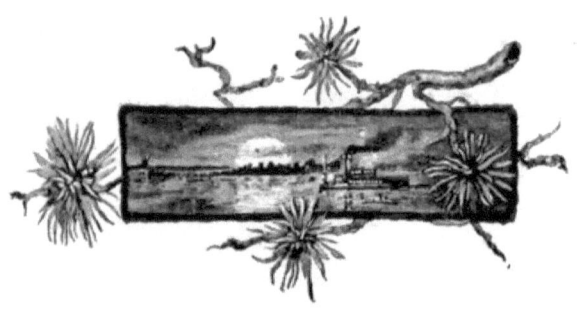

ACROSS NORTH DAKOTA.

E. V. SMALLEY writes as follows in the *Northwest Magazine:* North Dakota is essentially a prairie State. In the extreme northern part there is a region of low hills covered with a light growth of timber, and in the extreme western part are the Bad Lands with their picturesque buttes and deep ravines; with the exception of these two regions and the bold bluffs which everywhere skirt the Missouri river, the whole area of the State may be described as prairie. In the east the surface is almost level; just undulating enough to carry the drainage off in small streams flowing into the Red river of the North. Further west in the country drained by the Sheyenne and James rivers, the prairies lie in long, rolling stretches like the swells of a quiet sea, with here and there a hill dominating the landscape. Still further west we come to the region known as the Coteaux, the full name of which, on the early maps, was Plateau du Coteaux du Missouri. Here there are no streams, and the country may be described as hilly prairie with small lakes and ponds in the depressions which receive the drainage. The crests of the hills are covered with boulders, but their sides and the valleys among them furnish excellent plow land.

West of the Missouri river the country is broken by ranges of hills and buttes crowned with sandstone, and is drained by a number of small rivers flowing into the

Missouri; this is the country of both farmers and stock raisers, and is underlaid with seams of lignite coal, which crop out from the sides of the bluffs and afford cheap and abundant fuel for the settlers. Most farmers find their own winter supply of coal by opening up a vein in a convenient hillside and loading their wagons with a few hours' work with pick and shovel.

Still further west comes the singular region known as the Bad Lands, where the surface of the earth has been torn up by floods and devastated by fires burning the coal veins, and where the landscapes are so strange and weird, that they seem to have been dropped down from the moon. This is a cattle country and is one of the best stock ranges in the Northwest.

The width of North Dakota from east to west is about 350 miles. The settlement, which is tolerably dense in the extreme eastern part, becomes sparser and sparser as you go west until you reach the region of the great cattle ranges in the extreme western part of the State. Speaking in general terms, the land east of the James river is either actually occupied by settlers or owned by non-residents, but some districts may be found where there is still vacant land open to homestead entry, and there is a great deal of land on the market at very moderate prices, which formerly belonged to the railroad grant. West of the James river there is not a single county in which good homestead tracts may not be found for original entry; the opportunities are just as good to enter land in these regions as they were ten years ago, and the opportunities in the older settled portions of the State to purchase land are equally good; in fact, land is what the State has a great surplus of. Every county invites new settlers; if the newcomer wants to go into one of the Red River valley

Plowing on a Bonanza Farm.
[By permission of Harper & Brothers, New York.]

counties where wheat farming has been steadily pursued with success for ten, twelve or fifteen years, he must expect to pay a fair price for land, ranging from $6 to $10 an acre for wild land up to $20 or $30 for cultivated farms. The further west you go, the cheaper you find the land to be, because the country is newer and settlement is sparser, and for a further reason, that the rainfall diminishes as you go west. Crossing the State from east to west, you pass through a strictly agricultural region with abundant rainfall for general farming; then you come into a country where farming combined with stock-raising pays best, for the reason that a large wheat yield is not as certain as in the Red River valley. In the extreme western part of the State the country is a cattle and sheep country. But even there wheat farming has been carried on successfully by men who thoroughly understand the business. For example, at Taylor, ninety-four miles west of Bismarck, is a farm which has been cultivated for eight years, and which has averaged during that period fourteen bushels of wheat to the acre—a better average than Minnesota or Wisconsin can show for the same period. So also in the Coteaux country, which is especially adapted for sheep and cattle, there are long valleys and broad depressions in the general level where the record for wheat crops for the past ten years is almost as good as that of the Red river counties. It is, therefore, not possible to divide the State into strictly defined belts or districts and to say that in one grain-growing is the proper industry, in another mixed farming, and in a third stock-raising. There will be exceptions in each of such districts not only of individual farms, but of whole townships and of still larger areas. The main fact to be kept in view in any effort to understand the condition of North Dakota, is that there is scarcely any waste land in the State, and further that there is a great deal of excellent land not yet tilled, and open to settlement on advantageous terms and under circumstances of climate and facility of rail communication to near markets that ensure the prosperity of the practical farmer and stockman.

In looking at the condition of the North Dakota population to-day a thoughtful man will wonder that so great a degree of comfort has been achieved in a little more than a decade by people who for the most part brought nothing with them. The cities, towns, villages, farms, public institutions, school houses and churches—in fact the whole apparatus of civilized life—have been created out of the dormant wealth-producing capacity of what was a few years ago a bare prairie. When men go into new mining districts or new lumber districts they take large capital with them to buy machinery and employ labor; but the settlers in new prairie regions take hardly anything beside their teams and plows, their wives and babies. They have a hard struggle with nature for a time, but if the soil and climate are favorable and there are outlets to market for their products they win the fight in the end. It is not an exaggeration to say that at least nine out of ten of the North Dakota farmers, who today own comfortable homes, broad acres, implements and stock, came into the country with no capital but their muscles and their habits of patient industry. Others can follow them with only a small part of the effort and privation they had to go through when the country was new.

Now what about the North Dakota climate? The writer has known it well in all seasons for ten years. Let us begin with the winter, which is popularly supposed in the East to be bleak and frigid. Winter in North Dakota lasts four months, commencing about the middle of November, up to which time the weather is bright and agreeable. The snow fall is not as heavy as in Wisconsin or Northern New York. There is a good deal of solid, cold weather with a below-zero temperature, and with bright skies and still air. A blizzard is simply a snow storm with a wind blowing. It has no dangers save in unsettled regions where it may be difficult to reach shelter. As the country fills up with settlers one hears less and less of blizzards. There is good sleighing all winter and farmers are not tied up at home by bad roads or bad weather nearly as much as in Illinois or Iowa. When the snow melts in the early spring the roads dry up in two or three days under the prairie breezes and become in excellent condition for travel. There is absolutely no season of mud, either in spring or fall. Farmers in the old prairie States and in such clay regions as Ohio and Indiana will appreciate how much this condition adds to the comfort of life and to the actual money earning capacity of men and teams. The spring is a brief season of rains and sunshine and of springing grass and flowers, settling down into the long, sunny summer, about the end of May. In summer there are two or three spells of high temperature, with the thermometer marking well up into the nineties, but this heat is felt much less than a like temperature in the moist climate of the Pacific coast; and, besides, the breezes, which blow constantly, make it less serious and the nights are cool. One of these hot spells usually comes in June, one in July and one in either August or September, but rarely in both those months. The autumn is the delightful season of the year, with its cool days, its wealth of blue and yellow flowers, its garnered grain, and with the hum of the threshing machines

[Seeding on a Bonanza Farm. By permission of Harper & Brothers, New York.]

sounding all through the land. Usually the clear, exhilarating weather is prolonged almost to the first of December, interrupted only by a slight dash of snow in late October or early November. To sum up, North Dakota has a good, healthful climate all the year round—a climate favorable for labor, and for plant and animal growth.

North Dakota is the best wheat country of all the prairie States, for the reason that the soil and climate are favorable to the rapid growth and perfection of the best quality of wheat known—the so-called No. 1 Hard. You can't raise this king of wheat much south of the southern boundary of North Dakota. Indeed, the hard wheat region is practically limited to Northern Minnesota, North Dakota and Manitoba. North Dakota is also a good country for barley, rye, flax and potatoes, and Indian corn of varieties that mature early is successfully grown. It is a superb stock country, on account of the abundance of nutritious native grasses, the dryness of the winter atmosphere and the almost entire absence of cold, wet, chilling storms. The conditions for wool growing are as favorable as for raising cattle and sheep for the markets of the Twin Cities and of Chicago. It is a peculiarly healthful country, because of the stimulating quality of its air and the entire absence of malarial influences. Thousands of the most successful citizens migrated to the State on account of broken constitutions, feeble health or lingering disease and have regained more than their old energy and vitality.

Fargo. (251 miles from St. Paul; population, 10,000.)—This city, the county seat of Cass county, North Dakota, 242 miles west of Lake Superior, is situated on the western bank of the Red river, which, though a very tortuous stream, is the constituted boundary line between the States of Minnesota and North Dakota. This is the largest city in North Dakota, and is often called the metropolis of the Red River valley. The importance of Fargo is largely due to the railroad system of which it is a central point. The arrivals and departures of passenger trains number twenty-six daily. There is a rail connection east, west and southwest by the Northern Pacific line, another northwest and southeast by the lines of the Great Northern, and south by the Fargo Southern, operated by the Chicago, Milwaukee & St. Paul Company, while the Moorehead & Northern affords a northerly route on the eastern bank of the Red river. The steam navigation of the river is not as important a feature in the traffic movement of the town as it was a few years ago, but is still of considerable value, furnishing cheap transportation to the farmers in the immediate vicinity of the river banks. The growth of Fargo began when the Northern Pacific reached the Red river, late in 1871; but it was very slow until the large wheat farms in the vicinity, opened as a rather hazardous experiment by Oliver Dalrymple, had demonstrated the remarkable fertility and great agricultural value of the Red River valley. Fargo is a lively type of a new Western town, with all the modern improvements, such as daily newspapers, waterworks and electric lights. It suffered a severe disaster in the summer of 1893, when almost the entire business district and hundreds of dwellings were destroyed by fire, but it was rapidly rebuilt and few traces of the calamity can now be seen. Broadway, the chief business street, presents an attractive array of new business blocks of uniform height. Fargo is an important center of higher education, having the State agricultural college, and a growing Congregational college. The court house and high school are conspicuous edifices. A good deal of flour milling is done and the Northern Pacific divisional shops employ many mechanics. The wheat fields come close up to the western suburbs of the town.

Bonanza Wheat Farms.—Greene and Dalrymple, small stations west of Fargo, and Casselton, a little further on, are in the midst of the so-called bonanza farm district. A peculiarity of wheat-growing in North Dakota is the grand scale upon which it is frequently conducted. Prior to 1875 it was declared, upon high army authority, that beyond the Red river the country was not susceptible of cultivation; in going west from that stream to the James, there was some fair land, but much that was useless; and thence to the Missouri there was little or no available area, except the narrow valleys of the small streams; in fine with the exceptions named, that the country was practically worthless. This sweeping statement gained wide publicity, and caused much hesitation with respect to undertaking the cultivation of the Dakota prairies. But Messrs. Geo. W. Cass and Benjamin P. Cheney, both heavy capitalists, and directors in the railroad company, having faith in the fertility of the land determined to test its capacity for wheat production. They first bought, near the site of the present town of Casselton, 7,680 acres of land from the railroad company, and then secured the intervening Government sections with Indian scrip, thus obtaining compact farming grounds of enormous area. Mr. Oliver Dalrymple, an experienced wheat farmer, was engaged to manage the property; and in June, 1875, he turned his first furrow, plowing 1,280 acres, and harvested his first crop in 1876. The acreage was increased in each succeeding year, until in 1882 there were not less than 27,000 acres under cultivation. This immense farm does not lie in one body. One part of it, known as the Grandin farm, is situated in Traill county,

Harrowing on a Bonanza Farm.
[By permission of Harper & Brothers, New York.]

thirty miles north of Casselton. The entire area embraced by the three tracts is 75,000 acres. Farming operations conducted on so gigantic a scale seem almost incredible to persons who are only familiar with the methods of the older and more settled States. In managing the affairs of a "bonanza farm" the most rigorous system is employed, and the cost of cultivation averages about $1 per acre less than on smaller estates. The plan adopted by Mr. Dalrymple and all the other "bonanza" men is to divide the land into tracts of 6,000 acres each, and these are subdivided into farms of 2,000 acres each. Over each 6,000 acres a superintendent is placed, with a bookkeeper, headquarters building, and a storehouse for supplies. Each subdivision of 2,000 acres is under the charge of a foreman, and is provided with its own set of buildings, comprising boarding houses for the hands, stables, a granary, a machinery hall and a blacksmith's shop, all connected with the superintendent's office by telephone. Supplies of every description are issued only upon requisition to the several divisions. Tools and machinery are bought by the car load from manufacturers; farm animals are procured at St. Louis and other principal markets; stores of every description for feeding the army of laborers, are purchased at wholesale; and the result of the thorough system and intelligent economy in every department is found in the fact that wheat is raised and delivered at the railroad at a cost varying little from thirty-five cents per bushel. The net profit on a bushel of wheat is seldom less that ten cents, and the average yield per acre may safely be put at fifteen bushels, although it often exceeds that quantity.

On this great farm, or, rather, combination of farms—the 20,000 acre tract at Casselton—400 men are employed in harvesting, and 500 to 600 in threshing. Two hundred

and fifty pairs of horses or mules are used, 200 gang plows,
115 self-binding reapers, and twenty steam threshers.
About the 1st of August the harvester is heard throughout
the length and breadth of the land, and those who have
witnessed the operation of securing the golden grain will
never forget the scene. The sight of the immense wheat
fields, stretching away farther than the eye can reach, in
one unbroken sea with golden waves, is in itself a grand
one. One writer describes the long procession of reaping
machines as moving like batteries of artillery, formed *en
echelon* against the thick-set ranks of grain. Each machine
is drawn by three mules or horses, and with each gang there
is a superintendent, who rides along on horseback, and
directs the operations of the drivers. There are also
mounted repairers, who carry with them the tools for repairing any break or disarrangement of the machinery.
When a machine fails to work, one of the repairers is
instantly beside it, and, dismounting, remedies the defect in
a trice, unless it prove to be serious. Thus the reaping
goes on with the utmost order and the best effect. Traveling in line together, these 115 reaping machines would cut a
swath one-fifth a mile in width, and lay low twenty miles
of grain in a swath of that great size in the course of a
single day. "Carleton," a correspondent of the Chicago
Tribune, described the reaping scene thus:

"Just think of a sea of wheat containing twenty square
miles,—13,000 acres,—rich, ripe, golden–the winds rippling
over it. As far as the eye can see there is the same
golden russet hue. Far away on the horizon you behold
an army sweeping along in grand procession. Riding on
to meet it, you see a major general on horseback,—the
superintendent; two brigadiers on horseback—repairers.
No swords flash in the sunlight, but their weapons are

monkey-wrenches and hammers. No brass band, no drum beat or shrill note of the fife; but the army moves on—a solid phalanx of twenty-four self-binding reapers—to the music of its own machinery. At one swath, in a twinkling a path of 192 feet has been cut and bound—the reapers tossing the bundles almost disdainfully into the air—each binder doing the work of six men."

Casselton (271 miles from St. Paul; population, 1,500), is a thriving town, the situation of which is very advantageous, being in the midst of one of the finest wheat raising districts in the Dakotas. Tourists who wish to visit some of the bonanza farms will find this the most convenient stopping place. The hotel accommodations are good and teams can be had to drive to the farms.

Wheatland (277 miles from St. Paul; population, 500). —This town is established upon the dividing ridge that separates the magnificent black soil of the Red River valley from the undulating prairie beyond toward the Sheyenne, and is supplied with general stores, hotels, etc. It is the trading point for numerous small farmers, and also the headquarters for several large bonanza-farm interests in the vicinity.

Buffalo (287 miles from St. Paul; population, 500).— Buffalo is an incorporated village, and the trading point for farmers in its vicinity, the exports being principally wheat, oats and potatoes. It has an altitude of 575 feet above the level of **Fargo**. The surrounding country is an even prairie as far as the eye can reach. The first settler came to Buffalo in 1878. In the vicinity of the town are three bonanza farms.

Tower (293 miles from St. Paul; population, 800).— This town, named in honor of Charlemagne Tower, of Philadelphia, Pa., a former director of the Northern Pa-

Harvesting on a Bonanza Farm.

[By permission of Harper & Brothers, New York.]

cific railroad, is on the western edge of Cass county. It
was laid out in April, 1879. A school called Tower University is controlled by the Baptist denomination. The
Northern Pacific railroad, in boring a well at Tower,
struck a vein of water at a depth of 670 feet. The water
is soft, not very cold, sweet and pleasant to the taste, and
its medicinal properties are said to be similar to those of the
springs at Saratoga. Many persons who use the water say
that it works on the stomach and kidneys in a beneficial
manner, and tones up the entire system.

Valley City (308 miles from St. Paul; population 2,000),
is the county seat of Barnes county. It lies in a deep valley surrounded by an amphitheatre of hills, which rise to a
height of 125 feet or more on every side of it. Circling
round the valley is the beautiful Sheyenne river, a stream
at this point fully seventy-five feet in width, running over
gravelly beds, and fringed with sturdy oaks, elms and other
woods. The Northern Pacific railroad enters the town
on its eastern side by a winding passage through the bluffs
for a distance of several miles, and emerges on the steepest part of the line between Fargo and the Missouri river.
The town is furnished with a fine water-power by a fall of
ten feet in the river within the limits of the city proper.
The Sheyenne river, to which the town owes much of its
prosperity, is one of the few important rivers in North Dakota. It rises in the northern part of the Territory, in the
vicinity of Devil's Lake, and describes a tortuous course of
nearly 100 miles before it reaches Valley City. Its waters
are generally clear, and abound with fish, and its banks are
skirted with timber. Along its shores in former years
roamed the savage Sioux, and many a bloody conflict has
taken place between warrior tribes within sight of its
wooded slopes. One of the North Dakota Normal schools

is located at Valley City and occupies a handsome building in a natural park south of the river. The "Soo" road, a Canadian Pacific line, running from the Sault Ste. Marie, Mich., to Pasqua, Assiniboia, crosses the Northern Pacific near Valley City.

Prairie Farming.—The cultivation of the soil in a prairie country is, in some of its processes, very different from the methods pursued elsewhere, and has given rise to at least two technical terms, which are known as "breaking" and "backsetting." Premising that the prairie soil is free from roots, vines or other obstructions, and that the virgin sod is turned from the mould-board like a roll of ribbon from one end of the field to the other, a fact is presented which farmers who are accustomed to plow among stones, stumps and roots, can scarcely grasp. But the sod thus turned is so knit together by the sturdy rootlets of the rank prairie grass that a clod of large size will not fall apart even though it be suspended in mid-air. To "break" or plow this mat, therefore, it is necessary to cut it, not only at the width of the furrow it is desired to turn, but underneath the sod at any thickness or depth as well. An ordinary plow could not endure the strain of breaking prairie soil, so plows called breakers have been constructed to do this special work.

Usually, three horses abreast are employed, with a thin steel, circular coulter, commonly called a "rolling coulter," to distinguish it from the old-fashioned stationary coulter, beveled and sharpened for a few inches above the point of the plow to which it is attached. A furrow is broken sixteen inches wide and three inches thick, and the sod, as a rule, is completely reversed or turned over. Each team is expected to break sixteen miles of sod, sixteen inches wide and three inches thick, for a day's task. By cutting the sod only three inches thick, the roots of the grasses, under the action of heat and moisture, rapidly decay. The breaking season begins about the 1st of May, and ends about the 1st of July. The wages of men employed at this kind of work are $20 per month and board. The estimated cost of breaking is $2.75 per acre, which includes a proportionate outlay for implements, labor and supplies. But the ground once broken is ready for continued cultivation, and is regarded as having added the cost of the work to its permanent value. The "broken" land is now with propriety termed a farm.

"Backsetting" begins about the 1st of July, just after breaking is finished, or immediately after the grass becomes too high, or the sod too dry, to continue breaking with profit. This process consists in following the furrows of the breaking, and turning the sod back, with about three inches of the soil. In doing this work, it is usual to begin where the breaking was begun, and when the sod has become disintegrated, and the vegetation practically decomposed. Each plow, worked by two horses or mules, will "backset" about two and a half acres per day, turning furrows the width of the sod. The plows have a rolling coulter, in order that the furrows may be uniform and clean, whether the sods have grown together at their edges or not. The "backsetting" having been done, there only remains one other operation to fit the new ground for the next season's crop. This is cross-plowing (plowing crosswise, or across the breaking or backsetting), or so-called fall plowing, which is entered upon as soon as the threshing is over, or on damp days during the threshing season. A team of two mules will accomplish as much cross-plowing in a day as was done in backsetting —two and a half acres. The wages for backsetting and fall plowing are also $20 per month and board, or $1.50 per acre to hire the work done.

The virgin soil having been broken, backset and cross-plowed, is now ready for seeding. This, ordinarily, begins from about the middle of March to the 1st of April, and is often not finished until the 1st of May. Instead of the old style of hand sowing, a broadcast seeder is used, one of which machines will sow twelve acres a day. Fifty-two quarts of clean Scotch Fife seed wheat are used to the acre. The cost of sowing the ground is seventy-five cents per acre, and the average cost of the seed wheat, upon the larger farms, has been $1.50 per acre. Seeding having been carefully attended to, the harrowing or covering process demands close attention. The grain must be evenly covered, at a uniform depth, to insure a good stand, healthy growth, and even maturity. On the so-called bonanza and systematically conducted farms, one pair of harrows usually follows each seeder, going over the ground from one to five times, according to the condition of the soil, until it is well pulverized, the seed evenly covered, and the surface reasonably smooth.

Harvesting on the large farms begins about the 1st of August. Self-binding harvesters, one to every 160 acres, are employed, and one driver and two shockers are required to each machine. The wages during the harvest season are $1.50 to $2 per day and board.

The work on a wheat farm only occupies a few weeks in the year, and the business is attractive on that account, apart from the profits. After the plowing and seeding are finished, the farmer can look on, and see Nature grow and ripen his crop, until the harvest time comes. By the end of August the year's work is practically done. Expensive farm buildings are not required; for the grain may be threshed in the fields, and hauled immediately to the nearest railroad station. Very little fencing is needed on a wheat farm. Frequently the cultivated portion is left unenclosed, and a barbed wire fence is put around the pasture lot to secure the cattle.

Sanborn (320 miles from St. Paul; population, 500).—This is the diverging point for a branch road which runs to Cooperstown, thirty-six miles distant. There are a number of alkaline lakes near the town, which are great resorts of wild ducks. In a low range of hills about five miles south of the place ancient pottery has been excavated, showing that this region was once the home of a race less savage than the wild red men, who knew nothing of the fashioning and burning of clay.

Lake Eckelson.—The railroad crosses a large, shallow alkaline lake 323 miles from St. Paul. This lake is seven miles long and three-quarters of a mile wide and is a favorite resort for duck hunters.

Jamestown (343 miles from St. Paul; population, 3,000). —This is an active town, and is the commercial centre of an extensive region of country. It is the county seat of Stutsman county, and is situated in the midst of a rich agricultural region which is equally well adapted to wheat-raising and stock-growing. The town stands on a dry plateau on the east bank of the James, and is surrounded by ranges of sloping hills. The drainage is excellent, and the health conditions are remarkably good. Jamestown is the junction of the Jamestown & Northern Railway, extending north to Leeds, 108 miles, where it reaches the main line of the Great Northern railroad. The James River Valley railroad runs to Oakes, sixty-nine miles south of Jamestown.

The North Dakota Insane hospital, a public institution

costing over $100,000, stands on the hill about a mile south of the town. The two principal public school houses cost respectively $14,000 and $15,000. The Jamestown college, established by the Presbyterians, is a handsome brick edifice standing on the bluffs overlooking the town. There is a reading room and a circulating library. Jamestown is the headquarters of the Dakota division of the Northern Pacific railroad. The railway buildings here, including the round-house and machine shops, cost about $100,000.

The North Dakota Insane Hospital.—This institution ranks with the best and most progressive of its class in the country. The system is one of patient kindness coupled with only as much restraint as is absolutely necessary. The hospital is a home and not a prison for the demented. In either of the wards the visitor might well suppose himself to be in some first-class family hotel, so pleasant are the rooms, with their numerous pictures and their pretty furniture, so neat the halls and so quiet the behavior of the inmates. Many of the patients have the free range of the grounds and are employed in light labors about the farm and house. There are many forms of agreeable evening entertainments devised, including concerts and dances, to relieve the tedium of asylum life. Books and magazines are plentiful; some of the women inmates have house plants and birds, and some of the men carry on little mechanical employments for which they have a fondness. There is no effort to apply iron-bound rules and methods to all the inmates. Each case is studied separately, its history carefully looked up and a plan of treatment followed which promises a permanent cure. It is surprising how many cases of pronounced dementia yield speedily to a regimen in which good and sufficient food, physical comfort and cheerful surroundings are almost the only features. Perhaps the poor lunatic finds himself or herself for the first time in years seated at a bountiful table and lodged in a good clean bed, as well as freed from the special cares and annoyances that have brought on the brain sickness. In such cases nature promptly rebounds from its depression. The first step towards a cure is to make the patient feel cheerful and comfortable, and to secure good digestion and good sleep. The institution comprises eight separate brick structures, one containing the power and heating plant, one being the general office building, one the kitchen and laundry, and five the ward buildings. All the ward buildings are connected with each other and with the office building and the kitchen by semi-subterranean passages. These long corridors are profusely decorated with etchings, engravings and colored prints, and so are the patients' sitting rooms and bed rooms.

North of Jamestown can be found the "Hawk's Nest," where General Sibley had the Sioux corraled at one time. There are several battlefields in the vicinity, where fierce conflicts took place between the troops and the Sioux.

The Coteaux.—The country between the valleys of the James and Missouri rivers, traversed by the Northern Pacific line, is a high, rolling plateau, the general elevation of which, above these two streams, is about 400 feet. This region is generally known as *The Coteaux*. Its correct geographical name, as given it by the early French settlers, was *Plateau du Coteau du Missouri;* but this has been shortened into *Coteaux*. The Coteau country is open prairie, with an occasional small plat of timber on the shores of the lakes. It has no streams, the drainage all going into lakes and ponds. Most of the soil is deep and rich, and farming is successfully carried on. The region is also admirably adapted for stock-raising and wool-growing, pasturage being excellent, and the numerous natural meadows in the valleys and around the lakes and ponds furnishing an abundant supply of hay. From the western margin of the plateau, where it begins to dip toward the valley of the Missouri itself, the country is generally known as the Missouri slope.

Dawson and **Steele**.—These places, distant from St. Paul 394 and 402 miles, are the chief towns of the Coteaux country, and have a population of about 500 each, and are active centers of local trade. Steele is on the highest land on the line between the Red and the Missouri rivers. There are a number of lakes north and south of these towns which are visited in the fall by sportsmen from Chicago, St. Paul and Minneapolis. Wild geese resort to these lakes in great numbers on their annual migratory flights from the far North to the South. In fact, this is the best goose-hunting region in North Dakota.

. **Bismarck** (444 miles from St. Paul; population, 2,500). —This is the capital of North Dakota, and the county seat of Burleigh county, on the east side of the Missouri.

There is something fine and commanding in the situation of Bismarck, standing, as it does, on hills that overlook the course of the great river of the Northwest— the Missouri. Twenty or thirty miles of the tawny stream, with its bordering belts of cottonwood forest, can be seen from almost any street crossing in the town, and from the crests of the hills the great steel railroad bridge shows— the only railway crossing on the Missouri between Sioux City and Great Falls, a distance, following the bends of the stream, of fully two thousand miles. The group of

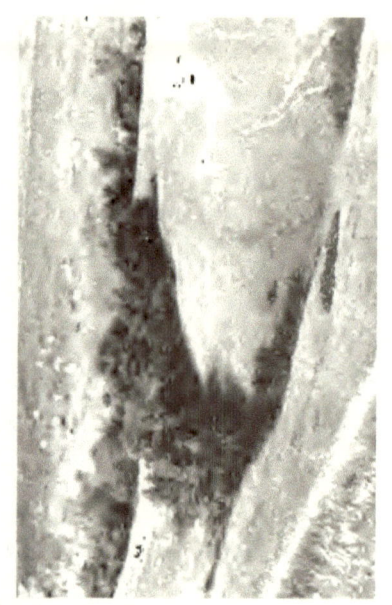

buildings, scarcely seen in the distance beyond the bridge, is the town of Mandan. That white speck on the bluffs far down the river is Fort Abraham Lincoln, a spot of sad memories, for it was from this post that the gallant Custer set forth with his cavalry on the ill-fated expedition that ended in the annihilation of his regiment.

When you enter Bismarck by rail from the east the first noble structure that you see is the State penitentiary, a solid red brick edifice surrounded by a very tall, white board fence, on which little sentry boxes are perched. Then you notice, on a brown hill slope far out beyond the limits of suburban growth, an enormous object of uncouth shape, looking like an exaggerated brick pile. This is the unfinished capitol building, and its peculiar appearance comes from the fact that it presents to the town the dead wall of the central structure, which is to be joined in the future, according to the architect's plan, to the wings of an imposing dome-surmounted edifice. Go up to the front of the building and you find that the wing built by the subscriptions of the people of Bismarck and presented by them to the old Territory, is of itself a structure of liberal proportions, and a visit to its interior will show that it is large enough for all the present needs of the economical government of a young State.

The business streets of Bismarck stand on the "second bench" above the Missouri, but the river is a long way off across a stretch of nearly two miles of hay bottoms and cottonwood groves. Following the railroad westward to the bridge, also about two miles away, you will notice that the stream here runs at the foot of the bluffs, and that the bottoms are on the other side. Here is the steamboat landing from which boats leave for the upper river, following its sinuous course as far as Fort Benton. This was the only highway of travel to the mines of the Northern Rockies until the railroad was built. Its importance as a channel of commerce has greatly diminished in late years, but it is still the only avenue of communication with a great deal of pastoral country lying along both sides of the stream, and the river traffic is still a valuable feature in the trade of Bismarck. With a fuller development of the river country the business of steamboating will considerably increase, and Bismarck has a right to look upon the broad, muddy river as one of her sure resources for future growth. The residence streets of the town climb gentle slopes from this level "second bench" back to the summits of the hills, and there are few dwellings so situated as to miss the superb outlook over the river and the valley which is the special pride of Bismarck people.

The business streets exhibit an unusual number of substantial three-story brick blocks for a town of 2,500 inhabitants, and the size of the stores and the stocks they carry show that the trade of the place is not wholly a local one. It reaches far out, in fact, going away up the river as far as the steamboats run, and down the river to farming settlements and stock ranches, and back into the country east of the river for a long distance.

The United States land office for the western part of North Dakota is located at Bismarck, and here settlers can get full information as to the tracts still open to homestead entry. The town is an interesting place for the Eastern tourist to visit. He should take time to talk with the old settlers about its romantic early history, and to drive out over the hard, elastic prairie roads to see the farms and stock ranches. The country is all attractive, and it is a very big, broad country, with plenty of room in it for new people.

Fort Abraham Lincoln.—From Capitol hill, in Bismarck, can be plainly seen the white walls of Fort Abraham Lincoln. This military station lies five miles distant by the road, on the high bluffs on the west side of the Missouri, and not far from Mandan. It was attacked on five different occasions during the years 1872-73, by the Sioux, with an aggregate loss of eight killed and twelve wounded on the side of the troops; but the repulsed Indians suffered more severely. The gallant and ill-fated Gen. Geo. A. Custer passed the last two years of his life at this post, and it was from this post that he set out with his regiment in 1876 on the expedition which resulted in the massacre of his entire command. One of the friends of the deceased general, in describing the incidents of Custer's busy life, gives a glimpse of his room at the old fort in the following words: "It was pervaded by an air of luxury and good taste, although the furniture was of the plainest, and much of it old and worn. But over every old chair or sofa, covering all deficiencies, were beautiful furs and skins that money could hardly purchase,—the spoils of Custer's rifle; and all around the walls hung grand heads of buffalo."

The Great Bridge Over the Missouri River.—This superb bridge was opened for traffic with appropriate ceremonies on the 1st of October, 1882. Prior to that time the river was crossed by means of a large transfer steamer, specially constructed for the purpose of carrying trains of cars. Owing to the strong current and constantly shifting sand-bars in the channel, the ferriage by steamboat was always tedious, and the Northern Pacific Railroad company never intended that so slow a transfer of its trains should be anything but a temporary arrangement.

The bridge proper consists of three through spans, each measuring 400 feet between centers of end pins, and two

approach spans, each 113 feet. It is a high bridge, the bottom chord of the three main spans being placed fifty feet above the level of the highest summer flood, thus giving room for steamboats to pass at all navigable stages of the river, the bridge allowing practically four feet more room than many of the bridges on the lower Missouri. The variable channel and the high bluff on the east side were sufficient reasons for adopting the high bridge plan in preference to the low bridge with a draw, and the violent action of the ice added to the force of these reasons. The east end of the east approach span is supported by a small abutment of granite masonry founded on the natural ground of the bluff. The west end of the west approach span is upheld by an iron bent, resting on two Cushing cylinders, which are supported by piles driven into the sand-bar. The three long spans are supported on four granite piers, which are of unusual size, with long, raking ice breakers, shod with steel. They are fashioned so as to cut readily the large sheets of ice upon the breaking up of the river in the spring, and to afford the least possible obstruction to the moving mass of broken ice which follows. Their stability far exceeds any force which the ice can exert.

Each of the main channel spans measures 400 feet, divided into sixteen panels of twenty-five feet each. The trusses are fifty feet deep from center to center, and twenty-two feet apart. The pedestals, end posts, top chords, and ten center panels of the bottom chord, and all the pins and expansion rollers, are of steel. All other parts in the main are of wrought iron, except the ornamental work, which is of cast iron. Each long span contains 600,950 pounds of wrought iron, 348,797 pounds of steel, and 25,777 pounds of cast iron, the total weight of each span being 975,524 pounds. The steel used was manufactured under the most rigid inspection, and subjected to extraordinary tests before it was placed in position. The extreme height from the bottom of the deepest foundation to the top chord of the bridge is 170 feet. The floor of the structure is formed of oak timbers, nine inches square and fifteen feet long, with spaces of six inches between. On this floor are laid the steel rails of the track.

The **West Missouri Country**, which is the region in North Dakota bounded on the east and north by the Missouri river, on the west by the Montana line, and on the south by South Dakota, is the best watered region in the two States of North and South Dakota. Within that region are the Little Missouri, the Knife, the Heart, the Little Heart, the Cannon Ball and the Grand rivers, to say nothing of many smaller streams tributary to those mentioned. These streams are running all the year. They get their waters from some hidden springs and do not depend upon local rains. The water that feeds them comes from the Rocky Mountains along strata that are shallow. Morton county, of which Mandan is the county seat and only town of any considerable size, extends some seventy-odd miles by rail westward from the Missouri river, and averages about fifty miles in width. There were over 400,000 bushels of hard wheat raised in the county in 1891, which would give $100, if sold at market price, to every man, woman and child within its borders.

Mandan (450 miles from St. Paul; population 2,000).—It lies on the west bank of the Missouri, nestled in the lowlands between that great stream and the Heart river, just after the railroad bridge is passed. On three sides it is inclosed by low ranges of hills, and the fertile Heart River valley here broadens into a wide, circular plain. Up to

1879, when the extension of the railroad west of the Missouri river was begun, the sight of Mandan was occupied by Indians, while buffaloes ranged on the neighboring hills. Even as late as the period named, the warlike Sioux had here a series of skirmishes, which culminated in a pitched battle with the Arickarees, or Rees, as they are commonly termed, a branch of the Mandan tribe. It is now a trading point for the Sioux on the great Standing Rock Reservation, forty miles south, which is divided by the boundary line between North and South Dakota, and was the scene in the winter of 1890 of those bloody battles between the United States troops and the Indians which the reader will recall.

The principal thoroughfare, Main street, which runs parallel with the railroad, is divided from the track along its entire length by a wide, open space that is set apart for a city park. This being the terminus of the Dakota division and the beginning of the Missouri division of the railroad, there are, at Mandan, extensive machine shops, round-house, freight buildings, and every other appliance for the transaction of railroad business, a large number of workmen being employed.

Fuel is supplied in abundance—both wood and coal—by the timber which skirts the rivers, and by the mines, which are worked to great advantage, on the line of the railroad westward. The coal is delivered by the car-load at a low price. Much attention is given in Morton county to stock and sheep raising, to which the country and climate are well adapted.

Near Mandan are points of interest dating from prehistoric times. A short distance south of the city are mounds which have been formed by successive layers of camp refuse, heaped together and burned by recurring prairie fires. In these stratifications are found stone weapons, arrow-heads, household implements, pottery, trinkets, and bones of men and animals. The Indians deny all knowledge of these mounds, the presence of which offers a fine field for archæological and ethnological research. The Mandan *Pioneer,* describing some of the discoveries, said:

"Two miles from Mandan, on the bluffs near the junction of the Heart and Missouri rivers, is an old cemetery of fully 100 acres in extent, filled with bones of a giant race. This vast city of the dead lies just east of the Fort Lincoln road. We have just spent a half-day in exploring this charnel house of a dead nation. The ground has the appearance of having been filled with trenches piled full of dead bodies, both man and beast, and covered with several feet of earth. In many places mounds from eight to ten feet high, and some of them 100 feet or more in length, have been thrown up, and are filled with bones, broken pottery, and vases of various bright-colored flints and agates. The pottery is of a dark material, beautifully decorated, delicate in finish, and as light as wood, showing the work of a people skilled in the arts, and possessed of a high state of civilization. Here is a grand field for the student, who will be richly repaid for his labors by excavating and tunneling in these catacombs of the dead. This has evidently been a grand battle field where thousands of men and horses have fallen. Nothing like a systematic or intelligent exploration has been made, as only little holes, two or three feet in depth, have been dug in some of the mounds; but many parts of the anatomy of man and beast, and beautiful specimens of broken pottery and other curiosities, have been found in these feeble efforts at excavation. Who are they, and from whence did they come, dying, and leaving only these crumbling bones and broken fragments of their works of art to mark the resting place of a dead nation? Five miles above Mandan, on the opposite side of the Missouri, is another vast cemetery, as yet uexplored.

"How long have these bones and remains laid in this cemetery, is a question which readily suggests itself. The fact that there are no existing tribes on the plains having any knowledge of pottery would indicate that the mounds had existed for a very long time. And yet there are found near the surface, and again down to a depth of nine, ten or fifteen feet, well-preserved bones, which look as if they had not been buried more than five or ten years. Then, again, the fact must be borne in mind that there are no tribes existing that will own to any knowledge of these mounds. The Indians simply say they are spirit mounds, concerning which they know nothing. It seems strange that they should have been forgotten, even within a period of 100 or 200 years, since the Indians have very tenacious memories for traditional matters. The sexton of this cemetery appeared to have a very peculiar way of doing his work. It seems that human bodies were buried, then an accumulation of grass and brush was thrown over them and set on fire. This is proved by the fact that above the bodies will be found from two to three inches of ashes. Then it looks as if the living folks had remained in the vicinity long enough to cover the dead remains with broken pottery and bones of animals. The whole would then be covered with layers of rubbish, such as would be cleared away from the tents of the people as a sanitary precaution, Broken pottery, and fragments of bones and ashes in layers, go to make the funeral mounds complete.

"In the ashes are found charred corn-cobs, burned bones

and charred meat. All the large bones that are found are broken, with the exception of the human bones. Judging from appearances, this was not only a great cemetery, but a great banqueting place also."

Prairie Dogs.—After leaving Mandan, the railroad passes through the fertile valley of the Heart river, which tortuous stream it crosses at frequent intervals, before reaching Marmot, the next station, nine miles westward. Marmot is situated on a high plateau near the confluence of the Heart and the Sweet Briar rivers. The station derives its name from the fact that a prairie dog village existed here before the railroad appeared. As the train advances westward these curious little animals are more abundant, their antics affording a great deal of amusement to passengers. Colonel Richard I. Dodge, in his book, "The Plains of the Great West," writes that this "well-known animal is badly named, having no more of the dog about him than an ordinary gray squirrel. He is a species of marmot, and burrows in the ground, as do wolves, foxes, raccoons, skunks, and all the smaller animals on the treeless plains. He lives on grass and roots, and is exceedingly prolific, each female bringing forth several sets of young each year. He is not excellent eating, but the young are as good as the common squirrel, and when other flesh meat is not to be had, they make no unwelcome addition to the bill of fare. I regard the prairie dog as a machine designed by nature to convert grass into flesh, and thus furnish proper food to the carnivora of the plains, which would undoubtedly soon starve but for the presence in such numbers of this little animal. He is found in almost every section of the open prairie, though he prefers dry and arid to moist and rich localities. He requires no moisture and no variety of food. The scanty

Indian Camp on the Line of the Northern Pacific Railroad

grass of the barest prairie appears to furnish all that is requisite for his comfortable existence. Though not in a strict sense gregarious, prairie dogs yet are fond of each other's company, and dig their holes in close vicinity. Such a collection is called a town, and they sometimes extend over immense areas. The numbers of inhabitants are incalculable. Cougars, panthers, wildcats, wolves, foxes, skunks and rattlesnakes all prey upon them without causing any perceptible diminution of their immense numbers."

The west bound train makes a steady climb of twenty-eight miles after crossing the Missouri river, through a rather rough country, and stops at New Salem, in the midst of a rich grain and grazing region. The immediate outlook is not particularly inviting, the best lands being hidden from view by broken ranges of low hills. These lands are not remote, by any means, as might be imagined, but lie chiefly within easy distance of the town. The cultivated sections are more or less scattered. Though a fair percentage of the lands are productive in one form or another, the desirable spots are far from being generally occupied by either crops or live stock. A colony of Germans from Illinois settled down in the neighborhood in 1883 and '84, made good farms of the virgin soil, and are now almost without exception in comfortable circumstances. These Germans still form the largest portion of the inhabitants of the region. Some Americans are located here and there who have been equally prosperous, one season's crops alone making them independent. Fine vegetables are grown in the vicinity, and the extent of the dairy product is something remarkable.

Sims (36 miles west of Mandan) was built principally in 1883 by the N. P. Coal company, that developed that year the coal mines opened in '78. Three companies have opened mines, shipping, during the winter season, from 200 to 250 cars a month. The coal is a superior quality of lignite, easily mined from veins seven feet in thickness. It is shipped east to Mandan, Bismarck, Jamestown and intermediate points, and to towns on the Jamestown & Northern and the James River valley branch. It can be delivered at those points so much more cheaply and quickly than Eastern coal, that a steady demand exists for it, and a reliable, profitable market is found near at hand. This lignite burns steadily, makes an intense heat and creates no soot.

A great stretch of country, admirably adapted for grazing, extends to the north and south of the Northern Pacific railroad in Oliver and Morton counties, which should be made productive. An abundance of Government and railroad land is obtainable any where in the neighborhood of Sims, which is well watered by three running streams, emptying into the Little Muddy, which in turn delivers its waters in the Heart river fifteen miles south. Almost any number of sheep or cattle ranches could be located on these lands and made highly profitable by careful management. The railroad lands are offered on terms which anybody could comply with, and in many sections they would produce grain.

Hebron is a settlement composed in great part of colonists of the German Evangelical faith, from Illinois and Wisconsin, and German-Russians, who migrated from the Province of Besserabia in Russia to avoid military conscription, and to find homes in a free country. These people are thrifty and industrious and make the best of the resources of the country. Many of them build substantial houses from the prairie turf, with good roofs thatched with straw,

They understand the care of cattle and the raising of grain, and although they arrived with very little money, they are, as a rule, in comfortable circumstances. The road here crosses a branch of the Big Knife river, which makes a handsome and fertile valley.

Gladstone (549 miles from St. Paul; population 500).— This town was laid out in the spring of 1882 by a colony from Ripon, Wisconsin, on the north bank of the Green river, and named in honor of the great English statesman. The situation of the town is pleasant, and the surrounding country for many miles is settled. At Lehigh, between Gladstone and Dickinson, are great fields of coal of a good variety for heating and cooking purposes. This coal is apparently of a recent formation, and emits no smoke or disagreeable odor, but burns like wood and equally as fast. It is shipped as far east as Fargo.

The farming community of the eastern portion of Stark county, composed mostly of Russians, supply themselves with the native coal, found either upon their own or neighbors' farms, without any cost but that of digging it from the side of the bank, build their own houses of native stone—or rubble—plaster and fill in the chinks and cracks with an excellent plaster, made from the clay and sand, farm the little valleys, herd their stock on the range of table lands, work hard and grow rich and contented. A number of Russians who live in this part of Stark county have money on deposit in the bank, own their farms, cattle and sheep, free from mortgage, to the value of thousands of dollars. They were very poor, eight or ten years ago.

Dickinson (110 miles west of the Missouri river and 560 miles from St. Paul; population, 1,000), is an active town in the valley of the Heart river. The ground on the outskirts of the town gradually slopes to the south, giving a fine

Buffalo Hunting in Early Days.

opportunity for drainage. Being the end of a freight division of the N. P., there are railroad shops and a roundhouse here. Dickinson is the county seat of Stark county. The tributary country is well watered, and the rainfall in spring and summer is sufficient to insure good crops. Many thousands of acres are already under cultivation, and there are excellent stock ranges within thirty miles of the town. The coal beds in the immediate vicinity produce a good quality of lignite, and a fine grade of clay for brickmaking, and sandstone for building purposes is found in the neighboring bluffs.

Between Stark county's western boundary and Dickinson is the limit, practically, of North Dakota's tillable soil. But there is no limit to the grazing lands. Stock growers thrive everywhere west of the Missouri river—in the grain sections of Morton and Stark counties, and in the Bad Lands to the west. In the country round about Dickinson only a small part of the land has been cultivated, stock raising having always been the chief occupation of the residents. A few miles west of Dickinson may be said to be the extreme western point where crops can be profitably raised without irrigation until Eastern Washington is reached.

The "**Bad Lands**."—At Fryburg the train suddenly leaves the beautiful rolling prairies, and enters a long cut on a down grade, presently emerging upon a region, the startling appearance of which will keep the vision alert until the Little Missouri river is reached, fourteen miles beyond. Here are the Bad Lands, sometimes called Pyramid Park, which show that the mighty forces of water and fire, fiercely battling, have wrought a scene of strange confusion. Buttes, from 50 to 150 feet in height, with rounded summits and steep sides, variegated by broad horizontal bands of color, stand closely crowded together. The black and brown stripes are due to veins of impure lignites, from the burning of which are derived the shades of red, while the raw clay varies from a dazzling white to a dark gray. The mounds are in every conceivable form, and are composed of different varieties of argillaceous limestone, friable sandstone and lignite, lying in successive strata. The coloring is very rich. Some of the buttes have bases of yellow, intermediate girdles of pure white, and tops of deepest red, while others are blue, brown and gray. There are also many of these elevations which, in the hazy distance, seem like ocean billows stiffened and at rest.

Between these curiously shaped and vari-colored mounds there are sharp ravines and gulches, which are often the beds of shallow streams. Here and there are broader spaces, covered with rich grass, and flecked with a growth of ground juniper of delicious fragrance. No trees worthy of the name are seen; but a fringe of gnarled and misshapen pines occasionally presents itself along the water channels. In ages long ago, however, dense forests existed in these Bad Lands. There is evidence of this primeval growth in the abundant petrifactions of tree stumps, four to eight feet in diameter, which are in portions translucent as rock crystals, and susceptible of as high a polish. Fine specimens of fossil leaves, of the Pliocene age, changed by the heat of the burning lignite into a brilliant scarlet, but retaining their reticulations perfect, are also found. The coal, still burning, gives a plutonic aspect to the whole region, one fiery mass not far from the railroad being easily mistaken at night for an active volcano, the cliffs having close resemblance to volcanic scoria. Among the many other fossil remains are oysters, clams and crustaceans,

The seeker for geological curiosities has here a fine field in which to work.

The term Bad Lands, as applied to this region, is a gross misnomer. It conveys the idea that the tract is worthless for agricultural and stock-raising purposes. Nothing could be wider from the truth. The fact is, the soil possesses fertilizing properties in excess, and the luxuriant grasses which here flourish, attract herbivorous game animals in large numbers. The designation "Bad Lands" is derived from the times of the old French *voyageurs*, who, in their trapping and hunting expeditions in the service of the great fur companies, described the region as "*mouvaises terres pour traverser*," meaning that it was a difficult region to travel through with ponies and pack animals. This French descriptive term was carelessly translated and shortened into "bad lands," and thus has resulted a wholly false impression of the agricultural value of the country.

The entire region, geologists tell us, was once the bed of a great lake, on the bottom of which were deposited, for ages, the rich clays and loams which the rains carried down into its waters. This deposit of soil was arrested from time to time sufficiently long to allow the growth of luxuriant vegetation, which subsequently decayed, and was consolidated by the pressure of succeeding deposits, transforming itself into those vast beds of lignite coal which abundantly meet the need of the country for fuel. The various strata thus deposited are all of recent origin, and, being without cementing ingredients, remain soft, and easily washed by the rains. When at last this vast lake found an outlet in the Missouri, the wear and wash of these strata, under the action of rain and frost, were very great. Hence the water-courses, especially the minor ones,

Pyramid Park Scenery.

where the wash has not had time enough to make broad
valleys, have precipitous banks, and high inclosing bluffs,
with curiously furrowed and corrugated sides usually bare
of vegetation, and showing only the naked edges of the
rich soils of which they are composed. The tops of these
bluffs and buttes are on the general level of the whole
country, and are equally as fertile. This is shown by the
hotel garden at the Little Missouri, where, in the very heart
of the "Bad Lands," and on the summit of the highest
bluff, a level spot was chosen and planted, which annually
yields heavy crops of vegetables, the potatoes alone producing as many as 300 bushels to the acre. But these Bad
Lands, misnamed as they are, form a very small part of
the country,—they are conspicuous from the fact that the
chaos of buttes is so curious and fantastic in form and
beautiful in varied color. From the railroad, which naturally follows the valleys between these strangely formed,
isolated mounds and hills, the view of the broad, open
country which lies on a level with their tops, is shut off.

Prof. N. H. Winchell, of Minnesota, who accompanied
Gen. Custer as geologist on his Black Hills expedition in
the summer of 1874, thus describes the general formation
of this region :

"Although I call these bad lands (for so they are
generally known among the men who have before crossed
here), they are not so *bad* as I had been led to expect from
descriptions that I have read. There is no great difficulty
in passing through them with a train. There are a great
many bare clay and sand buttes, and deep, perpendicular
cañons, cut by streams in rainy seasons ; but there are also
a great many level and grassy, sometimes beautiful valleys,
with occasionally a few trees and shrubs. There is but
little water in here, the most that we have found being due

to recent rains. The tops of a great many of the buttes are red and often they are overstrewn with what appears like volcanic scoria. This, I am satisfied, arises from the burning of the lignite, which occurs in nearly all these lands, there being one large bed of it, and sometimes two distinct beds in the same slope. The lignite is ignited by fires that sometimes prevail over the plains, set by Indians, and when fanned by the strong winds that sweep across them, produce a very intense heat, fusing over the underlying beds and mixing their materials in a confused slag, which, although generally of a reddish color, is sometimes of various colors. The clay makes a very hard, vitreous or pottery-like slag, and is sometimes green or brown. Iron stains the whole with some shade of red."

James W. Foley, Jr., in a letter to the *Northwest Magazine*, gives the following description of "The Capital," a decidedly novel feature of the Bad Lands:

"The original of the view of 'The Capital' stands, grim and imposing, in the center of a decidedly level tract of land, like some huge monument upon its pedestal. As is readily observed from a mere glance at the picture, the diameter of the stump proper exceeds that of the pillar, and, from its inclined position upon its support, the stump would seem easily displaced. Nevertheless it remains firmly imbedded in the soil underneath, and defies the efforts of winds of almost cyclonic force to dislodge it.

"Scattered here and there over its surface are masses of crystalline formation, which sparkle and glisten beautifully in the sunshine, and which, in connection with its other curious characteristics, give to the whole formation the appearance of some statue of a giant warrior, whose jewel-bedecked helmet flashes with the glints of refracted sunshine.

"While there exist, scattered in reckless abundance, throughout the length and breadth of the famous Bad Lands, innumerable stumps and trunks of petrified trees, such freaks of capricious nature as this are very rare; and it is well worth the time of any one with an eye to the artistic, to visit and satisfy himself as to the truth of the existence of such a curiosity.

"The most plausible theory as to the slow change from a once solid foundation to the present insecure support, and the theory which is generally accepted by those who have seen for themselves, is, that the tree, the stump of which now remains, originally grew upon a conical elevation. In the course of time, this elevation, being composed of but a sandy, clayey soil, has been eroded by the action of the elements; and, of course, the lower part of the hill having been more sensible to the action of water, was washed away first, until the shape was changed from conical to cylindrical.

"If, on some summer evening, you stand upon some neighboring hill-top and look down upon its statuesque outline, you are seized with an indefinite feeling of awe; and the very fact of its curious position inspires you with an indescribable respect for Nature and her wonderful works."

Medora, situated in the midst of the Bad Lands, surrounded by high bluffs and appearing strangely out of place in this land of solitude and freaks, is 600 miles from St. Paul and 18 east of the Montana line. The town was built primarily by the Marquis de Mores, a Frenchman of considerable note and gigantic projects, great wealth and enterprise, early in the '80s, for the accommodation of the men employed in his big beef slaughter and packing houses, which may be seen from the train. They have

Buttes in Pyramid Park

been unoccupied for several years, as have the few storerooms and dwelling houses. There were at one time nearly 500 people living in the town and on the Marquis' adjoining cattle ranch. He spent several hundred thousand dollars trying to establish a profitable business in the supplying of dressed beef, shipped in his own refrigerator cars, to the Eastern markets, but was finally forced to abandon the idea by the opposition of more powerful interests which were jeopardized by this enterprise.

Cattle Raising in the Bad Lands.—Hon. Theodore Roosevelt, of New York, who owns a cattle ranch near Medora, in an article in the Bismarck *Tribune*, wrote as follows on the subject of cattle raising in the Bad Lands:

"Roughly speaking, the stretch of country known among cattle men as the 'Dakota Bad Lands,' occupies the western portion of North Dakota, from the Black Hills region on the south, to the Missouri on the north; that is, it comprises the country drained by the Little Missouri river, and the waters running into it. This river runs in long loops, which enclose fertile bottoms, through a narrow valley, bounded on each side by a line of jagged buttes, back of which stretches a mass of very rough and broken hill country, rent and cleft in all directions by deep, winding ravines, and narrow, cañon-like valleys. Creeks open into the river every few miles. At certain seasons their beds hold foaming torrents, while during the rest of the year they are either perfectly dry, or consist merely of strings of small, shallow pools, with here and there a deep spring hole. Some of the alluvial river bottoms are thickly timbered with cottonwood, and in a few of the ravines there is a growth of pine and cedar. The Bad Lands proper extend back for from five to twenty miles, when we come out on the level prairie, which gives the cattle fine feed in summer, but offers them no shelter whatever from the bitter winds of winter.

"The herds of the stockmen now graze fifty miles north, and many times that distance south, of the railroad. The cattlemen through the Bad Lands have formed themselves into a stock association, and most of them, in addition, have joined the great Montana stock association. Their round-up takes in all the country along the Little Missouri, from Box Alder creek on the south to below the Big Beaver creek on the north, including the ranges of some fifteen or twenty stock outfits along a river front of nearly two hundred miles. Each such outfit may have from 500 to 10,000 head of stock, and from 10 to 100 head of ponies with which to herd them. There is plenty of timber for building purposes; the home ranch of each outfit consists of a log house, or shack, containing one or many rooms, according to the way the inmates appreciate comfort and the decencies of life; near by is a log stable and outbuildings, a strong, high, circular horse corral, with a snubbing post in the center, and further off the larger cow corral, in which the calves are branded, etc.

"The country is covered with a growth of short bunch grass, which cures on the stalk into excellent hay for winter feed; it is very nutritious, and upon it range cattle become as fat as stall-fed oxen. Over most of the land there is nothing but this grass, and the bitter, grayish green sage brush; except for a few weeks in spring, when the first growth forms a mantle of green, the whole land is colored a monotonous, dull brown, which, joined to the extraordinary shape and bizarre coloring of the water-worn buttes, gives the landscape a look of grim and forbidding desolation, although this very look of loneliness, sameness and vastness, also gives it an intense attraction for some men, including myself. This forbidding aspect of the land, however, completely belies its real character; the dull, barren-looking country, clad with withered brown grass, in reality offers as fine grazing as can be found anywhere in the West, while the cliffs and broken valleys offer almost perfect shelter to the animals in the winter. The loss among cattle during the winter, no matter how severe the weather, is surprisingly small, always excepting, of course, half-starved 'pilgrims,' or cattle put on the range late in the fall, and in poor condition. The rainfall is slight, and the snow rarely covers the ground to any depth. The water supply back of the river is scanty, and the country is wholly unfit for agricultural purposes; recognizing which fact, the last legislature very wisely repealed the herd law, in so far as it affected the western tier of counties, and the cattle men are now free from the fear of being sued by every unscrupulous adventurer who palms himself off as a granger, and declines to fence in his few acres of grain or vegetables. The scantiness of the water supply is no harm to the cattle men, as in summer the beasts keep within a few miles of the river, principal creeks or large water holes, and thus leave a great stretch of back country over which they have not grazed, and which affords them excellent winter feed when ice has closed up all the ponds and streams, and they are obliged to slake their thirst by eating snow.

"Each ranchman puts up a certain amount of hay for winter use for such horses as he constantly rides, to help out any sick animals which he finds, etc. So far, all this hay has been wild, and has been cut on the tops of the great plateaus; but the time is rapidly approaching when the ranchmen will be obliged to fence in large patches of ground and raise a hay crop—by preference, alfalfa, if on further trial it proves that it will grow.

Driving Cattle from the Range to the Railroad.

"The excellence of the Bad Lands as a country for fattening steers has been proved beyond all doubt; as yet it is too early to say definitely how it will turn out as a region for raising stock. Last year the calf crop was very light; but it is believed that this was mainly due to the very insufficient number of bulls on the range, as a number of the outfits have yet to learn that it is criminal folly to expect to get along with the same proportionate quantity of bulls loose on the range as would do on an Eastern farm. There will always be a lack of calves until the supply of bulls is much more ample than at the present time. Still, appearances indicate a much larger calf crop this year than was the case last. Along the river, as a whole, the steers greatly out-number the female stock. Horned cattle, and also horses, do excellently; but all efforts at sheep-raising have so far been flat failures,—for which the cattle men are sincerely grateful. The sheep have in each case died by the score and the hundred, but a small percentage surviving the first winter. Many of the ranchmen and small stock owners have now brought out their wives, and the country, which four years ago was an empty wilderness, or with straggling bands of Indians and parties of hunters, is now settled by a thriving and prosperous class of men, and in many spots a most pleasant home life is growing up. The ranchmen are hearty, open handed and hospitable. The cow boys are a fearless, generous, good-natured set of men, much misrepresented in some Eastern papers. Of course, there are fools in all classes, and the fool variety of cow boy likes to come into town and get drunk, and go about yelling and shooting in the air, firing at the car wheels of a passenger train, or perhaps shooting off the hat of some well-dressed stranger who looks small and timid. But, if a man keeps away from drinking saloons, does not put on airs, and at the same time, shows that he does not intend to stand any nonsense, he can safely reckon upon first-class treatment in cow-boy land."

Little Missouri is a small village just across the river from Medora. There is a coal mine on the bluffs close at hand. There is an abandoned military post a quarter of a mile from the place. Soon after leaving the Little Missouri river the country westward becomes less rough, although the railroad passes through many cuts and ravines. Gradually, however, the feature of the landscape is that of broad, rolling prairie, marked here and there by isolated buttes.

Sentinel Butte is a prominent object on the left hand, not far from the track. The top of this eminence is visible on clear days at a distance of thirty miles, but looks only to be about three miles off, so deceptive is the luminous atmosphere. This region abounds in moss agates, specimens of which are found near the foot of the buttes, of great size and beauty. A well-known army officer, who was at one time stationed here, secured a sufficient number of these agates so large that they were converted into dessert knife handles and served as a unique and handsome present to a lady on her wedding day.

Sentinel Butte, in spite of its precipitous faces, as seen from the railroad, is easy of access on the side remotest from the track. On its summit there is half an acre of level ground. Buffalo were very partial to this elevation, and sometimes resorted to it in so large numbers that many were crowded over the brink. The bones of these animals lie in heaps at the foot of the precipice, whitened by the weather. One mile west of Sentinel Butte station, the boundary between North Dakota and Montana is crossed. The line is marked by a tall pole, upon which is nailed a fine pair of antlers.

SEVEN HUNDRED MILES IN MONTANA.

The State of Montana.—This beautiful State, named on account of its mountainous character, is one of the largest in the Union, being surpassed in area by Texas and California only. It averages 275 miles from north to south, and 550 miles from east to west, stretching through 12° of longitude, and from 104° to 116° west of Greenwich, and lies for the most part between the forty-fifth and forty-ninth parallels of north latitude. Its southern boundary is in about the latitude of St. Paul, Minn., and its northern line joins the British possessions. The Northern Pacific railroad runs through the State from the southeast corner almost to the northwest corner, a distance of a little over 700 miles.

The mean height of Montana above the ocean level is estimated at 3,900 feet, the greatest elevation among the mountain peaks being 11,000 feet, and the lowest, on the Missouri river, being about 2,000 feet. Of the 93,000,000 acres contained within the limits of the State, two-fifths are mountainous and three-fifths valley or rolling plains. The water-shed between the Atlantic and the Pacific oceans, the main chain of the Rocky Mountains, traverses the western portion of Montana in a course of a little west of north, leaving about one-fourth of the entire State on the western slope and three fourths on the eastern. In the central part of the State are the Bull, Belt, the Little

Rocky and other smaller mountain ranges, which, with many lateral spurs and detached groups, give that great diversity of rocky ridges, broad plateaus and pleasant valleys which render the country extremely picturesque. The highest summits are those of the Peaks of Gallatin, about 100 miles south of Bozeman and plainly visible from the car windows as the train runs down the Gallatin valley west of that town. These peaks have an altitude of over 11,000 feet. Next highest is the Lo Lo peak in the Bitter Root range, which can be seen from Missoula. Montana is well supplied with rivers. Her great watercourses are Clark's Fork of the Columbia and the Missouri river, the latter with many important tributaries. The Clark's Fork drains 40,000 miles of the State, and flows into the Columbia river; while the Missouri and its tributaries, the Milk, the Yellowstone, the Teton, the Marias, the Judith, the Musselshell, the Jefferson, the Madison and the Gallatin carry off the waters of double that area. These rivers are navigated by steamboats a distance of 1,500 miles within the limits of the State. Montana has a number of beautiful lakes, the largest of which is Flathead, in Missoula county, ten by thirty miles in size. The cataracts of the Missouri river between the town of Great Falls and the town of Fort Benton are the most striking scenic features in Northern Montana. There are three principal falls, the Black Eagle, the Rainbow and the Great Falls; and three minor falls are within a distance of twenty miles. The height of the Great Falls is eighty feet, that of the Rainbow fifty feet, and that of the Black Eagle fifty feet.

The agricultural lands of Montana lie mainly in the valleys of the large rivers and their affluents. These valleys, usually old lake basins which have received the wash from the surrounding mountains, have an alluvial soil which has proved to be very fertile. The land has generally a gentle and regular slope from the higher ground which separates the valleys from the foot-hills, and this is a fact of great importance in its bearing upon irrigation. So uniform is the slope that, in almost every instance, when water is conducted by means of a ditch from any stream it may be made to flow over every foot of land in the valley below. The uplands (or bench lands, as they are commonly termed) are simply continuations of the valleys at a higher elevation. They frequently look like artificial terraces of enormous size, rising one above the other; and where the quantity of water in the stream above admits the irrigation of the bench lands, they are also found to be very productive. Beyond these terraces are the foot-hills, with rounded tops and grassy slopes, and behind these loom up the mountains, crowned with a scanty growth of pine and fir, although the slopes and valleys are always destitute of these varieties of timber. There are no deciduous trees, either, excepting groves of cottonwood and willows along the water-courses, and occasional copses of quaking asp in wet places on the sides of the mountains. Only in the extreme northwestern part of the State is a very large body of magnificent timber, covering mountains and plains alike.

Eastern Montana, stretching from the base of the Rocky Mountains to the boundary of the Dakotas and embracing an area of 90,000 square miles, is divided into three belts of nearly equal size by the Missouri and Yellowstone rivers. On the west and south are mountains timbered with pine and fir, and from them issue many streams, which abundantly water the country. The ground is covered with a rich growth of bunch grass, which makes the region an excellent stock range. But the large area of grassy rolling table lands in the northeastern part of the State is pre-eminently the place for cattle-raising and sheep husbandry. The resources of the entire State are varied and very valuable. Millions of acres of good agricultural land are awaiting development; but, owing to the light rainfall, irrigation is generally necessary.

Mining has always been, and probably will continue to be, the leading industry. The Drum Lummon mine, at Marysville, near Helena, has probably produced more gold than any other mine in the world. The Granite Mountain mine, at Phillipsburg, in Western Montana, is the most valuable silver mine in the world. The mines at Butte, which furnish the ore for the great smelters and reduction works at Anaconda, are the most productive copper mines in the world, and yield a great deal of silver. Besides these famous mines, there are many other rich deposits of ore which yield large annual returns to the companies working them. **Considerable** placer gold is still obtained by hydraulic processes, and a good deal is taken out of the old gulches by individual miners working with sluice boxes and quicksilver. Montana's total annual yield of precious metals is over $30,000,000.

The **stock-raising** interest of Montana ranks next in the value of its annual product to the mining interest. Cattle, **sheep** and horses are raised in great numbers on the plains and on the well-grassed foot-hills of the mountain ranges. The cattle and sheep are marketed chiefly in St. Paul and Chicago. The wool goes mostly to Boston. Montana horses have won a high reputation for speed and endurance, and are shipped as far east as New York City.

Historical.—The history of Montana has not been destitute of stirring incident. Before 1861 there were no settlements, and the only whites who had visited the region were trappers, missionaries and the members of various military exploring parties. Public attention was first directed to the Territory at about the period named by the discovery of gold in paying quantities in Deer Lodge county. The report brought an irruption of miners from all the Western States, among whom were some of the wildest and most reckless characters, whose names and misdeeds figure in the early annals of the Territory. In 1862 the rich placers at Bannack were discovered. In the following year a party, returning from an unsuccessful attempt to reach the Big Horn Mountains by way of the Gallatin river, whence they were driven back by the Crow Indians, camped for dinner on Alder creek, near the site of Virginia City. Here one of the number, William Fairweather by name, washed a few pans of gravel, and was surprised to obtain about $2 worth of gold to the pan. The news soon spread, and numbers flocked to the place, which has since yielded $60,000,000 of gold, half of which was taken out during the first three years after the discovery. The next important placer diggings were found in 1864, at Last Chance gulch, where Helena now stands, and at Silver Bow and German gulches, at the head of the Deer Lodge valley. Subsequently mines of great richness were found at various other points, and the excitement upon the subject ran high.

The fame of the diggings caused a large immigration, and, with the honest and deserving gold hunters, there was also a rush of the vilest desperadoes from the mining camps of the Western States and Territories. This ruffianly element served as a nucleus around which the evil-disposed gathered, and soon was organized a band of outlaws which became the terror of the country. These banditti included hotel keepers, express agents, and other

Eagle Butte, near Glendive, Montana.

seemingly respectable people, Henry Plummer, the sheriff of the principal county, being their leader. The roads of the Territory were infested by the ruffians, and it was not only unsafe, but almost certain death, to travel with money in one's possession. One writer affirms that "the community was in a state of blockade. No one supposed to have money could get out of the Territory alive. It was dangerous to cope with the gang; for it was very large and well organized, and so ramified throughout society that no one knew whether his neighbor was or was not a member." The usual arms of a "road agent," writes Prof. Dimsdale, in his history of "The Vigilantes of Montana," "were a pair of revolvers, a double-barreled shot-gun of large bore, with the barrels cut down short, and to this was invariably added a knife or dagger. Thus armed, mounted on fleet, well-trained horses, and disguised with blankets and masks, the robbers awaited their prey in ambush. When near enough, they sprang out on a keen run, with leveled shotguns, and usually gave the word 'Halt! throw up your hands, you ——— — ———!' If this latter command were not instantly obeyed, that was the last of the offender; but in case he complied, as was usual, one or two of the ruffians sat on their horses, covered the party with their guns, which were loaded with buckshot, and one dismounting, disarmed the victims, and made them throw their purses on the grass. This being done, a search for concealed property followed, after which the robbers rode away, reported the capture, and divided the spoils."

At last the decent citizens organized a vigilance committee in self-defense. The confession of two of the gang put the lovers of law and order in possession of the names of the prominent ruffians, who were promptly arrested. Twenty-two of the miscreants were hanged at various places, after the form of a trial, between December 21, 1863, and January 25, 1864, five having been executed together in Virginia City. This summary justice so stunned the remainder of the band that they decamped. From the discovery of the bodies of the victims, the confessions of the murderers before execution, and from information sent to the vigilance committee, it was found that certainly 102 people had been killed by the bandits in various places, and it was believed that scores of unfortunates had been murdered and buried, whose remains were never discovered. It was known that the missing persons had set out for various places with greater or less sums of money, and were never heard of again. After this wholesome justice had been meted to the murderers, law and order prevailed, the lawless element leaving the Territory, and the honest and enterprising remained to develop the mining and other natural resources. Congress provided for the admission of Montana as a State in the act passed at the session in 1889, which also provided for the admission of North Dakota, South Dakota and Washington.

Beaver Creek Valley.—Just west of the Bad Lands the Northern Pacific enters Montana and soon reaches the pretty valley of Beaver Creek, from which more cattle are shipped to Eastern markets than from any other district in the State. Mingusville, 635 miles from St. Paul, is the shipping station for the valley, and is a typical cow-boy town. Most of the buildings are drinking saloons and small taverns.

Glendive Creek.—After leaving Beaver Creek valley the road crosses a low divide and strikes Glendive creek, which it follows twenty miles, to the Yellowstone river. On either side of a narrow valley are curious bluffs, with seamed sides of dark and light brown earthy strata, and an occasional vein of lignite, and grotesque, jagged summits.

Glendive (666 miles from St. Paul; population 1,500). —Glendive is the first place of any prominence in Montana that is reached by the railroad. It is the county seat of Dawson county, the largest county in Montana, and is the terminus of the Missouri division and the beginning of the Yellowstone division of the railroad. The town is in latitude 47° 3' N., and longitude 104° 45' W., and lies 2,070 feet above the ocean level. Situated on the south bank of the Yellowstone, ninety miles from the junction of that stream with the Missouri at Fort Buford, N. D., Glendive occupies a broad plain, which slopes gently toward the river, and is sheltered by a range of curiously shaped clay buttes, distant about half a mile from the stream, and rising abruptly to a height of nearly 300 feet above its level. These buttes are not unlike those seen at the Bad Lands of the Little Missouri, only here the subterranean fires have not burned so fiercely as further east, and the river seems to have stopped the combustion, for across the water there is a large expanse of excellent soil. The site of the town was selected and laid out under the supervision of Gen. Lewis Merrill, U. S. A., who adopted the name of Glendive for his projected city, in remembrance of Sir George Gore, an eccentric Irish nobleman, who spent the winter of 1856 in hunting buffalo in this vicinity, and who originally applied the designation to the creek. Glendive was founded in 1881. A little irrigated farming is done in the valley, but the place is almost wholly a cattle town, being supported mainly by the trade of the stock ranchers. It is a good point to stop and study the range cattle business.

The scenery just beyond Glendive is imposing. The railroad skirts the river, and bluffs tower several hundred feet above the track. *Eagle Cliff* is especially noticeable, for its height, and the heavy engineering work which was necessary in constructing the railroad at this point.

The Yellowstone Valley.—The railroad follows up the Yellowstone valley from Glendive to Livingston, a distance of 340 miles. In its characteristics the Yellowstone river more closely resembles the Ohio than any other American stream. Its waters, unlike those of the Missouri, are bright and clear, except when discolored by the freshets of its lower tributaries. The stream runs over a bed of gravel through permanent channels, and among thousands of beautiful islands, covered with heavy timber. It is navigable during a good stage of water for more than 250 miles, from its confluence with the Missouri at Ft. Buford to a point above the mouth of the Big Horn river, by steamboats of two or three hundred tons.

The Yellowstone has many tributaries along that part of its course which is traversed by the railroad, especially on its south bank.* After leaving Glendive, the first important stream coming in from the south is the Powder river, so called by the Indians from its inky-black water, stained by the long course it runs through the alluvial soil flanking the Black Hills and Big Horn mountains. Here the valley of the Yellowstone broadens, and the country behind the bluffs is better and richer than before. On the north side of the Yellowstone, between Powder and Tongue rivers, several small streams come in which drain the divide between the Yellowstone and the Missouri. The next river of consequence on the south side is the Tongue, with a good but narrow valley, already well settled by farmers and herders. About thirty miles westward of the Tongue another affluent of considerable volume is the Rosebud, flowing from the south. Fifty-six miles beyond is the Big

Horn river, the largest tributary of the Yellowstone, draining the whole eastern slope of the Rocky Mountains from the Yellowstone southward to the Platte. The next important stream is the Clark's Fork of the Yellowstone, which must not be confused with the other and more important Clark's Fork of the Columbia.

The Yellowstone winds from side to side of the valley, and along most of its course westward presents a very picturesque appearance. Bluffs of what are called "Bad Lands" inclose it, showing their precipitous faces against the stream, first on one side then on the other, as the river winds from bluff to bluff, leaving always opposite the bluffs a considerable valley on either side of the stream. The width of the Yellowstone valley throughout its entire length scarcely exceeds three miles; sometimes it narrows to not more than two miles, and again it widens to seven. At the heads of the lateral valleys are fine sites for stock ranches or grazing farms, the same luxuriant grass covering the whole country. Clear, pure water is to be found every few miles in running streams and springs, along which are fringes of oak, ash, elm, box elder and cottonwood, with occasional pines and cedars in the ravines. Before reaching the Big Horn the valley becomes somewhat broader, and for many miles on the north side of the river, beginning at a point opposite Fort Keogh, are ranges of bluffs which finally recede in height and gradually dissappear. Along this part of the river the rough, broken water-shed of the Musselshell, the Missouri and the Yellowstone, called the Bull Mountains, is drained by three small streams, which have considerable valleys of fertile soil. The streams are Frozen Creek and the Big and Little Porcupine. The Yellowstone above the Big Horn runs through a comparatively narrow valley, which broadens only at a single point. The Clark's Fork bottom lies in this part of the valley, on the north side of the Yellowstone, extending from the rocky bluffs east of the old settlement at Coulson, near the site of Billings, to the hills which put into the river from outlying spurs of the Rocky mountains, some thirty-five miles westward.

The traveler, passing through the Yellowstone valley, except during the months of May and June, when vegetation is vividly green, is apt to rebel against the withered look of the grass. Lowland and highland alike are clothed with a russet garment, which the heat of summer has spread over them. The mountains appear like colossal hay-mows with the lush growth of bunch grass surging up their slopes, cured as it stands by the sun into the best of hay, upon which herds fatten all the year round. The valley has the same sere tone, and the fringe of dark pines on the brow of the hills does not relieve, but only serves to emphasize, the prevailing tone of the landscape. To an artist eye, however, the many shades of grey make the landscape peculiarly attractive. A prominent Eastern artist visiting the Yellowstone valley a few years ago, explained his delight at the scenery by saying, "Greens are common everywhere, but where else can you find such lovely greys!"

Iron Bluff (676 miles from St. Paul).—Large quantities of shell boulders are found in the vicinity. These consist chiefly of shells, which are mixed with small quantities of silica and alumina. The sides of the bluffs and the ravines running back into them from the river are remarkably rich in marine fossils. Entire fossilized fishes have been found with the iridescence of the scales still perfect, and every little hillock yields a quantity of perfect shells.

Fallon (695 miles from St Paul) is at the mouth of O'Fallon creek. It is the depot for the beautiful and fertile valley running 100 miles south, which has attracted many ranchmen and stock-raisers.

Batchford (715 miles from St. Paul; population, 100) is the depot for the Powder River valley region. Ten miles east of Ainslie, at the Powder river crossing, was fought a battle between the Indians and United States troops; and for several miles along the banks of the Yellowstone, the graves of the soldiers who died of their wounds on their march up the river, can be seen.

Miles City (745 miles from St. Paul; population, 2,000) is the only town on the Northern Pacific line between Superior and the Rocky mountains which did not owe its origin to the building of the road. It was a flourishing frontier trading post three years before the Northern Pacific reached the Yellowstone valley. Its business was originally, to a large extent, with buffalo hunters; but, after the extermination of the buffalo, the immense grazing country surrounding it was rapidly occupied by stockmen. There are over 700,000 cattle on the ranges tributary to the town. Miles City is the county seat of Custer county, and is a compact, well-built town. Nearly all the business houses are constructed of brick. Groves of cottonwood trees and thickets of wild rose bushes add much to the attractiveness of the place. The town enjoys a large trade from the surrounding cattle and sheep ranges and has, besides, a rich irrigated valley right at its doors, that of the Tongue river. Fort Keogh, an important military post two miles west, furnishes a good deal of business to its merchants.

Explorations of the Yellowstone.—The first recorded exploration of the Yellowstone valley was that made by

Captain William Clark, U. S. A., who was associated with Captain Meriwether Lewis, U. S. A., in the command of the famous Lewis and Clark expedition, fitted out in 1804, under authority of President Jefferson, to explore the region west of the Mississippi river, and extending to the Pacific coast. This vast territory known as "the Louisiana purchase," and subsequently as the Province of Louisiana, was ceded to the United States by Napoleon Bonaparte in 1803, for the nominal sum of $15,000,000. The heroic band of explorers numbering only thirty-two men set out from St. Louis on the 14th of May, 1804, ascended the Missouri river a distance of 2,858 miles from its mouth, and striking across the Rocky mountains and other ranges westward, reached the mouth of the Columbia river on the 7th of November, 1805. On the 23d of March in the following year, the dauntless explorers entered upon their return journey, recrossing the Rocky Mountains on the 3d of July. The expedition now resolved itself into three parties, one of which followed the eastern base of the mountains northward to the mouth of the Marias river, where it united with the second party, commanded by Captain Lewis, that had gone directly down the Missouri. The third detachment under Captain Clark pushed eastward until it struck the Yellowstone river, and then followed this stream 400 miles to its confluence with the Missouri, near which point the three parties again united. After an absence of nearly two years and a half, the expedition arrived at St. Louis on the 23d of September, 1806, having lost only a single man by death. This was one of the most brilliant and successful explorations ever made. By its means a mass of accurate information respecting the country was gathered, the practical value of which has continued to the present day. The result of the expedition was at once to open up the newly acquired territory to the enterprise of the great fur companies, who established trading posts with the Indians at many points. Aside from the trappers, however, no whites settled in Montana until the breaking out of the gold excitement in 1862. Then, and even for many years afterward, the settlements were confined to the extreme western portions of the Territory, which were the most accessible, the eastern half long remaining a wilderness, in absolute possession of the Indians. Only since the year 1853, at which time the Government sent out an expedition under command of the late General I. I. Stevens, to explore the region lying between the forty-seventh and forty-ninth parallels, with a view of reporting upon the feasibility of the northern route for a railroad from Lake Superior to Puget Sound, has the Yellowstone valley been brought to public attention. Since the date named a number of expeditions, both Government and private, have passed through the valley from time to time, and their records of experience and adventure are of the highest interest. But it is not within the plan of this book even to outline the more important features of any of these exploring expeditions. The space at command will only admit of the narration of a few of the more important facts connected with the various conflicts between the Indians and the United States troops, of which this valley was the scene between the years 1873 and 1877.

During the period in question the aborigines strove hard to keep possession of their favorite country. But civilization, repeating the history which has marked its progress in every land, was not to be kept back, and the fierce struggle for supremacy between the white race and the red man, resulted in the final disappearance of the latter from the Yellowstone valley.

. The railroad was finished to the Missouri river toward the close of 1872; but the actual surveys and locations for the roadway had been made as far west as the Powder river, 250 miles beyond. An escort of troops always accompanied the surveying parties, and minor engagements between these small detachments and the Indians were of common occurrence. During 1873 these attacks became so bold and frequent that it was necessary to transfer an additional regiment of cavalry from the Military Department of the South for the purpose of holding the hostile red men in check, and a supply depot was established on Glendive creek, where that stream empties into the Yellowstone.

A Fight with **Indians at Tongue River.**—In the summer of 1873 an army expedition, consisting of about 1,700 men, under the command of Major General D. S. Stanley, was sent out from Fort Rice, on the Missouri river, to explore the Yellowstone valley in the interest of the railroad. In due time the expedition reached the Yellowstone river, and marched for several days up that stream. The country eventually proved so rough and broken that in many places serious delays were encountered in finding a practicable route for the long and heavily laden wagon trains. These serious embarrassments were only overcome by sending out each morning, some distance in advance of the main column, two companies of the Seventh cavalry, under command of the late General Custer, whose duty it was to seek and prepare a practicable road. In carrying out the plan which already had been for some days followed successfully, Gen. Custer left camp on the 4th of August, with a force of ninety-one men, guided by Bloody Knife, a young Arickaree warrior. At a point nearly opposite the mouth of Tongue river, plainly in sight of the railroad, Gen. Custer encountered a force of Sioux outnumbering his own command over five to one. After a hard fight the Indians were driven off the field. For a week afterward, as the exploring party pursued its march, it entered upon a series of sharp skirmishes with the large force of Indians, who, however, were invariably repulsed, although the troops did not escape many severe casualties.

In 1874 and 1875 the Yellowstone valley enjoyed comparative quiet, although there were hostile bands of Sioux roaming over the valleys of the Big Horn and Powder rivers, and the entire Western frontier was ravaged by them. In June, 1875, a steamboat expedition, consisting of seven officers and 100 men, commanded by Col. Forsyth, of Lieut-Gen. Sheridan's staff, ascended the Yellowstone a distance of 430 miles, selecting sites for military posts at the mouth of the Tongue and Big Horn rivers, in order to better deal with the Indians. This expedition returned without encountering any hostile red men.

On February 21, 1876, an expedition left Fort Ellis, near Bozeman, under command of Major Brisbin, numbering 221 officers and men for the succor of a party of citizens, who were besieged by Indians at Fort Pease, near the confluence of the Big Horn with the Yellowstone. The original party consisted of forty-six men, who defended themselves desperately in a stockade until the relief column of troops arrived. Six persons were killed, eight wounded, and thirteen escaped during the night, leaving only nineteen in the stockade, who were rescued by the troops.

Later, 1876, the Government was compelled to send out a force against certain wild and hostile bands of Indians who were roaming about Dakota and Montana, not only attacking settlers and immigrants, but also making war upon the Mandans and Arickarees, who were friendly to the whites. To this class belonged the notorious Sitting Bull, who was not a chief, but only a "head man," and whose immediate followers did not exceed thirty or forty lodges. Another disaffected chief was Crazy Horse, an Ogallala Sioux, who properly belonged to the Red Cloud agency, and whose band comprised, perhaps, 120 lodges, numbering about 200 warriors. These bands had never accepted the agency system, and would not recognize the authority of the Government. They had been notified, however, by the Department of the Interior, that they must, before the 31st of January, 1876, retire to the reservations to which they were assigned, or take the alternative of being brought to subjection by the military power. Every effort, meanwhile, to pacify these bands, proved unsuccessful. They refused to come into the agencies, settle down and be peaceable. A strong force of troops was, therefore, set in motion to subdue them. On the 1st of March, Col. J. J. Reynolds, with a force of 883 men, moved out from Fort Fetterman, on the North Platte river, in search of the hostiles, and, after marching through deep snow and suffering great hardship, reached the mouth of the Little Powder river on March 16th, at which point he attacked and defeated a large village of Sioux and Northern Cheyennes, under Crazy Horse, destroying 105 lodges and a great amount of ammunition and supplies, and capturing a large herd of animals. The troops, however, had suffered so much from the severity of the weather, that they were compelled to return to Fort Fetterman to recuperate.

Operations were resumed by this force toward the end of the following May. On the 29th of that month, a column of 1,000 men, under the command of Gen. Crook, again left Fort Fetterman, and on the 13th and 17th of June, the Indians were discovered in large numbers on the Rosebud. Here a desperate fight took place, lasting several hours, resulting in the flight of the Indians, after heavy losses. The casualties to the troops in this engagement were nine killed and twenty-one wounded. From the strength of the hostiles who attacked Gen. Crook's column, it now became apparent that not only Crazy Horse and his small band had to be fought, but also a large number of Indians who had re-enforced them from the agencies along the Missouri, and from the Red Cloud and Spotted Tail agencies, near the boundary line between Dakota and Nebraska. Under these circumstances Gen. Crook deemed it best to await re-enforcements and supplies before proceeding further.

The Massacre of Custer's Command.—Simultaneously with Gen. Crook's operations, Gen. Terry had concentrated 400 infantry and 600 of the Seventh Cavalry, the latter under Gen. George A. Custer, at Fort Lincoln. With this force he left the fort on the 17th of May, and reached the mouth of the Powder river on the 7th of June, where a supply camp was established. From this point six troops of cavalry, under Major Reno, scouted up the Powder river to its forks, and across the country to the Rosebud, following down the last named stream to its mouth, definitely locating the Indians in the vicinity of the Little Big Horn river. During Maj. Reno's scout the force under Gen. Terry moved up the south bank of the Yellowstone, and formed a junction with a column consisting of six companies of infantry and four troops of cavalry, under Col. Gibbon, which had marched from Fort Ellis eastward, along the north bank of the Yellowstone to a point opposite the Rosebud. On June 21st, after a conference with Cols. Gibbon and Custer, Gen. Terry, who was in supreme command, communicated the following plan of operations: Gibbon's column was to cross the Yellowstone near the mouth of the Big Horn, march up this stream to the junction with the Little Big Horn, and thence up the latter, with the understanding that it would arrive at the last-named point on June 26th. Custer, with the whole of the Seventh cavalry, should proceed up the Rosebud until the direction of the Indian trail found by Reno should be ascertained. If this led to the Little Big Horn, it should not be followed; but Custer should keep still further south before turning toward that river, in order to intercept the Indians should they attempt to slip between him and the mountains, and also in order, by a longer march, to give time for Col. Gibbon's column to come up. On the afternoon of June 22d, Custer's column set out on its fatal march up the Rosebud, and on the morning of the 25th he and his immediate command were overwhelmed and pitilessly slaughtered by the Indians, who were concentrated in the valley of the Little Big Horn, to the number of over 2,500 fighting men. The harrowing details of the massacre are mainly a matter of conjecture. No officer or soldier who rode with their gallant leader into the valley of the Little Big Horn was spared to tell the tale of the disaster The testimony of the field where the mutilated remains were found showed that a stubborn resistance had been offered by the troops, and that they had been beset by overpowering numbers. The bodies of 204 of the slain were buried on the battle ground. The battle ground has been marked by a monument by the United States Government. It is about thirty miles south of the railway station of Custer, near the mouth of the Big Horn river. The important military post of Fort Custer was established near the battle-field not long after the massacre occurred.

The Brilliant Work of Gen. Miles.—After this calamity had befallen the expedition, additional troops were sent to the scene of operations as rapidly as they could be gathered from distant posts, but too late to be of immediate use. The exultant Indians had already broken up their organization, and scattered far and wide as bands of marauders, placing themselves beyond the reach of punishment in a body. In the autumn most of the troops were withdrawn from Montana, leaving only a strong garrison, under the command of Gen. Nelson A. Miles, who was then colonel of the Fifth infantry, to occupy a cantonment at the mouth of the Tongue river (now Fort Keogh). Through the energy and bravery of this command, the Yellowstone valley was soon entirely rid of the Indians. On October 10th a train of ninety-four wagons, with supplies, left Glendive for the cantonment at at the mouth of the Tongue river, and was beset the same night by Indians, seven or eight hundred strong, under Sitting Bull, who so crippled it that it was forced to turn back to Glendive for re-enforcements. These obtained, it resumed its journey, the escort numbering eleven officers and 185 men, in the hope of getting the much-needed supplies to the garrison. On the 15th the Indians attacked once more, but were driven back at the point of the bayonet, while the wagons slowly advanced. In this way the train proceeded until the point was reached from which the return had been previously made. Here the Indians became more determined, firing the prairie, and compelling the wagons to advance through the flames. On the 16th of October an Indian runner brought in the following communication from Sitting Bull to Col. Otis, commanding the escort:

"YELLOWSTONE.

"I want to know what you are doing traveling on this road. You scare all the buffaloes away. I want to hunt in this place. I want you to turn back from here. If you don't, I will fight you again. I want you to leave what you have got here, and turn back from here. I am your friend, "SITTING BULL."

"I mean all the rations you have got and some powder. Wish you would write as soon as you can."

Col. Otis replied to this cool request that he intended to take the train through, and would accommodate the Indians with a fight at any time. The train moved on, the Indians surrounding it, and keeping up firing at long range. Presently a flag of truce was sent in by Sitting Bull, who said that his men were hungry, tired of war, anxious for peace, and wished Col. Otis to meet him in council outside the lines of the escort. This invitation was declined; but the colonel said he would be glad to meet Sitting Bull inside the lines. The wary savage was afraid to do this, but sent three chiefs to represent him. Col. Otis told them he had no authority to treat with them but that they could go to Tongue river and make their wishes known. After giving them a present of hard bread and bacon, they were dismissed, and soon the entire body disappeared, leaving the train to pass on unmolested.

On the night of the 18th, Col. Otis met Col. Miles with his entire regiment, who had advanced to meet the train, being alarmed for its safety. Learning that Sitting Bull was in the vicinity, Col. Miles at once pursued him, and overtook him at Cedar creek. Here an unsatisfactory parley took place, Sitting Bull refusing peace except upon terms of his own making. The council broke up, the

Indians taking position immediately for a fight. An engagement followed, the Indians being driven from the field, and pursued forty-two miles to the south side of the Yellowstone. In their retreat they abandoned tons of dried meat, quantities of lodge poles, camp equipage and broken-down cavalry horses. Five dead warriors were left on the field, besides those they were seen to carry away. The force of Col. Miles numbered 398 rifles, against opponents estimated at over 1,000. On October 27th over four hundred lodges, numbering about 2,000 men, women and children, surrendered to Col. Miles, and Sitting Bull, with his own small band, escaped northward. He was vigorously pursued; but the trail was obliterated by the snow, and the troops returned to the cantonment. Again, in December, a portion of the command, under Lieut. Baldwin, left their quarters in search of Sitting Bull, who was found and driven south of the Missouri, retreating to the Bad Lands. Less than two weeks afterward the same command surprised Sitting Bull on the Redwater, capturing the camp and its contents, the Indians escaping with little besides what they had upon their persons, and scattering southward across the Yellowstone. Meanwhile, Col. Miles, with his main command, numbering 436 officers and men, had moved against the Sioux and Cheyennes under Crazy Horse, in the valley of the Tongue river; and, after repeated engagements, lasting from the 1st of January to the 8th of the same month, over fields covered with ice and snow to the depth of from one to three feet, completely vanquished the hostiles, and required them to surrender at the agencies. After the surrender of Crazy Horse, the band of Sitting Bull, in order to escape further pursuit, retreated beyond the northern boundary, and took refuge upon British soil, where this troublesome Indian remained until the spring of 1883, at which time he returned to the United States and was assigned to the Standing Rock Indian agency in Dakota. In May, 1877, Col. Miles led an expedition against a band of renegade Indians, under Lame Deer, that had broken away from those who had surrendered at Tongue river. This band was surprised near the Rosebud; and while negotiations for a surrender were in progress, the Indians, either meditating or fearing treachery, began firing, and ended the parley. The fight was resumed, and the Indians were driven eight miles, fourteen having been killed, including the chiefs Lame Deer and Iron Star, and 450 horses and mules, and the entire camp equipage fell into the hands of the troops. This band was afterward pursued so hotly that it eventually surrendered at the Red Cloud and Spotted Tail agencies.

On the 18th of September, 1877, Col. Miles, having learned that the hostile Nez Percés, from Idaho, under Chief Joseph, pursued by Gens. Howard and Sturgis, were likely to reach the frontier before they could be overtaken, started out from his cantonment to intercept them. By a series of rapid marches on the flank of the hostiles, after traversing a distance of 267 miles, Col. Miles came up with the Nez Percé camp on the morning of September 30th at the Bear Paw mountains, and compelled its surrender after a desperate resistance, with severe losses on both sides.

The troops under the command of Col. Miles, in their operations during the years 1876 and 1877, marched no less than 4,000 miles, captured 1,600 horses, ponies and mules, destroyed a large amount of camp equipage belonging to the hostiles, caused the surrender of numerous bands, and cleared the country of upward of seven thousand Indians. By this series of brilliant successes not less than

Current Ferry over the Yellowstone

400 miles of the Yellowstone valley were opened to settlement.

Current Ferries.—On the Yellowstone river, as well as on many other Western streams, a method of ferrying is in vogue which presents some peculiarities to Eastern eyes. The swift current is used as a motor for swinging a flat-bottomed ferryboat over the river. An elevated wire cable is stretched from shore to shore. Pulleys, attached by stout ropes to either end of the boat, are geared to the cable. The craft is shoved off from the brink at an angle oblique to the current, and starts languidly, the pulleys moving spasmodically at first. Presently the full force of the tide is felt, and the pulleys spin along the cable, carrying the boat across at fine speed. Then reaching the slacker water near the opposite shore, the pulleys resume the jerky progress on their cable track, and the boat grates upon the beach or puts her broad nose gently upon the strand precisely where it is wanted. The steering is done by means of wheel, or rather, windlass, used to tighten or slacken the pulley ropes, and so get the proper angle of resistance to the current. These ferryboats scorn any suggestion of an ordinary rudder in the water. They are guided by the guy-ropes only. The ferry-men usually charge a dollar toll upon each horse and each wagon, which seems good pay for little labor. They lament, however, that the good old times are gone when five dollars was the ordinary tax for this service.

Fort Keogh (747 miles from St. Paul) is situated a mile and a half west of the Tongue river, and two miles from Miles City, in a beautiful and fertile portion of the Yellowstone valley. The fort was built in 1877 by Gen. N. A. Miles, and is the most important post in the Northwest, having a large garrison of infantry and cavalry, the numbers varying with the demands of other military stations on the frontier. Fort Keogh consists of a number of commodious barracks, hospital, school, chapels and other buildings, besides sixteen attractive cottage residences for officers and their families. The fort draws its supply of water from the Yellowstone, and feeds a pretty fountain in the square, about which the residences are arranged.

Rosebud (777 miles from St. Paul; population, 150) is situated at the mouth of the Rosebud river. The extensive valley of this stream is admirably adapted to cattle-raising and its plains are dotted with settlements.

Forsythe (790 miles from St. Paul; population 500).— The place is named in honor of Gen. James W. Forsythe, who was the first officer to land by steamer at the present site of the town, and for a long time it was known as Forsythe's landing. It is situated in a delightful valley immediately on the banks of the Yellowstone river, and is surrounded by trees and immense bluffs rising abruptly on the south and west. Forsythe is the end of a freight train division, and the supply point for the settlers of the Rosebud bottom, on the south side, and the Big and Little Porcupine rivers on the north side of the Yellowstone.

Big Horn (832 miles from St. Paul, at the mouth of the Big Horn river) is the diverging point for a country well adapted to stock-raising. The valley of the Big Horn is fertile, and its enclosing hills are covered with excellent grazing. The railroad crosses the turbulent waters of the Big Horn river about two miles from the mouth of that stream, by a bridge 600 feet in length. Passing over the narrow intervening valley, it presently penetrates the bluffs which hem in the Yellowstone river, by means of a tunnel 1,100 feet long, and emerges into the comparatively small Yellowstone valley beyond.

Big Horn River, Bridge and Tunnel.

Custer (838 miles from St. Paul).—The station is on the Crow Indian reservation; the town is on the opposite side of the Yellowstone, and is called Junction City. It has a population of about 200. Custer is the station for Fort Custer, thirty miles distant, one of the largest military posts in the West, and situated near the scene of the Custer massacre. The large buildings at the station were erected by the Quartermaster's department for storing army supplies. A daily stage runs from the station to the fort.

Pompey's Pillar (863 miles from St. Paul) is a mass of yellow sandstone, rising abruptly to a height of 400 feet, its base covering nearly an acre of ground. About half way up on the north side is an inscription, of which the following is a miniature *fac-simile*

W^m. Clark
July 25th, 1806

carved deeply in the rock by the explorer himself on his return journey across the continent. This inscription covers a space three feet long and eighteen inches high, and is surrounded by a border. It appears that Captain Clark and his party were coming down the Yellowstone river in a boat, when they were overtaken by a storm which suddenly burst upon them. After it had cleared, they landed to examine a very remarkable rock, situated in an extensive bottom on the right, a short distance from the shore. "This rock," wrote the explorer, "is nearly 200 paces in circumference, and about 200 feet high, accessible from the southeast only, the other sides consisting of perpendicular cliffs of a light-colored, gritty stone. The soil on the summit is five or six feet deep, of a good quality, and covered with a short grass. The Indians have carved the figures of animals and other objects on the sides of the rock. From this height the eye ranges over a wide extent of variegated country. On the southwest are the Rocky mountains, covered with snow. There is a low mountain about fifty miles distant, in a northwest direction, and at the distance of thirty-five miles the southern extremity of what are called the Little Wolf mountains. The low grounds of the river extend nearly six miles to the southward, when they rise into plains reaching to the mountains, and are watered by a large creek, while at some distance below, a range of highlands covered with pine, stretches on both sides of the river in a direction north and south. The north side of the river for some distance is surrounded by jutty, romantic cliffs, succeeded by rugged hills, beyond which the plains are again open and extensive, and the whole country is enlivened by herds of buffalo, elk and wolves." After enjoying the prospect from this rock, to which Captain Clark gave the name of Pompey's Pillar, and carving his name and the date of his visit upon the stone, the explorer continued on his route. For the better protection of Captain Clark's name against vandals, who have already tried to cut their own insignificant designations within the border containing that of the heroic explorer, the railroad company has caused a screen to be placed over the relic for its protection.

The Crow Indian **Reservation**.—The entire southern shore of the Yellowstone river, from a point not far from Forsythe westward to the Big Boulder creek, and extending south to Wyoming, was set apart by Congress, in 1868, as a reservation for the Crow Indians. This is one of the most fertile and best watered areas in Montana, including the valleys of all the large streams which flow into the Yellowstone above the Rosebud river. The reservation originally stretched along the Yellowstone for 250 miles, and had an average width of about 75 miles, but it has twice been cut down at its western end by arrangement with the Indians and is now only about half its original size. Upon this territory live about 3,000 Indians. They own 40,000 ponies, and are a very rich tribe from every point of view. The Crows have long been friendly to the whites; but they are far inferior to their old enemies, the Sioux, in intelligence, handicraft and bravery. Of late they have made some small beginnings in agriculture upon irrigated lands. Most of Eastern Montana was originally claimed by the Crows, who at one time were a great and powerful nation. That the country was highly appreciated by these Indians is evidenced by the words of Arrapooish, a Crow chief, to the fur trader, Robert Campbell, as told in "Captain Bonneville's Adventures," by Washington Irving.

"The Crow country is a good country. The Great Spirit has put it exactly in the right place. When you are in it, you fare well; whenever you go out of it, whichever way you travel, you fare worse. If you go to the south, you have to wander over great barren plains; the water is warm and bad, and you meet the fever and ague. To the north it is cold; winters are long and bitter, with no grass; you cannot keep horses there, but must travel with dogs. On the Columbia they are poor and dirty, paddle about in canoes, and eat fish. Their teeth are worn out; they are always taking fish-bones out of their mouths. To the east they live well; but they drink the muddy waters of the Missouri. A Crow's dog would not drink such water. About the forks of the Missouri is a fine country—good water, good grass and plenty of buffalo. In summer it is almost as good as the Crow country; but in winter it is cold, the grass is gone, and there is no salt weed for the horses. The Crow country is exactly in the right place. It has snowy mountains and sunny plains, all kinds of climate, and good things for every season. When the summer heats scorch the prairies, you can draw up under the mountains, where the air is sweet and cool, the grass fresh, and the bright streams come tumbling out of the snowbanks. There you can hunt the elk, the deer and the antelope when their skins are fit for dressing; there you will find plenty of black bear and mountain sheep. In the autumn, when your horses are fat and strong from the mountain pastures, you can go down into the plains and hunt buffalo or trap beaver on the streams. And when winter comes on, you can take shelter in the woody bottoms along the rivers; there you will find buffalo meat for yourself, and cottonwood bark for your horses. Or you may winter in the Wind River valley, where there is salt weed in abundance. The Crow country is exactly in the right place. Everything good is to be found there."

The Legend of Skull Butte.—The high and rugged elevation across the river to the left of the railroad, just before reaching Billings, is named Skull Butte. Tradition says that about seventy years ago several hundred lodges of Indians, belonging to the powerful Crow nation, were encamped on the river bottom, when small-pox broke out,

and the ravages of the disease were so fearful that in a
short time the tribe was decimated. To appease the anger
of the Great Spirit it was determined by the chief medicine
man that forty young warriors should offer themselves as
a sacrifice. Volunteers for this purpose were called for,
and soon the allotted number of braves, who had recently
passed through the ordeal of the "sun dance," and assumed
the status of warriors, presented themselves. With much
ceremony the preparation for the sacrifice was conducted,
and, after all the rites had been performed, the heroic
band mounted their ponies, forded the river, ascended the
steep heights opposite, and made themselves ready for their
fate. It was determined that they and their ponies should
be blindfolded, and, rushing at full speed to the steep edge
of the cliff, should plunge to the rocky strand hundreds of
feet below. The word was given, and the forty braves,
with tremendous shouts, urged their steeds to the brink of
the cliff, and all went down to their destruction. For years
afterwards, bleaching skulls and bones of men and horses
were found around the base of Skull Butte.

The railroad crosses to the north side of the Yellowstone upon a substantial truss bridge, near the old settlement of Coulson, at the foot of Skull Butte.

Billings (892 miles from St. Paul; population, 2,500) is
named in honor of the late Hon. Frederick Billings, once
president of the Northern Pacific Railroad company. It is
situated at the foot of Clark's Fork bottom, on a beautiful
plain, sloping down to the Yellowstone river, in the heart
of a fertile and picturesque valley, and is the county seat
of the new county of Yellowstone. The town was founded
in the spring of 1882. Among the noticeable buildings are
the handsome brick church edifice, the gift of Mrs. Billings;
a large bank building, constructed in part of stone quar-

ried in the neighboring cliffs, and a number of substantial brick business blocks. This is the terminus of the Yellowstone division, and the beginning of the Montana division, of the railroad. The company has built a substantial round-house, shops, etc., for the purpose of a division terminus. The Clark's Fork Bottom ditch, thirty-nine miles long, terminates at Billings, and is the longest of six canals which irrigate in the valley above the town, and have converted what was practically a desert in 1882, into a beautiful farming region. Billings is a supply and trading post for a large extent of farming and grazing country within a radius of over 100 miles. It also receives the trade of the Stinking Water district, Wyoming Territory, a large and prosperous tract of country. The town possesses extensive cattle yards, and is one of the principal cattle-shipping points in Montana, great numbers of cattle being driven here for shipment from the Musselshell and Judith ranges. The Yellowstone river affords a fine water power. Large shipments of wool are made from here, and a good wool market is established.

Montana Stock and Sheep Raising.—Abundance of nutritious grasses, mildness of climate and markets easy of access, are a combination of advantages which render Montana famous as a cattle-raising region. Montana steers command the highest prices in the Chicago cattle mart, and the Northern Pacific railroad, with over 700 miles of track within the Territory, affords ready transportation from the grazing fields to the East. All the better varieties of grass do as well in Montana as elsewhere; but the most valuable of the native grasses is the bunch grass. This grows most luxuriantly upon the high, rolling plains, of which a large part of the surface of the Territory consists. It begins to renew itself in the early spring, before the

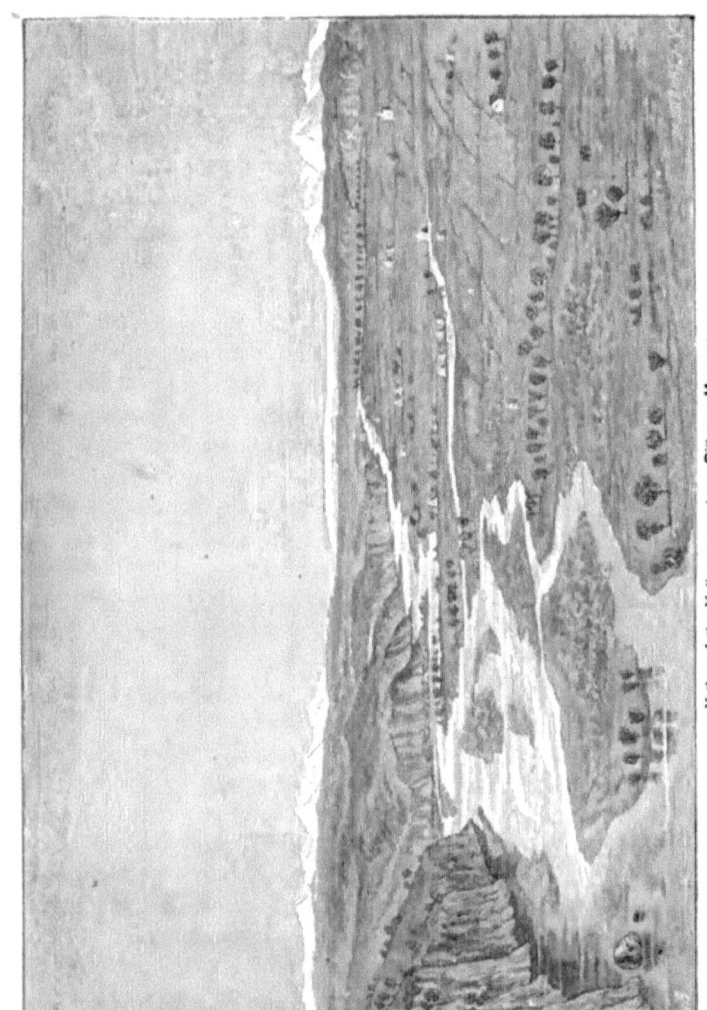

Valley of the Yellowstone above Billings, Montana.

ground is yet free from frost, rapidly attains its growth, is early cured, and stands as hay through the remainder of the year until the succeeding spring. Throughout the winter months it perfectly retains its sweet and nutritious qualities. The manner of its growth is similar to that of the short, curly and quickly cured buffalo grass of the plains. It stands in detached clusters or bunches, between which are visible interstices of bare ground. Its clusters, however, are finer, denser, of much taller growth, and cover the ground more closely and compactly than the tufts of buffalo grass. A single acre of bunch grass is fully equal to three acres of average buffalo grass in the quantity it furnishes of actual sustenance for cattle. It is, moreover, a stronger nutriment than ordinary plains vegetation, being unexcelled by the best cultivated grasses, timothy hay or clover.

The railroad, except where the main line crosses the mountain ranges, follows a system of valleys unsurpassed in their broad, beautiful and fertile surfaces, and extending across the Territory from east to west. These valleys are free to all for pasturage purposes. Over these great natural ranges the herds roam at will, being separated, or "rounded up" by their owners only twice a year—in the spring to brand the calves, and in the fall to choose the fat steers for market. The principal cattle ranges of the Territory, aside from the great valley of the Yellowstone, are on the headwaters of the Little Missouri, in the southeast; the valleys of the Powder, the Tongue, the Rosebud, the Big Horn (still in possession of the Crow tribe of Indians), and the Clark's Fork, which meet the Yellowstone region from the south; the great valley of the Sun river, the broad basin of the Judith, the magnificent valley of the Musselshell, all situated northward of the Yellowstone and intermediate between the Bull, Belt, Big Snowy and Little Rocky ranges; the valleys of the East and West Gallatin, Madison and Jefferson rivers, adjacent to the eastern bases of the Rocky mountains; and the intramontane country of the Clark's Fork of the Columbia, westward.

The customary way of managing a band of cattle in Montana is simply to brand them and turn them out upon the prairie. Under this careless management some steers are lost, which stray away or are stolen. A more careful system is to employ herders, one man for every 1,500 or 2,000 head of cattle, whose duty it is to ride about the outskirts of the range, follow any trails leading away, and drive the cattle back, seeking through neighboring herds, if there are any, for cattle that may have mistaken their companionship. At the spring round up a few extra men have to be employed for several weeks. No human being dare go among the cattle on foot. If he did he would be gored or trampled to death at once. The animals are only accustomed to horsemen, of whom they are in wholesome terror; but the sight of a person on foot instantly causes a rush toward the strange appearance, and death is certain to him who fails to find a place of refuge. In starting a new herd, cows, bulls and yearlings are bought; but calves under one year old running with the herd are not counted.

The average cost of raising a steer, not counting interest or capital invested, is from sixty cents to one dollar a year, so that a four-year-old steer raised from a calf and ready for market costs about $4. A herd consisting of yearlings, cows and bulls, will have no steers ready for the market in less than two or three years. Taking into account the loss of interest on capital invested before returns are received, besides all expenses and ordinary losses, the average profit of stock-raising in Montana during the last few years, has been at least thirty per cent. per annum. Some well-informed cattlemen estimate it at from thirty to forty per cent. A flock of sheep containing 1,000 head and upward, in good condition and free from disease, are procurable in Western Montana for from $2 to $3 per head. They must be herded summer and winter in separate flocks of not more than 2,000 or 3,000 each, must be corraled every night, and guarded against the depredations of dogs and wild animals. Hay must be provided to feed them while the ground is covered with snow, and sheds must be erected to prevent them from severe storms. They must, however, be raised by themselves. Cattle and sheep do not live together on the same range. The latter not only eat down the grass so closely that nothing is left for the cattle, but they also leave an odor that is very offensive to the others for at least two seasons afterward. But, notwithstanding that the cost of managing sheep is greater than that of handling cattle, the returns from sheep-raising are quicker and larger. While a herd of young cattle begin to yield an income only at the expiration of three years, sheep yield a crop of wool the first summer after they are driven upon a range, and the increase of the band is much greater than that of cattle, being from seventy-five to 100 per cent. each year. The wool is of good quality, free from burs, and brings a good price on the ranch, agents of Eastern houses being always on hand eager to buy it. The profits of sheep-raising are generally estimated at a higher figure than those of cattle-raising. The lowest calculation is based upon a net profit of from twenty-five to thirty-five per cent. on the whole investment, although occasionally larger returns reward the fortunate stockman.

There are few large bands of horses in Montana; but breeding these animals is beginning to receive attention. Breeders estimate that fifty brood mares and a draught stallion, costing in all $2,500, placed upon a stock ranch where the proprietor does his own herding, will in the course of five years be worth $10,000. Horses are more hardy than sheep or cattle, being better able to endure cold weather, and to "rustle," or paw through the snow that covers their pasturage. But they are so much more valuable than other species of stock that most owners prefer to have their bands either fenced in or carefully herded. The best horse farms are those in small valleys, ten or twelve miles long, on whose sides the foot-hills extend up to high mountains. By fencing across the ends of such a valley the horses are prevented from straying.

The Cow Boys.—As the train passes through the Yellowstone valley, it is no uncommon sight to see herds of sleek cattle contentedly grazing on the russet hills. Sometimes, also, droves of one or two thousand are noticed slowly advancing in a broad column from the direction of the distant mountains on their way to the railroad shipping stations. Such a drove is kept well in hand by a number of herders, picturesquely garbed in sombreros, gray shirts and leather breeches called "chapps," each man being armed with revolver, bowie knife and a rawhide whip, and well mounted. If the drove of cattle has made a march of several hundred miles from the range, it will be pioneered by a large band of ponies, carrying camp equipage and supplies, and serving as remounts for the cow boys. These latter are usually brawny, clear-eyed fellows, civil enough to answer questions in spite of the fact that every fibre of both man and horse seems strained to its utmost tension in keeping the wilder and straying members of the drove within the bounds of the horned column.

Grand Mountain Views.—In passing up the valley, westward of Billings, there is a prospect from the car windows which combines more striking features of beauty and grandeur than could hardly be found elsewhere nearer than Switzerland. Beyond the smiling valley and the winding, glistening river, to the westward and southward, rise white, gigantic masses of mountains. These snowy ranges are so lofty, and, in some conditions of the atmosphere, so ethereal, that the surprise of an Eastern tourist, who had never seen high mountains before, was quite natural. Standing on the platform of a Pullman car, his eye caught the white, gleaming bulwark on the western horizon. "Conductor, those clouds look very much like mountains," he said. "Clouds; what clouds?" replied the conductor, looking around the clear blue sky. "Out there; just ahead of us." "Those are not clouds; they are the mountains at the head of the valley." "Good gracious!" exclaimed the traveler, who had got his conception of mountains from the Alleghanies or the Adirondacks. "Those white things way up in the sky mountains! Well, well, this is worth coming all the way from New York to see."

Laurel (908 miles from St. Paul, 13 miles west of Billings) is the junction point of the Rocky Fork and Cooke City railroad, which runs to the important coal mining town of Red Lodge, 44 miles distant at the foot of the mountains seen on the southern horizon.

Park City (914 miles west of St. Paul; population, 250), at the head of the Clark's Fork bottom, is the centre of a large tract of agricultural land, the very last worthy of mention before the rough approaches to the Rocky mountains are entered. Citadel Butte, three miles northeast of the town, commands from its summit, 400 feet above the plains, a fine view of the snowy peaks to the westward.

Trout Fishing on the Big Boulder.

Piscatorial.—The Yellowstone river, beyond its confluence with the Big Horn, flows with a strong current through a valley of varying breadth, and is fed by many beautiful mountain streams. Here trout are in abundance and give excellent sport.

Stillwater (932 miles from St. Paul).—This is an old trading post for Indians and hunters. The old Crow Indian Agency buildings are situated about twelve miles south of Stillwater. The agency has recently been removed to the Little Big Horn river, near Fort Custer. At this point the railroad crosses to the south side of the Yellowstone river, the bridge being known as the second crossing.

Big Timber (973 miles from St. Paul; population, 700). —This town is located near the mouth of Big Boulder creek, which flows into the Yellowstone from the south, and facing the mouth of Big Timber creek, which enters the river from the north. An extensive grazing country in the valleys of the Big Boulder, the Yellowstone and the Big Timber, is tributary to this point, and the town is one of the most important wool shipping stations in Montana. It is also the supply point for a gold mining district lying on the flanks of the Snow mountains at the head of Boulder creek.

Springdale (988 miles from St. Paul) is the station for Hunter's Hot Springs, about two miles distant across the Yellowstone.

Hunters' Springs.—These celebrated hot springs are situated eighteen miles east of Livingston, at the foot of the Crazy mountains, on the north bank of the Yellowstone, one mile and three-quarters from the stream. They were noted for their wonderful healing virtues years before they became accessible by railroad, and, in fact, if the traditionary reports of the aborigines may be credited, have been famous among all the Northern tribes from time immemorial. All the Indians in friendly relations with the Crows—within whose country the springs were situated until their reservation lines were fixed by the Government

—had for generations made pilgrimages to this natural sanitarium with their invalids, pitching their tepees around the fountains for the relief of their sick, while their sorebacked ponies were healed by washing them in the healing waters below. Of course, the curative properties of the springs were the last hope for those at a great distance, whose afflictions had baffled the skill of their ablest "medicine men." No better proof than this of the healing properties of the water could be afforded, as the savage tribes acquire all their knowledge of the treatment of diseases from the experience of ages handed down from father to son. But there is abundant testimony, also, on the part of numbers of white men who have been restored to health by drinking and bathing in the water of these springs, that there was no superstition in the red man's faith in their remarkable curative powers. They are named Hunter's Springs in recognition of the fact that Dr. H. A. Hunter was the first white man to visit them and discover their medicinal qualities. The doctor being in advance of the train with which he was traveling, and a mile north of its direct course—his object in making the detour being to capture an antelope or deer for dinner—was attracted to the springs by the cluster of Indian tepees which had been pitched around them. Eight or ten different tribes were represented in the concourse. He boldly rode into the promiscuous camp, and his friendly salutations were responded to in a spirit of equal friendliness. Being a physician, he perceived, by the bright iron-stains upon the rocks, the strong sulphur fumes of the ascending vapors, and the white soda and magnesia coating of the vegetation growing out of the sedimentary deposits, the medicinal value of the waters. He reached the spot in the early part of July, 1864, his train being one of the first that entered the then newly discovered gold mines of Montana by way of the Big Horn valley. Whoever may visit the now famous springs, and feast his eyes upon the beauties of the surrounding scenery, will not wonder that Dr. Hunter at once relinquished his bright hopes of winning fortune in the gold mines, and resolved, that, if any white man during his lifetime should become possessed of these healing fountains, he himself should be that man. The clay all around the springs is a blue, adhesive, argillaceous formation, thickly studded with pyritic iron, some of the cubes shining with a gold-like luster; and in close proximity to the hot water fountains there are copious springs, from which flow streams of pure water—as cold in the hottest weather as ordinary ice water.

Hunter's Springs are from 3,000 to 4,000 feet above the sea-level, and from 50 to 100 above the Yellowstone river. Their temperature ranges from 148° to 168° Fahrenheit, and they discharge at least 2,000 gallons a minute—sufficient to accommodate all visitors, without the necessity of pumping. The water, hot or cold, is palatable, many who had used it while under treatment being regularly supplied with it by express, ordering it by the cask. The surrounding geological formations indicate that the springs have been flowing for many centuries. A chemical analysis shows sulphur to be the predominating constituent; but the water also contains magnesia, arsenic, iodine and lime.

The soil near Hunter's Springs is highly productice, under irrigation, being enriched with gypsum and other strong mineral fertilizers. Everything is produced in the gardens of this section that is cultivated in the States of Ohio, Indiana and Illinois. It is one of the best grazing localities in the Yellowstone valley, the whole face of the country being heavily grassed.

A Fine Country for Sportsmen.—Back in the bluffs, within easy walking distance of Hunter's Springs, there are still many antelope; wild hares, ducks, geese and other

small game abound in the vicinity. Deer are occasionally "jumped up" in the groves in the Yellowstone, near the springs; and it is seldom that the sportsman walks far along its banks without having the opportunity to wing a goose or duck. Elk are numerous in the mountains a few miles out. Few rivers are more thronged with trout than the Yellowstone. The angler must be unskillful indeed who fails to capture a handsome "string" in a couple of hours' fishing. The largest trout will weigh fully three pounds. Good coal has been found within two miles of Hunter's Springs, but the adjacent country has been only superficially prospected for minerals. Springdale station is about three miles from this place, and there is telephonic communication between the two points. Mails arrive and depart daily. Hacks are at the station on the arrival of every train to take tourists and invalids to the springs. There are distinct bath houses for the well and the sick, for male and female, and some of the tubs or tanks are large and deep enough for plunging and swimming. Visitors who prefer vapor baths are also accommodated; the medicated vapors coming up freshly from the steaming waters, are regulated to any degree of temperature by cold-air jets.

Livingston (1,007 miles from St. Paul; population, 2,000).—This place is an important passenger division and branch railroad terminus. It was founded in 1882. Here the main line makes its third and last crossing of the Yellowstone river, leaving the valley, along which it has run a distance of 340 miles westward from Glendive, and passing through the Bozeman tunnel, in the Belt range of mountains, to the Gallatin valley beyond. The river at this point makes an abrupt turn, flowing from its sources in the mountains far to the southward, through the world renowned region of the Yellowstone National Park. Three miles from Livingston the high mountains of the Yellowstone or Snow range open their portals just wide enough to allow the river an outlet, and through the cañon thus cut by the stream the branch railroad to the Yellowstone

Gate of the Mountains, near Livingston.

National Park is laid. Livingston is situated on a broad, sloping plateau on the left bank of the Yellowstone river, directly at the foot of the Belt range. Large engine houses, machine and repairing shops, and other buildings for the use of the railroad are situated here, on a scale only second in magnitude to those at Brainerd. Veins of fine bituminous coal have been opened eight miles distant, from which coke is made for the smelters at Helena and Butte, and ledges of good limestone are in the immediate neighborhood. The Clark's Fork silver mines lie directly south, and the surrounding hills are occupied by cattle ranches. There is also much valuable mining territory on the Yellowstone river between Livingston and the northern boundary of the National Park. Travel to the Yellowstone National Park passes through Livingston, and a large business is done in furnishing supplies to tourists. Livingston is one of the most convenient places from which to leave for the Crazy mountains and the country adjoining them, which are the favorite breeding grounds of the elk. There is fine trout fishing in the vicinity of the town. The lofty mountain peak in prominent view south of the town is called Old Baldy, and is about 9,000 feet high.

Yellowstone National Park.—It does not come within the plan of this volume to describe the remarkable features of the Yellowstone National Park. It is believed that the convenience of the tourist has been best regarded by setting forth in detail the chief attractions of the park in a separate book.

Daily trains leave Livingston for Cannabar, on the northern boundary of the park, fifty-one miles distant. From Cannabar, tourists are taken in coaches to the Mammoth Hot Springs, which is the distributing point for travel through the park.

USEFUL INFORMATION FOR YELLOWSTONE NATIONAL PARK TOURISTS. Season June 15th to September 15th. Stop-overs on railroad and sleeping-car tickets of all classes are given at Livingston, Montana, June 15th to September 15th, to enable our patrons to visit Yellowstone Park, provided the limit of the original transportation ticket allows sufficient time.

The following excursion rates to the Yellowstone National Park were in effect during the season of 1899. It is probable that practically the same rates will continue during succeeding years. Our readers should therefore consider that figures quoted here are only approximate and should make inquiry of ticket agents before starting so as to get the exact rates.

$47.50 Round-Trip Ticket—St. Paul, Minneapolis, Duluth or the Superiors to Mammoth Hot Springs and return. This ticket covers rail and stage transportation from above named points to Mammoth Hot Springs; returning via Northern Pacific to any one of above named points, or via Billings and the Burlington & Missouri River R. R. to Omaha, Council Bluffs, St. Joseph, Atchison or Kansas City.

$5.00 and $49.50 Yellowstone Park Tickets, on sale at St. Paul, Minneapolis, Duluth, Ashland and Livingston. The $5.00 ticket covers railroad fare, Livingston to Cinnabar and return, and stage fare, Cinnabar to Mammoth Hot Springs and return. The $49.50 ticket includes railroad and stage fares from Livingston to Mammoth Hot Springs, Lower, Fountain and Upper Geyser Basins, Yellowstone Lake, Grand Canyon and Falls of the Yellowstone, and return to Livingston, and five and one-half days' board and lodging in the Yelowstone Park hotels.

$92.00 from St. Paul, Minneapolis or Duluth for tour of Park including all expenses south of Cinnabar. By purchasing one of the $47.50 tickets to Mammoth Hot Springs and return and one of the $44.50 tickets, which are on sale at Mammoth Hot Springs, for the tour of the Park, a rate of $92.00 can be secured covering all rail and stage fares, also accommodations in the hotels of the Yellowstone Park Association for five and one-half (5½) days.

$105.00 Round-Trip Ticket—St. Paul, Minneapolis, Duluth or the Superiors through the Park, returning via Monida, to the Missouri River Terminals, including hotel accommodations in the Park. This ticket covers rail transportation from St. Paul, Minneapolis, Duluth or the Superiors to Cinnabar, stage transportation Cinnabar to Mammoth Hot Springs, Lower Fountain and Upper Geyser Basins, Yellowstone Lake, Grand Canyon, Falls of the Yellowstone and Monida, six and one-quarter days' board and lodging between Cinnabar and Monida, and rail transportation from Monida via Oregon Short Line R. R. and Union Pacific to Missouri River Points, or via O. S. L. R. R., to Ogden, any line Ogden to Denver, thence via either the B. & M. R. R. R.; Union Pacific; A. T. & S. F. Ry., or Mo. Pac. Ry., to Missouri River terminals.

$85.00 Round-Trip Ticket—St. Paul, Minneapolis, Duluth or the Superiors through the Park, returning via Monida to Missouri River Terminals, excluding Hotel Accommodations. This ticket covers rail and stage transportation only, no meals or lodging being included therein; except in this regard covers the same tour as the $105.00 ticket. Limits, selling dates and other conditions, except as noted, are the same as covered by the $105.00 rate.

Over the Belt Range.—The Belt range runs parallel to the Main Divide of the Rocky mountains for about 150 miles and at an average distance from that divide of about forty miles. It is a bold and handsome range, wooded on its flanks with pine and lifting bare rocky ridges and peaks to an altitude of about 8,000 feet. The road begins to climb by a uniform grade of 116 feet to the mile soon after it leaves Livingston, and in an ascent of twelve miles reaches the west portal of the Bozeman tunnel, which is the highest point reached by the track between the Mississippi valley and the Pacific coast. The tunnel pierces the mountains a distance of 3,500 feet at an elevation of 5,572 feet above the ocean. The train runs down the western slope in the wild defile of Rock cañon, passing out into the broad, fertile valley of the West Gallatin at Elliston, near the military post of Fort Ellis, twenty-two miles from Livingston. The scenery in Rock cañon is remarkably grand and impressive. Enormous precipices of gray rock with castellated seams rise high above the dark forests which clothe the sides of the narrow ravine. The rocks have been worn by the action of the weather into many singular and fantastic shapes. At several places massive walls run up the mountain sides, so regular in their appearance that they seem to have been built by human hands.

Timberline, just west of the tunnel, is a shipping station for coal mines which furnish a good quality of bituminous coal, not as rich in carbon as Ohio or Indiana coal, but a good locomotive and domestic fuel.

Bozeman (1,032 miles from St. Paul; population, 4,500), the county seat of Gallatin county, is situated near the end of the Gallatin valley, at its narrowest point. North of the city the mountains are about three miles distant; but the range suddenly diverges in the same direction, and afterward the valley becomes twenty miles in width. Bozeman is the oldest established town on the line of the Northern Pacific railroad in Montana, the townsite hav-

---

Tourists are recommended to obtain a "Manual," for sale on the **trains**, descriptive of the Yellowstone National Park, profusely illustrated.

ing been laid out in July, 1864. In August of that year a well-known frontiersman, John Bozeman, reached the place in charge of a party of emigrants, who were so impressed with the beauty and fertile soil of the valley that they determined to go no further. The town was named in honor of this pioneer, who was murdered three years afterward by Indians in the Yellowstone valley. In 1865 a mill was put in operation, and two years afterward Fort Ellis, situated two and a half miles east of the town, was established, and garrisoned by three companies of the United States troops. The post was abandoned in 1887. The gradual increase of population in the Gallatin valley was soon evident, settlers coming in from the surrounding country, and making Bozeman their trading centre. The city presents a very attractive appearance with its many substantial brick structures, among which are business blocks, a four-story hotel, churches, graded schools, and a court-house, while on every side appear handsome residences and neat cottages.

Bozeman is the best stopping place for the traveler who wishes to see what can be done in Montana in irrigation on small farms. Well cultivated farms, supplied with water from mountain streams, extend up and down the valley for thirty miles. Here wheat ordinarily yields from 35 to 50 bushels to the acre, and oats from 60 to 100 bushels. There is never a failure of crops. The farmers are as a rule in independent circumstances. The scenery surrounding Bozeman is very picturesque. Thermal Springs, said to contain medicinal properties, are within an hour's drive. Matthews' Hot Springs, with a hotel and bath house, are seven miles distant. Mystic Lake, twelve miles from the town, covers about eighty acres, and is a beautiful sheet of water. On the mountains around Mystic Lake, and in the vicinity of Bozeman, are forests of stately pines. Bozeman has remarkable advantages as a summer resort. The air is cool and invigorating. The mercury seldom goes up as high as 85°, and the nights are always cool. There are numerous pleasant drives in the vicinity, and interesting excursions are made to the wild cañons of the Bridger and Gallatin mountains.

The Montana Agricultural College and Experiment Station is located at Bozeman.

Mountain and Valley Views.—After leaving Bozeman, the railroad traverses the broad, level valleys watered by the East and West Gallatin rivers. Farming is carried on by irrigation, the gentle slope of the valley being very favorable for the construction and management of ditches. The mountains on the east are the Belts, and the two high peaks on the near horizon are Mount Bridgeman and Mount Blackmore. On the south are the peaks of Gallatin, and on the west the Main Divide of the Rockies bounds the view.

A Big Barley Farm.—Manhattan (1,051 miles from St. Paul), is in the center of the largest barley farm in the world. The farm, which is seven miles long and five miles wide, is the property of a company of New York City brewers and other capitalists, who bought part of the land from the Northern Pacific company and the rest from settlers, and who have brought the greater part of it under ditches and are raising barley for making malt. This company owns the 150,000-bushel elevator and the large malt house at the station, and nearly all the other buildings in the villages. The farming operations are carried on scientifically, and have produced favorable financial results. Some of the plowing is done by steam, the gang-plow being hauled across the fields by a traction engine. In the early summer the growing barley, of different shades of green, gives a beautiful appearance to the landscape.

Logan (1,051 miles from St. Paul) is the diverging point for the line, by way of Butte, which rejoins the main line at Garrison, 125 miles distant. This is called the Northern Pacific and Montana branch, and is described under that head. Travelers holding through tickets have their choice of the two routes, via Helena or via Butte, the trains over the two lines joining and consolidating at Garrison. Each line has special scenic beauties and special interests in towns and mining industries.

The Three Forks of the Missouri.—Gallatin is the station for old Gallatin City, at the three forks of the Missouri, and for the new town of Three Forks. Gallatin City was formerly a commercial town of some importance, but is now merely a decayed hamlet of half a dozen buildings. Within a few hundred yards of this place there is a rocky elevation from which may be seen the meeting of the waters which form the Missouri river. The Madison and Jefferson unite about half a mile south of this promontory, and are joined by the Gallatin a short distance north of the rock. When Lewis and Clarke ascended the Missouri on their exploring expedition in 1806 they were unable to determine which of the three streams should be regarded as the Missouri, and therefore concluded to give a separate name to each. Later explorations showed that the Jefferson was in reality the main river, being considerably longer than either of the other two streams, and carrying a larger volume of water. Lewis and Clarke, therefore, robbed the Missouri of over 300 miles of its length, by confining its name to its course below the junction of the three streams which form it.

After leaving Gallatin the railroad enters a savage gorge

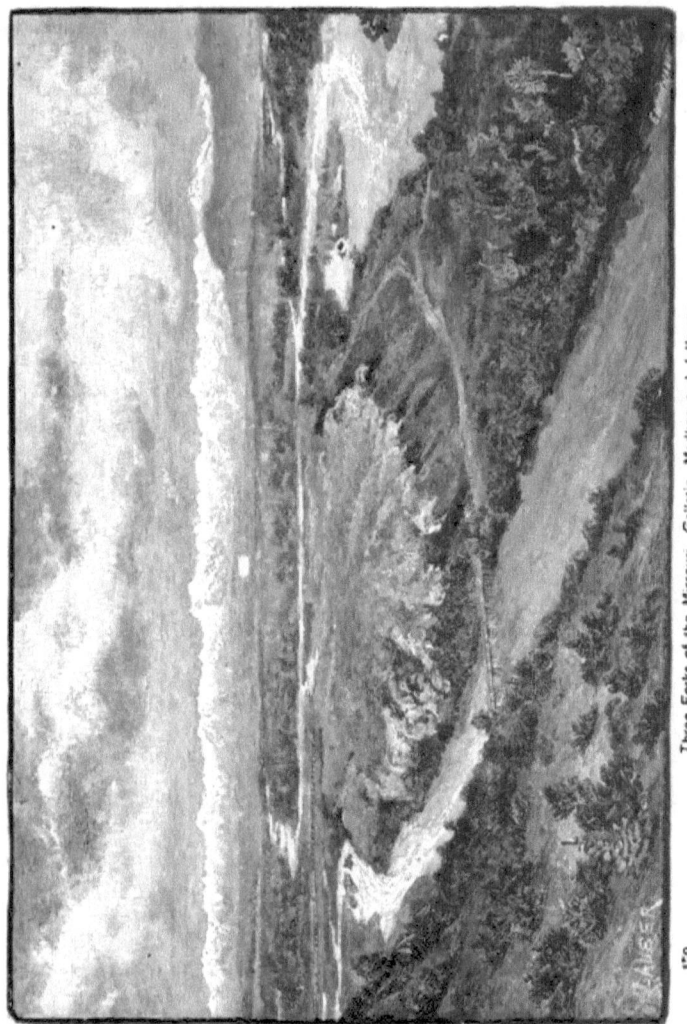

Three Forks of the Missouri—Gallatin, Madison and Jefferson

of weather-worn rocks showing stains of iron and copper, and rising to the height of several hundred feet above the track. On one side of the road runs the swift, clear current of the Missouri, and on the other tower enormous precipices. The scenery in this cañon is among the finest on the whole line of the road.

Toston (1,086 from St. Paul, population 200) is a town at the head of what is known as the Missouri valley. This name is locally applied to a stretch of rich bottom lands, about thirty miles long, and from three to five in width. There is a smelter at Toston which uses the ores found a few miles distant on the opposite of the Missouri river in combination with ores brought from the Cœur d'Alene mining district in Northern Idaho.

Townsend (1,097 miles from St. Paul) has a good situation near the centre of the Missouri valley, and is a place of considerable trade. The upper and middle portions of the valley are irrigated from small streams running out of the defiles in the Belt mountains, and the lower portion gets water from a ditch taken out of the Missouri. The town was established in 1883. There is a daily stage line at White Sulphur Springs, the county seat of Meagher county, forty miles distant, on the other side of the Belt mountains. White Sulphur Springs has a population of about 500, and is an important trading point for a large district of grazing country. The springs are renowned in Montana for their curative properties, and are much visited by invalids. Good hotel accommodations can be had. The Castle silver mines are also reached by stage from Townsend, a distance of sixty miles.

Gorges and Canyons.—Across the Missouri valley from Townsend, in a northeasterly direction, a series of deep gorges, or canyons, have been cut by the waters in the faces of the precipitous mountains. Crowning the summits of the first range skirting the valley is a gigantic ledge of lime rock. This ledge has been thrown up in places to a great height with almost vertical sides, which are partly smooth, partly seamed and gashed by ages of storms, and sometimes cut through from top to bottom by the streams, forming narrow gorges of fantastic shapes. Avalanche Canyon is of great note from its wild beauty and extensive and rich placer mines. This canyon received its name from the frequency of avalanches, or snow slides, which rush down its almost perpendicular sides in winter, sometimes completely filling the gorge. Hell Gate canyon, about two miles westward, while having a peculiarly suggestive name, amply merits the appellation. Perhaps in no other accessible spot in Montana is there as much rugged beauty in so small a space. The canyon forms the tortuous passage of a silvery stream through a series of gates cut in very high walls. These gates are so narrow that a man can span their width with extended arms. The walls are only a few feet in thickness, but of a surprising height. On each side of the main gorge are smooth fissures, called Devil's Slides, and every nook is filled with bright mosses and lichens.

Bedford (1,100 miles from St. Paul) is an old mining town, with a small hotel and a few business houses. Some placer mining is carried on in the neighboring gulch. In the early days of mining in Montana, there were two placer camps near Bedford, with the singular names of "Hog'em" and "Cheat'em."

Prickly Pear Junction (1,126 miles from St. Paul) is the point of divergence of the Helena & Jefferson County railroad, which runs to the important mining district of Wickes, on the eastern slope of the Rocky mountains, twenty miles distant, to Boulder; the county seat of Jefferson county, and the center of a productive silver-mining district, and also to Elkhorn, where there is one of the most productive quartz mines in the State. A large smelting plant is located at **Prickly Pear Junction** and is owned by Helena capitalists. Ores are brought by rail to these works from nearly all the mining districts of Central and Western Montana.

Helena (1,130 miles from St. Paul; population, 14,000). —Helena, the capital of Montana, is pleasantly situated at the eastern foot of the main chain of the Rocky mountains, in latitude 46° 30′ N., and longitude 112° 4′ west of Greenwich, on both sides of the famous **Last Chance Gulch**, from which at least ten millions of dollars' worth of nuggets and gold dust have been taken, and which still yields annually a considerable amount of the precious metal. So large was the influx of miners at this point in 1864, that the United States Government felt compelled to establish a postoffice for their accommodation. Until then the camp had been known as "Crab Town"; but a meeting was called for the purpose of selecting a better name, and the majority of those assembled decided upon christening it after Helen of Troy. It contains a handsome court house, built of Rocky mountain granite and sandstone, an auditorium for public gatherings, built by the city, a United States assay office, a college and a theater. It has electric street railways, water-works, large public school buildings, daily newspapers and many imposing structures used for banking and general business. There are a number of costly and handsome private residences. The leading hotels are the Helena, the Merchants and the Grand Central. The business center is about two miles

The Gates of the Rocky Mountains, Missouri River, near Helena, Montana.

from the railway station and is conveniently reached by electric cars. The traveler can get no adequate idea of the size or beauty of the city by what can be seen from the depot platform or the windows of the passing train. The Montana Central railroad, from Great Falls to Butte, runs through Helena, and the city is the diverging point of three branches of the Northern Pacific system, running to mining towns.

Helena is surrounded by mountains, rising one above the other until the more distant are lost among the clouds, forming a view of striking beauty and grandeur, which is visible from every part of the city. To the south and west these mountains recede in long, picturesque, timbered ridges, to the main range of the continental divide. The Missouri river is only twelve miles distant, and eighteen miles north of the city begins the famous canyon of the Missouri river, named by Lewis and Clark's expedition in 1805 "The Gates of the Rocky Mountains." Here the river has forced its way through a spur of the Belt mountains, forming cliffs, frequently vertical, from 500 to 1,500 feet high, which rise from the water's edge for a distance of twelve miles. A monumental column rising high above the general level of the walls of the canyon and plainly visible from Helena, is called the Bear's Tooth." Sapphires and precious garnets are mined on the gravel beaches along the Missouri just above the canyon.

The **Broadwater Hot Springs.**—About three miles from Helena and reached by two lines of electric railroad, is one of the finest natatoriums in the country, established by the liberality of the late Colonel Broadwater, a Helena millionaire. This immense oriental structure is 300 feet long by 100 feet wide. Comfortable dressing rooms surround the bath. The water flows over an artificial structure of rock work in two cascades, one of hot and one of cold water, which unite midway of the descent and form a single fall. The temperature of the hot water cascade varies from 110 to 140 degrees Fahrenheit. Around the Natatorium the grounds are prettily ornamented with fountains, flower beds, shrubbery and walks.

Across the Main Divide —About twenty-one miles from Helena the main range of the Rocky Mountains is crossed by the railroad at the Mullan Pass, so named after Lieut. John Mullan, U. S. A., who in 1867 built a wagon road from Fort Benton, Mont., to Fort Walla Walla, Wash., thus bringing these distant military posts into direct communication. Here there is a tunnel 3,850 feet in length, and 5,547 feet above the level of the ocean, lower by more than 2,500 feet than the highest elevation of the Union Pacific railroad, and 2,200 feet below the highest elevation on the line of the Central Pacific. The route from Helena to the Mullan Pass is through the charming valley of the Prickly Pear, across Ten-Mile creek, and up, past heavy growths of pine and spruce, and masses of broken boulders, the narrow basin of Seven-Mile creek, to the eastern portal of the tunnel. The scene from above reveals one of the most picturesque regions in Montana, in which mountain and valley, forest and stream, are conspicuous features. Describing this region, E. V. Smalley wrote:

"Approached from the east, the Rocky Mountains seem well to deserve their name. Gigantic cliffs and buttresses of granite appear to bar the way and to forbid the traveler's further progress. There are depressions in the range, however, where ravines run up the slopes, and torrents come leaping down, fed by melting snows. Over one of these depressions Lieut. John Mullan built a wagon road a score of years ago, to serve the needs of army transportation between the head of navigation at the Great Falls of the Missouri and the posts in Oregon. Mullan's wisdom in selecting the pass, which bears his name, was indorsed when the railroad engineers found it to be the most favorable on the Northern Pacific line. The road is carried up ravines and across the face of foot-hills to a steep wall, where it dives into the mountain side, runs under the crest of the divide through a tunnel three-quarters of a mile long, and comes out upon smiling green and flowery meadows to follow a clear trout stream down to a river whose waters seek the mighty Columbia. The contrast between the western and eastern sides of the Main Divide of the Rockies is remarkable. On the eastern slope the landscapes are magnificently savage and sombre ; on the western slope they have a pleasant pastoral beauty, and one might think himself in the hill country of western Pennsylvania, instead of high up on the side of the great water-shed of the continent. The forest tracts look like groves planted by a landscape gardener in some stately park, and the grassy slopes and valleys, covered with blue and yellow flowers, and traversed by swift, clear brooks, add to the pleasure-ground appearance of the country. What a glorious place this would be for summer camping, trout fishing, and shooting, is the thought of every traveler as he descends from the summit, with his hands full of flowers picked close to a snow-bank. Snow Shoe Mountain rises just in front, across a lovely, verdant valley. Powell's Peak, a massive white pyramid, cuts the clear sky with its sharp outlines on the further horizon, and a cool breeze blows straight from the Pacific Ocean."

Passing down the western slope the descent is made to the valley of the Little Blackfoot river. This valley is open and well grassed, with cottonwood on the stream and pine on the slopes of the hills. The river received its name from the Blackfeet Indians, who often passed down the valley in early days to make their raids upon the Flathead Indians. There is good ruffed grouse shooting in the valley, and also a great many blue grouse in the neighboring cañons. In October black-tailed deer are plentiful, and elk are also found in the mountains. Bear—black, grizzly and cinnamon—can be found.

The stations on the Little Blackfoot are Elliston and Avon, small towns which supply neighboring mines and ranches.

Garrison (miles from St. Paul; population, 200), in the valley of the Deer Lodge river, is the junction of the Montana Union railroad with the Northern Pacific. Garrison was named in honor of William Lloyd Garrison, the eminent leader of the anti-slavery movement in the days before the civil war. It derives its importance from the transfer of freights and other railroad business. The Montana Union railroad, owned jointly by the Northern and Union Pacific companies, runs up the Deer Lodge valley from Garrison to Deer Lodge, Anaconda and Butte.

Down the Hell Gate River.—After leaving Garrison, there are fine views of mountain scenery, especially on the left hand, where the snow-mantled peaks of Mount Powell appear.

Below the mouth of the Little Blackfoot, Deer Lodge river changes its name to Hell Gate river. The valley here rather abruptly narrows, its breadth for seven or eight miles scarcely exceeding a single mile, with mountains on the right hand and bold bluffs on the left; but it again becomes broader where the waters of Flint creek flow from the south and swell the volume of the river.

Gold Creek (1,190 miles from St. Paul) is the station for the old mining town of Pioneer, about three miles distant. On Gold creek the first discovery of gold within the present limits of Montana was made in 1862. At the mouth of the stream there are enormous bars of gravel and boulders produced by the hydraulic and sluice washings in the region above. There is still some placer mining done on this creek.

Near Gold Creek station the ends of the track of the Northern Pacific railroad, advancing from the east and the west, were joined in September, 1883. The event was made the occasion of a remarkable celebration, which was attended by many distinguished guests of the railroad company from England, Germany, and from the principal cities of the East, and also from the Pacific coast. The eastern guests arrived in four immense trains, and were joined by a fifth train loaded with guests from Portland and other towns on the Pacific coast. This opening excursion of the Northern Pacific was the most extensive and liberal affair of the kind known in railway annals. The first iron spike driven in the construction of the Northern Pacific railroad was used as the last spike, and was driven by Henry Villard, at that time president of the railroad company.

Drummond (1,202 miles from St. Paul; population 300) is the junction of the Drummond & Philipsburg railroad. Considerable sluice and hydraulic mining is done in the neighborhood, and the valley of Flint creek, which joines the river opposite the town, contains many well cultivated farms.

Through Hell Gate Canyon.—A short distance below Bearmouth the Hell Gate canyon is entered. This is, however, no narrow mountain pass, as its name would indicate, but, rather, a valley from two to three miles in width, extending a distance of forty miles to the junction of the Hell Gate river with the Big Blackfoot, after which it widens to unite with the valley of the Bitter Root, whereon Missoula stands. The scenery along the Hell Gate canyon is very fine often grand. Rock-ribbed mountains rise on either hand, their slopes black with noble specimens of yellow pine, and flecked in autumn with the bright gold of giant tamaracks. The stream itself is deep and swift, quite clear also, except where it receives the murky water of its many tributaries, which latter in summer are always coffee-colored from the labors of the gold washers in the mountains. Many islands covered with cottonwood and other deciduous growths, lie in the crooked channel, adding to the general picturesqueness. Two-thirds of the way down the canyon, Stony creek, a fine, bold mountain stream, enters from the southwest, after flowing eighty miles through the range between the Deer Lodge and Bitter Root valleys. The water teems with trout. The Big Blackfoot, Hell Gate's largest tributary, comes in from the east, with a valley eighty miles long and varying from half a mile to twelve miles in width, considered one of the finest grazing and agricultural sections in Montana. Many good quartz and galena leads have been discovered in the mountains, and the Wallace district, near Baker station, is especially promising.

There are several large saw-mills in the Hell Gate canyon, which obtain their logs from the canyon itself and from the neighboring mountains. The principal market for the lumber is in Butte, where it is in demand, not only for building purposes, but in large quantities for supports to roofs of the mines.

Bonner (1,248 miles from St. Paul; population, 150) is a saw-mill village near the crossing of the Big Blackfoot river. The mills at this place are the most important in Western Montana. Logs are floated down the Big Blackfoot river from the slopes of the main divide of the Rocky mountains.

Beaver Hill—A Legend.—In traveling between Deer Lodge and Missoula, twenty-eight miles from the latter place, at Kramer's Ranch, a remarkable ridge or tongue of land is seen stretching across the valley of the Hell Gate river from the east side, almost in the form of a beaver *couchant*. It is known as Beaver Hill, and it projects so near to the mountains on the west side of the valley as to nearly dam up the river, which is here compressed into a narrow, rocky channel. There is a legend connected with this hill, which is about as follows:

A great many years ago, before the country was inhabited by men, the valleys along the whole length of the river and its branches were occupied by vast numbers of beavers. There was a great king of all the beavers, named Skookum (which in Indian means "good"), who lived in a splendid winter palace up at the Big Warm Spring mound, whereon the State insane asylum is now situated. One day the king received word that his subjects down the river had refused to obey his authority, and were going to set up an independent government. In great haste he collected a large army of beavers, detachments joining him from every tributary on the way down. On arriving at the great plain now crossed by Beaver Hill, he halted his army, and demanded of the rebels that they pay their accustomed tribute and renew their allegiance. This they insultingly refused to do, saying they owned the river below to the sea, that it was larger and longer than that above; and, as they were more numerous, they would pay tribute to no one. The old king was able and wily, and immediately sent for every beaver under his jurisdiction. When all had arrived he held a council of war, and said, that, as he owned the sources of the great river, he would dam it at that point, and turn the channel across to the Missouri. This would bring the rebels to terms below, because they could not live without water. He so disposed his army that in one night they scooped out the great gulch that now comes in on the north side of Beaver Hill, and with the earth taken out the hill was formed in a night, and so completely dammed up the river that not a drop of water could get through. When the rebellious beavers below saw the water run by and the river bed dry up, they hastened to make peace, paid their tribute (internal revenue tax, perhaps) and renewed their former allegiance. So King Skookum had the west end of the dam removed, and ever since that time the river has run "unvexed to the sea." To commemorate the event, he had the earth piled up on the top of the hill to resemble a beaver in form, and it can be seen either up or down the river a long way. The Indians who first settled up the valley got this legend from the beavers, their cousins, more than a thousand years ago; for in those ancient times they could converse together, and did hold communication until some young and treacherous Indians made war on the beavers for their furs, when the beavers solemnly resolved never to converse with them again, and have steadfastly kept their word.

Missoula (1,255 miles from St. Paul; population 5,000) is the county seat of Missoula county and the junction of the Bitter Root Valley railroad and the De Smet and Cœur d'Alene railroad. It is beautifully situated at the western gateway of the Rocky mountains, on a broad pla-

Beaver Hill, Hell Gate Cañon, near Missoula, Montana.

teau on the north side of the Missoula river, near its junction with the Bitter Root and the Hell Gate, and commands a lovely view of the valley and the surrounding mountain ranges, that stretch away as far as the eye can see. This town used to be as isolated and remote a frontier post as could be found in the Northwest; but the railroad has converted it into a stirring place. It contains an opera house, well appointed hotels, railroad repair shops, handsome public school buildings, a female seminary, conducted by the Sisters of Charity, a hospital, also under the charge of the same sisterhood, and also a sanitarium of the Western division of the Northern Pacific railroad, conducted on the same plan as the sanitarium at Brainerd, Minn., which takes charge of sick and injured employes on the Eastern division of the road. It has many attractive and substantial business blocks and residences. There are also a flouring mill and saw-mills.

The fertile lands of the plain near by and the large and rich valley of the Bitter Root, already well settled, over eighty miles long, with an average width of about seven miles, besides other agricultural districts to the northward, all make a lively trade. The altitude of this region is about 3,000 feet. The climate is not as cold as in a similar latitude east of the Rocky mountains, and the soil produces readily a great variety of cereals, fruits and vegetables.

In clear weather a fine view of the Bitter Root range of mountains, including the highest summit of the range, Lo Lo peak, may be had from the train as it runs down the valley after leaving Missoula.

The country surrounding Missoula has been the scene of many fierce conflicts between the Indians. Before the whites inhabited the territory, the Blackfeet Indians ambushed Chief Coriacan, of the Flatheads, in a defile fourteen miles north of the city, with a portion of his tribe, and massacred nearly every man. A few years later the Flatheads avenged their chief's death by killing a like number of Blackfeet in the same defile, which now bears Coriacan's name.

Missoula county embraces the large and fertile valleys of the Missoula, the Bitter Root and the Jocko. The county is heavily timbered and is rich in mineral and grazing lands. It contains also many beautiful lakes, well stocked with fish and frequented by water fowl. Good trout fishing, as well as various other kinds, is obtained in the Missoula, the Bitter Root, Jocko, Lo-Lo, Flathead, Big Blackfoot and Pend d' Oreille rivers, and in numerous mountain creeks. The mountain goat is in abundance, and can be found in the vicinity. Fort Missoula, a garrison of the U. S. troops, is pleasantly situated about half an hour's drive from the town, in the Bitter Root valley.

To the Cœur d'Alene Mines.—Travelers who wish to go by the shortest route to the Cœur d'Alene mining towns should leave the main N. P. line at Missoula and take the De Smet and Cœur d'Alene branch, which crosses the Bitter Root range and runs to Mullan, Wallace and Wardner, Idaho, in the silver mining district. A description of this route will be found in the latter part of this volume.

The Coriacan Defile.—Leaving Missoula, the railroad passes westward across the northern edge of the plain, over a low and well-timbered divide, which separates the waters of the Missoula river (the continuation of the Hell Gate) from those which drain into the Flathead. Fourteen miles from Missoula the road enters the Coriacan defile, and crosses the Marent gulch by means of an iron bridge 866 feet in length and 226 feet in height. The Coriacan defile is surmounted by a grade of 116 feet to the mile, the whole length of the heavy grade being thirteen miles, ascending and descending. The track follows no valley, but proceeds along the faces of hills, which are covered with fir, pine and tamarack, down into the valley of the Jocko river, where the agency of the Flathead Indians is established.

Arlee (1,282 miles from St. Paul), named in honor of the chief of the Flatheads, is the station for the Flathead Indian agency. The agency buildings are in sight, about five miles distant, at the foot of the Mission mountains.

The Flathead Indian Reservation.—This reservation extends along the Jocko and Pend d'Oreille rivers a distance of sixty miles. It contains about 1,500,000 acres, which, if divided among the 1,200 Flathead, Pend d'Oreille and half-breed Indians who hold the tract, would give 5,000 acres to each family of four persons. A large part of the reservation consists of a mountainous area, with a growth of valuable timber; but there is also a fair quantity of fine grazing land, as well as many well-sheltered, arable valleys. E. V. Smalley visited the reservation in the summer of 1882, and gave the result of his observations in the *Century Magazine* for October of that year as follows:

"The Flathead agency is under the control of the Catholic church, which supports a Jesuit mission upon it, and has converted all of the inhabitants to at least a nominal adhesion to its faith. At the missions are excellent schools for girls and boys, a church, a convent, and a printing office which has turned out, among other works, a very creditable dictionary of the Kalispel or Flathead language. The agent, Major Ronan, has been in office over five years, and, with the aid of the Jesuit fathers, has been remarkably successful in educating the Indians up to the point of living in log houses, fencing fields, cultivating little patches of grain and potatoes, and keeping cattle and horses. The

Government supplies plows and wagons, and runs a sawmill, grist-mill, blacksmith shop and threshing machine for their free use. There is no regular issue of food or clothing; but the old and the sick receive blankets, sugar and flour. Probably nine-tenths of these Indians are self-sustaining. Some persist in leading a vagabond life, wandering about the country; but these manage to pick up a living by hunting, fishing and digging roots, and sell ponies enough to buy blankets, tobacco and powder. But even the best civilized, who own comfortable little houses, with plank doors and porcelain door-knobs, got from the Government, like to keep their canvas lodges pitched, and prefer to sleep in them in summer time: Farming is limited to a few acres for each family; but herding is carried on rather extensively. Thousands of sleek cattle and fine horses feed upon the bunch pastures along the Jocko and the Pend d'Oreille, on the Big Camas prairie, and by the shores of Flathead lake.   * * *   Probably there is no better example of a tribe being brought out of savagery in one generation than is afforded by the Flatheads and their cousins, the Pend d'Oreilles. Much of the credit for this achievement is, no doubt, due the Jesuit fathers, who, like all the Catholic religious orders, show a faculty for gaining an ascendancy over the minds of savages, partly by winning their confidence by devoting themselves to their interests, and partly, it may be, by offering them a religion that appeals strongly to the senses and superstitions. These Indians boast that their tribe never killed a white man. They are an inoffensive, child-like people, and are easily kept in order by the agent, aided by a few native policemen. Life and property are as secure among them as in most civilized communities. With them the agency system amounts only to a paternal supervision, providing implements and machinery for husbandry, and giving aid only when urgently needed. It does not, as upon many reservations, undertake the support of the tribe by issuing rations and clothing. Instead of surrounding the agency with a horde of lazy beggars, it distributes the Indians over the reservation, and encourages them to labor. It ought to result in citizenship and separate ownership of the land for the Indians. Many of them would now like deeds to the farms they occupy, but they cannot get them without legislation from Congress changing the present Indian policy. Practically, they control their farms and herds as individual property; but they have no sense of secure ownership, and no legal rights as against their agent or the chief. Some of them complain of the tyranny of the native police, and of the practice of cruelly whipping women when accused by their husbands of a breach of marriage vows—a practice established, it is charged, by the Jesuits; but in the main they seem to be contented and fairly prosperous. Among them are many half-breeds who trace their ancestry on one side to Hudson's Bay Company servants or French Canadians—fine-looking men and handsome women these, as a rule. They are proud of the white blood in their veins, and appear to be respected in the tribe on account of it; or perhaps it is their superior intelligence which gains for them the influence they evidently enjoy. Shiftless white men, drifting about the country, frequently attempt to settle in the reservation and get a footing there by marrying squaws; but they are not allowed to remain. The Indians do not object to their company so much as the agent."

Selish (1,292 miles from St. Paul) is the station for the Saint Ignatius mission. It was formerly named Ravalli, in honor of Father Ravalli, an eminent philanthropic missionary who labored among the Flatheads and their allied tribes for about forty years, and died in 1884. The Saint Ignatius mission, six miles from the station is, with the exception of the Saint Mary's of the Bitter Root valley, the oldest Catholic mission in the Northern Rocky Mountain region. It was established in 1854. It consists of a church, a school for girls, a school for boys, a dwelling for the missionary fathers, and numerous shops and mills.

Mission valley is one of the loveliest in Montana, and is well worthy the attention of tourists. The Mission mountains, which bound it on the east, are unsurpassed for grandeur of scenery in the entire Rocky mountain chain. They contain numerous canyons and waterfalls. Flathead lake is easily reached from the mission by a drive of about thirty miles over a good road.

The railroad follows the beautiful valley of the Jocko river to its confluence with the Flathead, forty-four miles from Missoula. The Flathead for the next twenty-five miles, until its waters are united with those of the Missouri, is now called the Pend d'Oreille river. Keeping along the left or southern bank of this stream for seventeen miles, the road sweeps around a grand curve, and crosses to the right bank over a fine truss bridge, which, with its approaches, is about 800 feet long. Eight miles beyond the crossing, the muddy waters of the Missouri, pouring in from the south, mix with the bright flood of the Pend d'Oreille, and the united streams now take the designation Clark's Fork of the Columbia. This name is retained, except where the river widens out into Lake Pend d'Oreille, 100 miles westward, until the waters mingle with those of the Columbia river, in the British possessions, northward.

Paradise Valley and Horse Plains.—Two small and charming valleys soon appear to vary the fine mountain views. They are Paradise valley and Horse plains, both celebrated among the Indians as wintering places for their ponies. Paradise valley is seven miles westward of the junction of the rivers. It is two by four miles in extent, and well deserves its name. Six miles beyond is Horse plains, a circular prairie, six miles across, containing a township of fertile land, situated in the midst of very wild scenery. High mountains stand around, and lend the warmth of spring, while their own sides are white with snows. These valleys are the only spots on the immediate line of the railroad for over a hundred and fifty miles that

Thompson's Falls, Clark's Fork of the Columbia, Montana

invite cultivation. The land of Horse plains produces everything desirable in a northern latitude, under irrigation; but in some seasons irrigation is not needed. At Horse plains there is a prosperous community of farmers and stock men.

Leaving Horse Plains, and crossing Clark's creek, with Lynch's buttes visible to the right, the railroad continues westward along the right bank of the river through an unbroken mountain region which affords magnificent views at every turn. The mountains tower on either side. There is no bench land, much less any fertile bottoms, though sometimes level spots of a few acres are heavily timbered. Room is not always found for the track, which is often blasted out from the points of the hills.

Thompson's Falls (1,357 miles from St. Paul; population 300) is beautifully located at the falls of the Clark's Fork river, has hotels, livery stables and a number of mercantile houses. The river furnishes a remarkable waterpower, which has not yet been utilized.

Grand Scenery.—Every where along the Clark's Fork of the Columbia there is magnificent scenery. Cottonwood grows close to the river, and firs and pines clothe the benches and mountain-sides, except where the latter are so nearly vertical that the forest cannot grow. Magnificent vistas are presented as the train moves along, changing and wearing new forms at every turn. The mountains are conical, and sometimes vertical, as where the river has cut through them with tremendous force. The constant succession of towering hills, grouped in wild array, is never wearying, and is sometimes startling in effect, as when some tributary from the north or south tears its way to the greater stream, and offers a vista. reaching far through the deep-worn canon or ravine, along which the heights are ranged as far as eye can see. One of the most striking of these side effects is where Thompson's river comes in from the north, and you look up the long and sharp ravine to catch a momentary glimpse, from the tressle bridge, of the foaming waterfall and the heights that wall it in.

Views on the Clark's Fork.—Reaching the second crossing of the Clark's Fork, there is seen a navigable stretch of water that was utilized by placing a small steamer on it at the time the railroad was under construction. East of the second crossing, the mountains close in upon the view, often abruptly. West of it the valley widens. There is no land to style it a valley; but the gorge is wider and the river less turbulent. The scenery has the same features, but in rather quieter lines, as the heights do not crowd the river so much. The road is now on the south side of the stream. West of Second Crossing, about ten miles, the track follows a high bench, and a view is shown of the river where its waters have cut a deep channel far below. Mountains on the north stand imminent, and make a striking picture.

Good Hunting and Fishing—Another feature of this mountain region, which is likely to attract the attention of lovers of sport, that abundance of game is found among all the ranges. There is no other region that can surpass it for the presence of wild and game animals, as well as birds and fish. Bears are very common; elk, caribou or moose haunt these mountains, and deer of various kinds abound. There are many of the fur-bearing animals, such otter, beaver and mink; while grouse, pheasants, ducks, geese and other fowl are plentiful in their season. The waters abound in the finest trout of several varieties, from the little speckled beauties of the mountain rills to the great salmon trout found in the larger streams and lakes.

After coursing along the northern and southern banks of the Clark's Fork of the Columbia for a hundred miles, the views of mountain and forest sometimes broadening,

Along the Clark's Fork.

sometimes narrowing, and the river alternately showing a wooded reach of smooth water and a stretch of tumbling breakers, the mountains again crowd together near Cabinet Landing. The stations are either for the convenience

Cabinet Gorge, on Clark's Fork.

of railroad employes or for the shipment of lumber, and in every other aspect are at present of not sufficient importance to be described. At several points on the line the track is carried across lateral streams by massive trestle bridges, the one over the deep gorge of Beaver creek being especially noticeable from its height and graceful curve. These frequent bridges, as well as many deep cuttings through the spurs of the mountains, attest the difficulties which the engineers were required to surmount in constructing the line.

South of this mountain range, stretching nearly across the State, is the Snake River plain, the surface of which is either level or gently undulating. Still further south is an elevated plateau, which merges in the southwest into an alkaline desert. Idaho is, on the whole, well watered. Its principal stream is the Snake or Lewis Fork of the Columbia, which, with its many affluents, drains about five-sixths of the State. This stream, generally confined within high walls of basalt, pursues a tortuous and tumultuous course, from its sources in Wyoming, of about 1,000 miles, interrupted by many falls of considerable height. It is only navigable from a short distance above Lewiston, near which city it leaves the State, to its junction with the Columbia river, at Ainsworth, less than 100 miles distant. The principal tributaries of the Snake river are the Salmon, the Boise, the Owyhee and the Clearwater, the Salmon river draining the central part of the State.

The arable lands of Idaho are estimated at ten per cent. of its area. There is a fine plateau in the northern part of the State, just north of the Snake and Clearwater rivers, which is an excellent grain country and a good fruit country. In the south there are good valleys which are cultivated by irrigation. The grazing lands of Idaho cover a great area, especially in the southern part of the State. All the level country of the Snake river plains is valuable for pasturage, as well as the mountain ranges to the south and southeast, which are covered with bunch grass.

The Territory was organized in 1863, having been cut off from Oregon, although a part of it was subsequently given to Montana, and the State was admitted to the Union. Its population by the census of 1890 was only 85,000 exclusive of the Indians, who number about 5,000. These Indians consist of the Nez Perces, Bannacks and Shoshones. The former, numbering 2,807, have a reservation of 1,344,000 acres on the Clearwater, near Lewiston, toward the northern part of the State. The latter two tribes, numbering 1,500, jointly occupy a reservation of 18,000 acres in the southeastern part of the State, on the Snake and Portneuf rivers. There is also a reservation near Lemhi, in the Salmon River mountains, where 677 Indians are reported as having their homes.

In Northern Idaho lie the Cœur d'Alene gold and silver mines, reached by Northern Pacific lines from both Missoula and Spokane. These mines are among the most productive in the United States. Precious metals are also mined at various points in the central and southern parts of the State.

ACROSS THE PAN HANDLE OF IDAHO.

The State of Idaho.—The Northern Pacific railroad passes over a very narrow strip of Northern Idaho—scarcely a degree of longitude—between the eastern end of Lake Pend d'Oreille and a point near Spokane, Washington. It is a forest country all the way, timbered with Rocky mountain pine, commonly known as bull pine, until the eastern edge of the Spokane plain is reached, beyond Rathdrum, and near the Washington boundary. This part of Idaho is called the Pan Handle, but a better name would be the Shank, for the shape of the State closely resembles that of a leg of mutton, of which the shank is the northern part, extending to the British Columbia line.

Idaho is bounded on the east and northeast by Montana and Wyoming, from which it is separated by the winding chain of the Bitter Root or Cœur d'Alene mountains. On the south it follows the forty-second parallel along the line of Utah and Nevada. On the west lie Oregon and Washington, and on the north the British possessions. Idaho is embraced between the forty-second and forty-ninth parallels of latitude, and between the 111th and 117th meridians of longitude, west of Greenwich. Its area is 86,294 square miles, or 55,228,160 acres. The northern part of the State is quite mountainous, some of the highest altitudes reaching 10,000 feet. Mountain and valley alike are covered with a dense growth of coniferæ. The principal ranges are the Bitter Root and the Salmon mountains, the latter traversing the central portion of the State.

Cabinet Landing.—At this point the Clark's Fork is confined in a rocky gorge, through which it dashes at tremendous speed. The columnar rocks that hem in the torrent are from 100 to 150 feet in height, their brows crowned with pines, and the romantic wildness of the gorge is of surpassing beauty. The bold fluted pillars of rock are not unlike those of the "Giant's Causeway" in Ireland. Cabinet Landing derives its name, in part at least, from the fact that here the Hudson's Bay company, in carrying up goods by boat from the foot of Lake Pend d'Oreille to Horse plains, was compelled to make a portage. From Cabinet Landing the train runs through solid rock cuttings, the walls of which tower far above the rushing, tumbling stream below. Clark's Fork, a station near the long railroad bridge over the Clark's Fork, affords some fine river views, and ten miles further the pleasant town of Hope, on the strand of Lake Pend d'Oreille, is reached.

Lake Pend d'Oreille.—This beautiful lake may be likened to a broad and winding valley among the mountains, filled to the brim with gathered waters. Reaching the lake, the railroad crosses the mouth of Pack river on a trestle one mile and a half in length, and skirts the northern shore for upward of twenty miles. The shores are mountains, but, wherever there is a bit of beach, it is covered with dense forest. The view of the lake from the car windows, with its beautiful islands and its arms reaching into the surrounding ranges, is superb. The waters stretch out south, and fill a mountain cove to the southwest before those of the Clark's Fork meet them. From this point the river makes the lake its channel, and passes out at the western end on its flow northward to meet the Columbia, just over the boundary line in British Columbia. The whole length of the lake, following its curves and wind-

Skirting the Clark's Fork.

ings, must be nearly sixty miles. In places it is fifteen miles wide, and in others narrows to three miles.

The circuit of the lake shore is full of surprises. The mountains are grouped with fine effect, and never become

Lake Pend d'Oreille, Idaho.

monotonous. Along the lake the most prominent features of civilization are the saw-mills, which supplied material for railroad construction, and are now employed manufacturing lumber for shipment. The forest is interminable; but, where the mountains are abrupt, the trees do not grow large enough and clear enough to make good lumber. The benches and levels along the streams are generally thickly studded with giant pines or firs, and these trees also tower in the ravines. These spots of good timber were selected as sites for saw-mills, and the carrying of lumber is now an important branch of traffic. The Northern Pacific road reaches its farthest northern limit at Pend d'Oreille, and thence turns south and west.

Hope, Idaho (1,428 miles from St. Paul; population, 500) is beautifully located on high ground on the northern shore of Lake Pend d'Oreille. It was formerly only a fishing and hunting resort, with a small hotel for sportsmen; but the removal of the Northern Pacific division terminus from Heron in 1888, and the discovery of mines of silver ore on the south shore of the lake, have caused considerable growth. Steamers cross the lake to the new mines, called Chloride and Weber. The landing for the mines is at the mouth of Gold creek, about thirty miles by water from Hope. The principal street of Hope is built on a narrow shelf on the mountain side overlooking the railroad and the lake.

Pack River (1,439 miles from St. Paul).—Near this station the Pack river enters Lake Pend d'Oreille, and from here an old fur-trading and mining trail leads to the Kootenai river, a distance of about thirty miles. The Kootenai is an eccentric stream, running first south, and making a long bend, and afterward flowing due north far into British territory. The Kootenai is navigable for 150 miles, for 100 miles of which it expands into a deep, narrow lake. Numerous large veins of galena silver ore are found along the shores of Kootenai lake and river, and are the basis of several important mining enterprises. A small steamer runs upon the Kootenai.

Sand Point (1,444 miles from St. Paul), on the shore of Lake Pend d'Oreille, is a place of importance on account of its being the point of junction with the Great Northern road, which gives access to the Kootenai valley and the Flathead valley on the east, and which runs down the Clark's Fork from the lake for about fifty miles before turning westward to Spokane.

Cocolalla (1,457 miles from St. Paul).—This station derives its euphonious Indian name from the bright sheet of water which lies near the track. The lake is several miles long, but not wide. On approaching it, a charming view of wave, wood and mountain will be caught. But we are passing out of Wonderland. Mountains no longer seem to overtop us. The train sweeps on toward the southwest, following a natural pass between the ranges, presently entering a valley a few miles wide.

Rathdrum (1,485 miles from St. Paul) is a small town situated on the northeastern verge of the great Spokane plain, has a population of 300. There is considerable good farming land near by, much valuable timber, and some excellent range for stock.

Hauser Junction (1,492 miles from St. Paul) is the point of the divergence of the Spokane Falls & Idaho railroad, which runs to Cœur d'Alene City on the lake of the same name, sixteen miles distant, there connecting with steamers on the lake and river to Mission, from whence there is a railroad to the Cœur d'Alene mining towns. Noble views of the Cœur d'Alene mountains which sur-

Lake Cœur d'Alene, Idaho.

round the lake, may be enjoying it from the car windows as the train crosses the plains between Rathdrum and Spokane.

FIVE HUNDRED AND TWENTY-FIVE MILES THROUGH WASHINGTON.

The Evergreen State.—The main line of the Northern Pacific runs for 525 miles in the State of Washington, entering it on the Spokane plain, near the crossing of the Spokane river, and leaving it at Kalama, where the trains are ferried over the Columbia river on their way to Portland, Oregon.

Washington is called the "Evergreen State" from its extensive forests of evergreen trees, and also from the fact that in the western part the winters are so mild that the grass remains green throughout the year. In situation it is the most northwestern of the States of the Union, being bounded by British Columbia on the north and the Pacific ocean on the west, while its southern line rests upon Oregon and its eastern line upon Idaho. Its length from east to west is about 360 miles and its width from north to south 240 miles. Its area is 69,994 square miles, of which 3,114 are water, leaving 66,880 square miles of land or 42,803,200 acres, about equal to the area of Ohio and Indiana combined. Washington Territory was organized in 1853, and at that time included much that is now Idaho. Its admission to the Union was provided for by the act of Congress passed in the winter of 1889. Its present population is not less than 500,000.

The Cascade mountains, a broad volcanic plateau, with many lofty, snow-clad peaks, rising high above the general level, divide both Washington and Oregon into two unequal parts, which differ widely in surface, climate and vegetation. Westward of this mountain chain, from forty to seventy miles, is still another and lower range, lying along the ocean shore, known as the Coast mountains in Oregon and the Olympic range in Washington.

Between these two mountain ranges spreads out the basin of Puget Sound, and the valleys of the Cowlitz, Chehalis, and other rivers. The entire region west of the Cascade mountains, including the slopes of these elevations, is covered with dense forests, mainly of coniferæ, which constitute a large source of wealth.

The climate of this section is mild and equable, with slight ranges of temperature, showing a mean deviation of only 28° during the year, the summer averaging 70°, and the winter 38°. There is an abundant rainfall, and the wet and dry seasons are well marked. The rains are more copious in December, January and March than at any other time. But the rain falls in showers rather than continuously, with many intervals of bright, agreeable weather, which often last for days together. Snow rarely falls in great quantities, and it soon disappears under the influence of the humid atmosphere. During the dry season the weather is delightful. There are showers from time to time; but the face of the country is kept fresh and verdant by the dews at night, and occasional fogs in the morning. The soil of the valleys of Western Washington is generally a dark loam, with clay subsoil, and in the bottom lands near the water-courses are rich deposits of alluvium. These soils are of wonderful productive capacity, yielding large crops of hay, hops, grain, fruits and vegetables.

The area east of the Cascade mountains, by far the larger portion of Washington, presents features in marked contrast to those which have been already outlined. This is not only true of the climate, but also of the soil and topography, fully warranting the popular division of the country into two sections, known as the coast region and the inland region which are essentially dissimilar in aspect.

The area east of the Cascade mountains extends to the bases of the Blue and Bitter Root ranges. A broad strip on the north is mountainous and covered with forest; but the greater portion embraces the immense plains and undulating prairies, 250 miles wide and nearly 500 miles long, which constitute the great basin of the Columbia river. Within the limits of this basin are a score of valleys, many a one of which is larger than some European principalities, all of which are well watered, and clothed with nutritious grass.

In the eastern section the temperature is decidedly higher in summer and lower in winter than in the western section—the average indicating respectively 85° and 30°. The rainfall is only half as heavy; but it has proved sufficient for cereal crops. From June to September there is no rain, the weather being perfect for harvesting. The heat is great, but not nearly so oppressive as a much lower grade would be in the Eastern States, and the nights are invariably cool. The winters are short, but occasionally severe. Snow seldom falls before Christmas, and sometimes lies from four to six weeks, but usually disappears in a few days. The so-called "Chinook," a warm wind which blows periodically through the mountain passes, is of great benefit to the country. It comes from the southwest across the great thermal stream known as the Japan

Distant View of Mount Tacoma

current, and the warm, moist atmosphere melts the deepest snow in the course of a few hours.

The soil is a dark loam, of great depth, composed of alluvial deposits and decomposed lava overlying a clay subsoil. The constituents of this soil adapt the land peculiarly to the production of wheat.

Agriculture is the leading industry, and wheat is the principal product of the entire country. Its superior quality and great weight have made it famous in the grain markets of the world. The entire surplus of the wheat crop is exported by sea to Liverpool and other European markets, from the shipping ports of Tacoma and Portland. Oats and barley also yield heavily. Hops are a very important product, and widely cultivated in the Puyallup and White River valleys on Puget Sound, and in Yakima county, east of the Cascade mountains. Vegetables of every variety, and of the finest quality, are produced. Fruits of many descriptions, all of delicious aroma and flavor, grow to a remarkable size. Among them are apples, pears, apricots, quinces, plums, prunes, peaches, cherries and grapes. Strawberries, raspberries, blackberries, gooseberries and currents are also abundant.

An important industry is the raising of cattle, sheep and horses. This is only second to agriculture, and is pursued in all parts of the Pacific Northwest. The horses are of excellent race, and excel in speed. Sheep husbandry has proved very profitable, especially among the Blue mountain ranges.

It would scarcely be possible to exaggerate the extent and value of the forests. East and west of the Cascade mountains there are large tracts of timber lands. The Blue mountains and eastern slopes of the Cascades are thickly clothed with pine timber, and west of the Cascade moun-

tains there is an inexhaustible supply. Perhaps the finest
body of timber in the world is embraced in the Puget
Sound district. The principal growths are fir, pine, spruce,
cedar, larch and hemlock, although white oak, maple,
cottonwood, ash, alder and other varieties are found in considerable quantities.

The mineral wealth of Washington is large and diversified. Coal takes a foremost rank among the mineral resources of the country. Immense beds of semi-bituminous and lignite coal are found west of the Cascade mountains, and also east of those mountains, in the Upper Yakima valley. This mineral exists in Oregon in different localities; but the coal fields of Washington are far more extensive. The principal mines are on the Puyallup, Carbon and other rivers flowing into Puget Sound, near Tacoma, Seattle and Whatcom, and also at the head of the Yakima valley, at Roslyn. Iron ores—bog, hematite and magnetic—exist in great masses, and are found in both Oregon and Washington.

Silver ore is successfully mined in the Colville valley, about 100 miles north of Spokane, and also at various points in the Okanogan valley and on the western slope of the Cascade mountains. Gold is obtained by washing auriferous earth on the Swauk and Te-anaway, small streams which flow into the Upper Yakima. Gold quartz is mined at Palmer mountain in the Okanogan valley. Copper has been found in the Peshastin range of mountains north of Ellensburgh. There are also extensive iron ledges in those mountains.

The waters of all the rivers of Washington flow into the Pacific ocean, the largest of which, the Columbia, is navigable for a distance of 725 miles. The Snake river comes next in importance, and there are many other streams nav-

Puget Sound is a beautiful archipelago, covering an area of over 2,000 square miles. Its waters are everywere deep and free from shoals, its anchorage secure, and it offers every facility that a great commerce demands.

There are several commodious harbors for vessels on the coast line, exclusive of those found at the mouths of the several rivers. At these places a thriving trade is carried on in lumbering, coal mining, fishing, oystering, dairying and agricultural products.

These waters abound in fish, of which many varieties are of great commercial value. Particularly is this the fact with regard to salmon. Extensive establishments for canning are carried on at several places on the Columbia river, where the business of salmon packing is the principal industry. The far famed reputation which the Columbia river fish has acquired secures it a large market in the Eastern States, and it is sold extensively in Australia, England and other European countries.

The remarkable variety of resources offered by this great new State, its peculiarly agreeable and healthful climate, its strikingly beautiful landscapes of snow-capped mountains, noble rivers, great estuaries of the sea, magnificent forests, charming lakes and fertile prairies, combine to make it a region particularly attractive to all who seek new homes in the great Northwest. The State is well supplied with railway facilities by four transcontinental lines —the Northern Pacific, Union Pacific, Great Northern and Canadian Pacific.

Spokane (1,512 miles from St. Paul), formerly called Spokane Falls, is the commercial capital of all of Eastern Washington and Northern Idaho, its trade territory extending from the western ranges of the Rockies on the east to the Cascade mountains on the west. It is a remarkable city on account of its rapid growth, the solidity of its construction and the picturesque features of its cataracts and river gorge, its mountainous surroundings and its handsomely improved streets. The entire business district was burned in 1890, but the immediate result was its rebuilding in a style of beauty and solidity not attained by old Eastern cities in a century of growth. The stately business blocks of brick and granite would do credit to a city ten times the size of Spokane.

Spokane was named for the river and the falls, and they bear the name of a tribe of Indians, the Spokanes, which formerly inhabited this region. The first settlement was made in the seventies by four men who took up claims that cornered at the falls. All of them became millionaires by the enormous appreciation of their property. When the Northern Pacific reached the place in 1880, building from the west, it contained about 300 people. Its present population is more than 35,000. Flour milling and lumber sawing were the first industries, based on the admirable water power of the numerous falls. As the agricultural lands of the south and west attracted population the town became a center of mercantile trade, which was greatly extended after the discovery of precious metals in the mountains on the east and north. The building of branch roads and a second transcontinental line confirmed and strengthened its position for general business and the further improvement of the water power attracted numerous manufacturing enterprises. The railway facilities comprise the main line of the Northern Pacific, three branches of the Northern Pacific running east to the Cœur d'Alene country, south through the rich Palouse farming country to Lewiston, at the junction of the Snake and Clearwater rivers, and west to the farming regions of the Big Bend country; the main line of the Great Northern, one of the branches of the

Oregon Railroad and Navigation Company, and the line of the Spokane and Northern. These various roads make of Spokane much the most important railway center in the Pacific Northwest.

Spokane has numerous electric roads climbing the steep hills south of the town. It has a Methodist college, a Catholic college and an excellent public school system, with a high school building of conspicuous dimensions and handsome architecture. The electric lights and electric cars are run with power generated at the falls. The leading hotel is "The Spokane." Four bridges span the river. The surroundings of the city are exceedingly picturesque, and there are many beautiful drives along the banks of the Spokane river and Hangman's creek, and across the beautiful flowery prairies north and east of the city.

The falls, seen when melting snows swell the flow and the banks are brimming with the hurrying flood, are a sight never to be forgotten. Basaltic islands divide the broad river, and the waters rush in swift rapids to meet these obstructions. A public bridge crosses from island to island. The width of the river is nearly half a mile. There are three great streams curving toward each other, and pouring their floods into a common basin. Reunited, the waters foam and toss for a few hundred yards in whirling rapids, and then make another plunge into the canyon beyond. Standing on the rocky ledge below the second waterfall, and looking up the stream, a fine view is obtained of the wonderful display of force. All things are weak and trivial compared with the tremendous torrent that heaves and plunges below, and the grand cascades that foam and toss above. Eternal mist rises from the boiling abyss, and sunshine reveals a bow of promise spanning the chasm.

Spokane Valley and Lake Cœur d'Alene.—One of the most singular districts of this country is the Spokane valley. It is thirty miles long, and three to six miles in width, surrounded by the western ranges of the lower Cœur d'Alene or Bitter Root mountains. The river rises in Cœur d'Alene lake, close under the timbered mountains, in Idaho, about ten miles south of the railroad. The lake extends south at least forty miles and has long arms reaching in among the mountains. A rich agricultural region lies close to it on the west. The rivers that drain the western water-shed of the Cœur d'Alene mountains pour immense volumes into the lake; but the Spokane river, the lake's only outlet, is comparatively small in size, with no tributaries of importance. Still, thirty miles below the lake, this stream becomes a great roaring cataract at the city of Spokane. The theory is advanced that the region around the lake and all the upper Spokane valley consists of a deep gravel deposit. Time has made for the lake a water-tight bottom, and a well, dug within a rod of its shores, will not furnish water, and no well can be dug in all the Spokane valley. The water furnished by the mountains soaks through this immense bed of gravel, making Spokane river, in its upper reaches, so puny a stream. Eight miles below the lake are the Post Falls, where the river flows between rocks very close together. Thirty miles below the gravel deposit ends and basaltic shores close in upon the stream. Gradually, as the lower valley is reached, the river is increased in volume as the flow is forced to the surface, and, at the falls, it is all gathered well in hand, and makes a tremendous leap, with a force far greater than would be believed after seeing Post Falls.

The Palouse Country,—Tourists and others who wish to see one of the best farming regions in the world should leave the main line at Spokane and take a train on the Spokane & Palouse road through the Palouse country, stopping at Palouse, Pullman and Moscow. Nothing can be seen of this region from the main line, and the traveler who does not visit it will get a very inadequate idea of the agricultural resources of Washington.

The name Palouse country is applied to the region drained by the Palouse river and its feeders. It begins about ten miles south of Spokane and stretches southward to the Snake river, which runs through a deep cañon and receives no drainage to mention from the country north of it. In fact, the Palouse drains the rolling, high plateau almost up to the brink of the precipice at the bottom of which flows the mighty Snake. The Palouse heads in the Cœur d'Alene mountains, and so do all the creeks that feed it. It has a course of about 150 miles. Its two main branches join at Colfax. Soon after it has collected all its waters it leaves the fertile country and comes out into the hot, dry, bunch grass plains. Then it tumbles down three hundred feet by a sheer descent into a crevice in the volcanic rock and soon after joins the Snake. The Palouse country means the fertile belt between the mountains on the east and the arid plains on the west, and between the forests that envelope the Spokane plain on the north and the cañon of Snake river on the south. Using round numbers we may outline it as one hundred miles long and thirty miles wide. There is no perceptible line of demarkation between the fertile country and the desert. One merges gradually into the other. The nearer the mountains the more rainfall; the further from the mountains the less rainfall, is the rule. As you go westward you descend steadily from an altitude of 2,800 feet, and as you descend the summer heats increase and the precipitation diminishes. The heads of grain are smaller and the stalks more slender and sparse. Finally the farms give way to stock ranches. Before you reach the falls of the Palouse you are in the great hot, dry basin that lies between the Columbia and the Snake.

The suface of the Palouse country is a succession of hills and ridges, covered with grass and wild sunflowers and lupins. The soil is a decomposed basalt, very rich in the ingredients that go to the making of all the small grains. Curiously enough, the hill slopes and summits have not been washed of their fertility for the benefit of the valleys. On the contrary they are just as rich as the depressions between them. The region is very young, geologically speaking, which may account for this circumstance. The granite has been overflowed by successive floods of lava, and the different layers of basalt thus formed can be clearly distinguished from each other in the outcroppings along the valleys of the streams and in the cañons of the Snake and Palouse. There is no timber except a few scattering pines on the hill slopes along the creeks, until you get back to the foot-hills of the mountains, which are covered with Rocky mountain pine, fir and tamarack.

The climate is as agreeable and healthful, taking the year round, as can be found anywhere in the United States. A short winter with moderate snowfall is followed by an early spring, beginning usually in February. In March the flowers are blooming and the plows going. There are usually three or four short hot spells in summer, but in those spells the nights are cool enough to make blankets requisite and the rest of the summer is breezy and comfortable. In the hottest days you do not feel the heat if you are in the shade. It appears that only the sun's rays are hot and that the air does not get heated up after the coolness of the night.

The melting snows and the June rains make the crops. After June no rain is expected until October. The farmer threshes his grain at his leisure and leaves the sacks in the field until he is ready to haul them to the railroad. Then, when the shipping season is at its height, the warehouses will not hold half the grain, and the sacks are piled high on the open platforms around the stations. In September and October, columns of dust arising from the roads show where the four and six-horse teams are on their way to the stations with their loads of grain. The dust is the only drawback to this wonderful farming country. But as it necessarily goes with a rich and easily tilled soil, the people put up with it without grumbling. The autumns are the crown of the year—cool, perfect days and nights, with a touch of frost. Much might be written about the remarkable grain crops of this region, but the story would repeat itself over and over again in accounts of reported yields of wheat, barley and oats, on the same lands, year after year, with never less than twenty-five bushels of wheat to the acre, and frequent crops of forty, fifty and even sixty bushels. If the land is allowed to lie idle after harvest it volunteers a crop the second year that would make Minnesota farmer rejoice. Volunteer crops of twenty bushels to the acre are not remarkable. A favorite wheat is the "Little Club," which has a stout stalk of moderate length, and a short, chubby head. Its growth is so even that the header is the popular reaping machine. Its knives are set to correspond with the growth of the grain in the field which it is to cut, and then, pushed before four horses, it clips off the heads and deposits them in the bin of a wagon following beside it. Binders are growing in favor, but probably three-fourths of the farmers prefer the header, because it will cut a great deal more in a day and puts them to no expense for twine.

Marshall (1,522 miles from St. Paul) is the diverging point of the road to the Palouse country, but the trains are made up in Spokane. The fertile region begins about five miles distant, beyond the forest belt through which the main line runs.

Cheney (1,529 miles from St. Paul ; population, 1,500). —This is an important wheat-shipping point, in the midst of a rich farming country, and is the station where the Central Washington branch diverges, which runs westward through the Big Bend country to Coulee City, 108 miles. The agricultural country tributary to Cheney consists of rolling and hilly plains, with a rich soil, highly productive of wheat, oats, barley, rye and potatoes. In its natural condition the surface of this region is covered with a flourishing growth of bunch grass, which affords excellent pasturage for stock. Cheney has an attractive situation in the midst of a grove of pine trees and on the borders of the prairie country. From the high ground north of the town there is a superb view southward over more than fifty miles of rolling prairie country to Steptoe butte, a conspicuous elevation on the southern horizon.

Sprague (1,554 miles from St. Paul; population, 1,000) is the county seat of Lincoln county.

that the railroad for hundreds of miles either way follows the banks of rivers or the dry beds of old water-courses. The traveler does not see any good, arable land as he journeys through it. At Sprague, looking eastward, there is a range of purple hills a few miles distant that are the western boundary of the fertile Palouse country. The level land between these heights and the railroad is rocky, with frequent ponds, and Lake Colville, two miles west of Sprague, lies along the road for eight miles.

The old water-courses are called coulées. The road follows them, from the time it leaves Spokane until it reaches the Columbia river at Pasco, for 100 miles. Timber is abundant east of Sprague, but not a tree is afterward seen before the Columbia river is sighted, over 100 miles beyond. The coulées are rocky and desolate. There are stations all along, every few miles, and the company has planted shade trees at each of them, to show that, desert as this region appears, it only needs water and care to make the land productive.

Ritzville (1,577 miles from St. Paul; population, 700) is the county seat of Adams county, and a point of departure for the agricultural and stock-raising country of Crab creek, north of the railroad, and in the Big Bend of the Columbia. It has a newspaper, two hotels, and a number of stores. Beyond Ritzville the country traversed by the railroad is mainly too dry for agriculture, but is covered with bunchgrass, and is valuable for stock-raising.

Connell (1,623 miles from St. Paul) is in the midst of a dry, unsettled country, and is important only as the junction of the Columbia & Palouse railroad running eastward, eighty miles, to Colfax, the county seat of Whitman county, whence it diverges into two branches, one running to Moscow, Idaho, and the other to Farmington, Washington. It is a branch of the Union Pacific system.

Northern Pacific R. R. Bridge over the Columbia River at Pasco.

Pasco (1,658 miles from St. Paul; population 500) was so named from the fact that the Northern Pacific passes over the Columbia river about two miles from the town, the word having been ingeniously coined by the engineers who constructed the line westward. Pasco is an important junction point for travel to and from the Walla Walla country, and to points on the Columbia river. The Northern Pacific has a branch crossing the Snake river on a huge steel bridge and running on to Wallula, 17 miles distant, where it connects with a line of the Union Pacific running west down the river to Portland and east to the numerous towns in the Walla Walla country. An independent road called the Washington & Columbia River railway connects at Pasco and runs trains to Pendleton on one line, and to Walla Walla, Dayton, Waitsburg, and other points in the fertile country south of Snake river by another.

West of the Columbia.—The Cascade division of the Northern Pacific is the most recently constructed of all the divisions of the main line. It was mainly built in the years 1885, 1886 and 1887, and the great tunnel under the Cascade mountains was completed in June, 1888. The road crosses the Columbia river between Pasco and Kennewick on a combination iron and wood bridge, which spans the broad, blue flood of this mighty stream just about the mouth of its principal affluent, the Snake river, and follows the valley of the Yakima river, which empties into the Columbia a few miles above Kennewick, all the way up to the source of the former stream in the Cascade mountains. Along the lower Yakima the country is dry and covered with sage-brush where not cultivated, but the soil is fertile and irrigating-ditch enterprises are fast converting the entire region into a thickly settled farming country. The beneficial effects of irrigation are seen as soon as the western bank of the Columbia is reached, and may be observed at almost every mile of progress up the Yakima valley to the foothills of the Cascade mountains.

For about thirty miles the road runs through the Simcoe Indian reservation, which is well settled and contains many irrigated farms and large stretches of verdant pasture land. Mt. Adams, one of the highest snow peaks of the Cascade range, is in plain sight from the train while passing across the Simcoe reservation. This mountain is over 9,000 feet high and its base is about fifty miles distant from the nearest point on the railroad. Passing Union Gap through a low mountain range the road enters a well-cultivated basin, where the Natchess and other tributaries of the Yakima furnish abundant water for irrigation. Continuing northwestward, the road winds for many miles through the profound and picturesque defiles of the Yakima cañon, and then emerges into the Kittitas valley, which is watered by the Yakima and numerous tributary streams, and is well settled by farmers engaged in raising grain and stock. Considerable placer-mining is done on the headwaters of the Tenaway and the Swauk, two large creeks which rise in the Peshastin mountains. These mountains run across the head of the Kittitas valley and present a magnificent spectacle of lofty rocky peaks crowned with snow, which can be enjoyed from many points on the railroad. The highest of these peaks is Mt. Stuart, which has an altitude of over 12,000 feet. The Peshastin range is a granite formation, entirely different in its geological character from the Cascade mountains, which are basaltic, and of which it seems to form a spur. Near the base of the Peshastin mountains lies an extensive coal field. The ascent of the Cascade mountains is made by the Northern Pacific road up remarkably light grades, the heaviest of which does

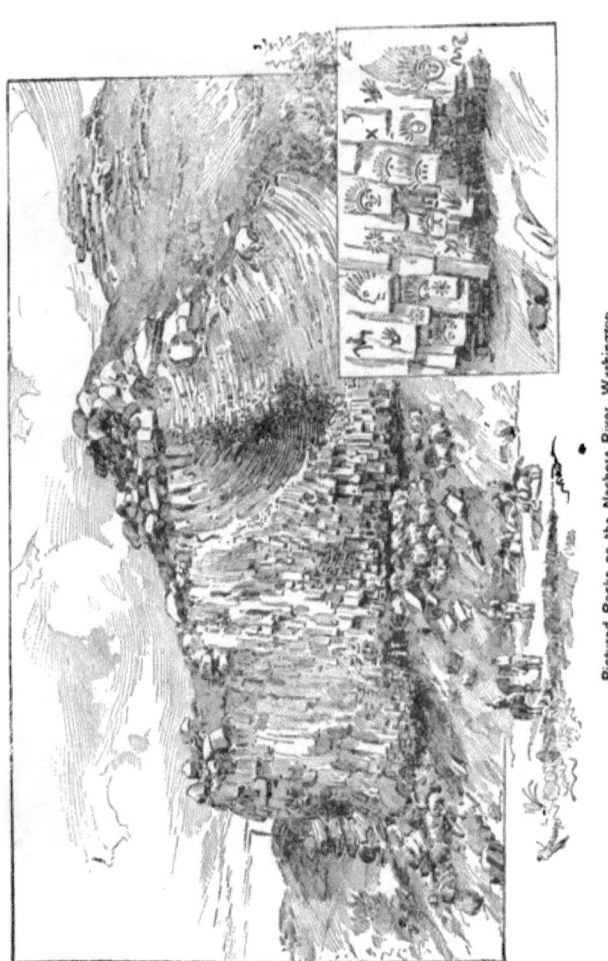
Pictured Rocks on the Nachess River Washington.

not exceed two feet to the hundred, or 116 feet to the mile.

Kennewick (1,621 miles from St. Paul) is the first station west of the river and is situated on a broad, fertile plateau, recently irrigated by a canal brought from the Yakima at a point about twenty-five miles distant. The town is becoming a center of small farming and fruit raising. The summers are long and warm, with a great deal of sunshine and hardly any rain, and the mellow soil is quickly responsive to water brought upon it by ditches, and produces extraordinarily rapid and perfect growths of fruits, vegetables, alfalfa, grass and small grains.

Prosser (1,698 miles from St. Paul) is a promising town at the falls of the Yakima river. These falls afford good waterpower for mills. The most important irrigating canal in the valley terminates on the north side of the river not far from the town, and another important canal has its intake gate on the river below the town. Prosser is the point of departure from the railroad to an extensive grazing and farming region, called "The Horse Heaven country," which lies just south of the low range of grassy mountains that rise immediately back of the town.

The Sunnyside Irrigated Lands.—After leaving Mabton, westward bound, a heavy belt of forest to the northward outlines the course of the Yakima river. Beyond and extending along the river for thirty miles is the rich "Sunnyside" country recently brought under cultivation by the Northern Pacific, Yakima & Kittitas Irrigation company, the largest completed enterprise of its kind in the State of Washington. This canal is so mammoth in its proportions that a small steamboat could navigate its waters, which have reclaimed the plain, and are turning it into a richly cultivated and densely settled community; for here the profits of agriculture are so certain and large that twenty acres is a large farm and "ten acres is enough." Thus, the isolation incidental to large Eastern farms is obviated and the entire 64,000 acres watered by the canal is already becoming a vast village of prosperous, progressive farmers, who, while securing the benefits of a new country, will enjoy all the advantages of schools, societies, etc., incidental to the more densely settled communities of the Eastern States. The apparently sterile sage-brush plain, tenanted by roving bands of cattle, is now changed by water's magic wand into a grand oasis of hop, fruit and grain fields interspersed with alfalfa, timothy and clover meadows. The soil and climate are found especially congenial to the hop industry, many farmers already having from five to twenty acres in hop yards which yield from one thousand to two thousand five hundred pounds per acre, depending upon the age of the yard. The season of picking, drying and baling profitably employs hundreds of men, women and children, who make a holiday of the task. No failure has been known, and the product shipped to London and New York brings a price which nets a profit of from $75 to $200 per acre to the fortunate owner. The soil, a decomposed basalt, is free from stones and so uniformly rich in quality for a depth of from fifty-five to eighty-five feet, that it is conjectured by scientists to be the sediment deposited by a lake which in prehistoric times covered the entire Columbia basin. This rich, mellow loam is suited to fruit raising quite as well as for the hop. The upper and older part of the "Sunnyside" is already occupied by prune, peach, apple and pear orchards amounting in the aggregate to several thousand acres now in full bearing, while in the newer sections, recently brought under the canal, the numerous young orchards set out within the year have made a growth of from five to eight feet, so long and congenial are the summers for plant growth. Here the farmer is his own rainmaker, and the certainty, variety and productiveness of the crops grown are in strong contrast to Eastern farming conditions.

Zillah, a thriving village recently started, is three miles from Toppenish, the nearest station on the railroad, on the northern bank of the Yakima river, which here culminates in majestic bluffs eighty-five feet in height. The headquarters of the canal company are at this place, and, in order to view the fruit and hop lands, which, though so near the railway, are not in sight, the stage should be taken from Toppenish to Zillah, and from thence the transformation from the range to thickly settled garden, fruit and hop lands can be observed. Another point, Mayhew, fifteen miles east of Zillah, is divided into fruit lots of one, two and five-acre lots, with wide streets, down which flow streams of clear water from the main canal between the sidewalks and roadway. An area of land four times as large as at Pasadena surrounds Mayhew, which, in consequence, will become an important fruit producing point. Mayhew is seven miles from Mabton, the nearest railroad station. Here the main canal courses along the slopes of a low range of mountains covered with bunch-grass to their summits and furrowed by ravines down which course streams of spring water. Settlement is rapid here, and many of the ten and twenty-acre farms are already in a high state of cultivation.

The Yakima Basin.—This is a highly fertile region, enclosed by low ranges of mountains which are covered with bunch-grass to their summits. It is watered by the Yakima and by its tributaries, the Nachess, Cowychee and the Attanum. The three smaller streams are fed by springs and melting snows in the Cascade mountains, and carry the largest volume of water during the hot season. They furnish abundant water for irrigation purposes to the lands along their banks. West of the Yakima river the basin extends for a distance of about twenty miles, and a large part of it is irrigated by a big ditch taken from the Yakima. This district is known as the "Moxee Country." The Yakima basin, like the lower Yakima valley, greatly resembles many of the California valleys. The winters are short and mild, and the summers long and sunny. The soil produces, under an inexpensive system of irrigation, very heavy yields of hops, wheat, oats, barley, Indian corn, millet, clover, timothy and vegetables of all kinds, and all fruits of the temperate zone grow to perfection. Grapes are beginning to be culivated for wine-making purposes, and it is believed that the valley will in time rival some of the best wine districts of California. Tobacco culture has been successfully tried in recent years, and a good grade of tobacco is raised for the manufacture of cigars. The land was originally occupied in large farms, but is now being cut up into small farms of from ten to forty acres each for the cultivation of fruits, vegetables, hops, tobacco, etc. On the neighboring foothills and mountain ranges there is a luxuriant growth of bunch-grass, and the raising of cattle, sheep, and horses is a profitable industry. During open winters stock feed upon the ranges without any care, but prudent farmers put up a small quantity of timothy or alfalfa hay for feed in case of severe snow storms.

North Yakima (1,747 miles from St. Paul; population, 2,500) is the county seat of Yakima county and the trade center for all the valleys embraced in the Yakima basin. It is an attractive and handsome town with good brick busi-

In the Yakima Canyon.

ness blocks and well-shaded streets. In each street, between the sidewalks and the roadways, run streams of clear water from which little ditches lead to the lawns and gardens. Travelers who desire to see irrigation farming on a large scale, are advised to visit the Moxee farm, just west of the Yakima river, about four miles distant from the town. This farm embraces about 2,000 acres under ditch and cultivation, and with an extensive stock range of many thousand acres. It is owned by a company in which Gardner Hubbard, of the Bell Telephone company, is the principal stockholder. Irrigation is carried on by both the flooding and small-ditch systems. Tobacco, hops, wheat, oats, corn, barley are the principal crops.

The Yakima Canyon.—After leaving North Yakima the railroad runs through a gap in a low mountain range, passes the outlet of the Wenass valley, another strip of agricultural lands along the Wenass river, and then enters the Yakima canyon, a profound gorge in the Umptanum mountains. The scenery in this canyon is peculiar and impressive. Some washing for gold is done by Chinamen along the banks of the river. The railroad emerges from the canyon into the great Kittitas basin.

The Kittitas Basin.—This is the largest in extent of the fertile valleys traversed by the Yakima river. It is about 20 miles long, with an average width of ten miles, and can all be seen from the railway platform at Ellensburg. It is bounded on the west by the Cascade mountains, above whose green heads can be seen the white top of the great snow peak, Mt. Tacoma. On the north the basin is bounded by the Peshastin and Wenatchee mountains. The former range is a mass of rock and snow, and its highest peak, Mt. Stuart, has an elevation of 10,000 feet above the sea, and resembles somewhat the famous Matterhorn of the

Swiss Alps. This region is rich in mineral wealth, containing coal, iron, copper, gold and silver. The Wenatchee mountains are timbered to their summits and reach to the Columbia river. The Umptanum mountains, which shut in the basin on the south, are about 3,000 feet high and are covered with bunch-grass. The Kittitas basin has an altitude about 800 feet greater than the Yakima basin, and the climate has more of a mountain character, the nights being cool and the summer days not as warm. The farming lands in the basin are irrigated by ditches taken from creeks running into the Yakima. They have a rich alluvial soil and produce heavy crops of small grains and vegetables. The raising of horses and cattle is the chief industry, and much attention is paid to blooded and grade stock. Cattle are shipped to the markets of the cities on Puget Sound and in British Columbia.

Ellensburg (1,784 miles from St. Paul; population 2,500) is the county seat of Kittitas county, and the headquarters of the Cascade division of the Northern Pacific railroad. Ellensburg is the trade center for the entire valley, and for the coal mining region at the head of the valley. The business streets were entirely burned over a few years ago, but were immediately rebuilt with substantial brick structures, all of a uniform height of two stories, which gives the town a remarkably handsome appearance.

Clealum (1,809 miles from St. Paul; population 300) is the junction of the short branch road which runs to the Roslyn coal mines.

Roslyn (1,813 miles from St. Paul and 4 from Clealum) is the terminus of the Roslyn branch, and has a population of about 1,600. It is the most important coal-mining point on the entire line of the Northern Pacific. The coal is a superior hard, black lignite, and is used for locomotive fuel and also for domestic fuel in all the towns of Eastern Washington. About 500 tons a day are mined.

Easton (1,822 miles from St. Paul), on the eastern side of the Cascade mountains, is a small railroad town at the commencement of the mountain grade.

The Great Tunnel.—The mountains are crossed at Stampede Pass, through the sharp comb of which a tunnel almost two miles long has been excavated. This tunnel is with one exception the longest in America, being surpassed only by the Hoosac tunnel in Massachusetts, which is three miles in length. The Hoosac tunnel was excavated from both ends and from a central shaft, but the mountain over the Cascade tunnel was too high to admit of a shaft, and the whole of the excavation was done at the ends. In view of this fact, and also of the wildness of the country, and the distance from sources of supplies, the Cascade tunnel may fairly be regarded as a greater work of engineering than the famous tunnel under the Hoosac mountains. During the progress of the work on the tunnel a switch back line was built over the summit of the Stampede Pass, with maximum grades of 290 feet to the mile, and was successfully operated for over a year, trains being hauled over the mountains by decapods or ten-wheeled engines, the heaviest ever built in America.

Weston (1,840 miles from St. Paul) is a small railroad town in the dense forests on the western slope of the Cascade mountains, at the foot of the mountain grade.

Along Green River.—After emerging from the tunnel the railroad descends by grades no steeper than those on the east side of the mountains into the valley of the Green river, in the midst of superb mountain scenery. Green river is a beautiful mountain stream, well stocked with trout, and flowing through dense forests of fir, cedar and spruce.

Eastern Slopes of Cascade Mountains, near the Stampede Tunnel.

Western Portal of Stampede Tunnel.

The Great Forests of Washington.—Here the traveler gets his first views of the dense forests of enormous evergreen trees which cover the whole country in Western Washington between the Cascade mountains and the Pacific ocean, except where the land has been cleared for farming along the valleys of the streams. A few small prairies here and there with a gravelly soil that will not support large trees, are the only spots in this region which nature left open.

An estimate of the forest area of Washington places the total at 23,558,000 acres, and the amount of standing timber is calculated to be about 400,000,000,000 feet, having a stumpage value at present of $270,000,000. The amount of merchantable timber per acre varies from 5,000 to 40,000 feet. In Chehalis county there are extensive districts that will average 32,000 feet per acre. The *Lumberman* has an article, the writer of which says that he has stood in a Chehalis forest and counted within a radius of 200 feet sixty-four trees, not one of which was less than four feet in diameter and from 200 to 400 feet in height, besides as many more smaller ones that would be termed "merchantable lumber." The secretary of the Board of Trade of Anacortes writes to the same journal that "16,000,000 feet of merchantable timber to the square mile in this county (Skagit) is not a high figure, when it is considered that there are many 40-acre tracts that will cut from three to four million feet each." A cedar tree from twelve to twenty feet in diameter, and from 150 to 350 feet high, the first limb being nearly or quite 100 feet from the ground, will cut a considerable number of feet of clear lumber, or quite enough shingles to fill several cars. While of course this is not average timber, it is not difficult to find such enormous trees, when occasion requires, in any of several of the counties of **Western Washington.**

Lake Kichelos, near the Summit of Cascade Range.

This forest region is beyond any question more heavily timbered than any other in the world. The stupendous growth of trees which covers it is accounted for by scientists by the great amount of rainfall, the absence of low winter temperatures, and the cool summers. All conditions are favorable to the development of vegetable life. Amid the gigantic trunks of the firs, cedars and spruces, there flourishes such a rank undergrowth that travelers who have penetrated the tropical forests along the Amazon say that the difficulties they encountered were not so great as those which must be overcome in going through these Washington woods.

Felling a Giant Fir.—Louise Herrick Wall, of Aberdeen, Wash., writes as follows in the *Atlantic Monthly:*

As we stood in the broad sunshine of the roadway the stillness took a far rhythmic pulse. It was the choppers once more at work upon a standing tree. We followed the sound, keeping to the fork of the skid road that led into the deeper forest, passed beyond the main group of loggers and the deep-breathing team, until we could hear the voices of the choppers.

As we came up the two men paused, and one said good-humoredly, "That's right! Come to see us fall this tree?" Then the axes swung again. Each man stood lifted up on a springboard, whose end was slipped into a notch cut in the base of the tree four or five feet from the ground. They always work above the ground this way, in order to escape the increased work of cutting through the great swell at the base. Standing with feet apart upon the springy perches, they were "under-cutting" the tree on the side toward which they wanted it to fall. The axes sent their pleasant reverberation up the straight, limbless trunk, communicating only a quiver to the plumed limbs two hundred feet above. Clean white chips were cleared out from the ⌳ shaped cleft of the undercut, and after a little measuring and squinting along the tree the men dropped down, and shifted their boards to notches in the opposite side of the tree from the under-cut. Then the long saw with handle at each end came into use. The men started carefully, holding the saw quite true that later it might not wedge. They drew it back and forth cautiously at first, until it penetrated the rough bark evenly and the teeth caught on the wood. A thin shower of pale sawdust floated down from either side, as the saw grated in and out and the loggers swayed slightly from hip to hip, their red-shirted arms moving with the iron regularity of piston-rods. Back and forth, back and forth, went the handle of the saw. It seemed an endless business for those two men to drive that edge of steel through twelve feet of solid, flawless wood. There is the dull monotony of machine-work in the sawing, different from the spirited rise and fall of the axes, and the sharp cracking away, beneath the telling blows, of great white chips, and our eyes wandered beyond the workers to the green stillness. Little clearing had been done at this point. The whole upper growth was of evergreens, and so dense that no speck of sky could be seen beyond their exalted tops—so dense that in this virgin forest the running elk throws his antlered head backward and from side to side to pass through the close phalanx of trees, and is sometimes wedged between their bodies and slowly perishes. Beneath the lofty canopy, supported upon its close, shaftlike columns, grew a matted tangle of underbrush and man-high elk fern, the pale green of the small-leafed huckleberry and salmonberry making a delicious note of freshness beneath the sombre grandeur of the dull green vault above. So dense is the overshadow-

A Glimpse of Green River.

ing of the evergreens that the air is moisture-laden in midsummer, and is seen through the vista of endless columns a vaporous blue, as of drifting incense. Upon the rough ground, muscular with plaited roots, mats of heavy moss, vividly green during the rainy season, lay in yellow patches.

The saw labored heavily as the weight of the tree began to settle upon the deeply imbedded blade; two steel wedges were driven a little way into the cleft, but although the weight was lifted the saw still moved hard. The men paused again, and one took the adjustable handle from his end of the saw, while the other drew the toothed blade half its length out toward him and spattered a liberal supply of kerosene oil from his bottle upon it; then pushing it back, the handle was readjusted. The men jerked up their trousers, wiped the sweat from their foreheads, and jumped heavily on their springboards to jar them back into place.

"All set!" called the older man, and once more the even grating, the piston-rod arms and the drifting drizzle of pale gold sawdust. Then the sound of the saw suddenly changed from the dry grate to a dull, soft mumble.

"Pitch!" exclaimed both men in a tone of deep disgust; and as they spoke, through the fine cleft the saw had made oozed a thick sluggish stream of turpentine, and crept down the side of the tree to the ground.

"There's barrels of it in this tree, and it's as slow as molasses in January."

But they settled themselves once more for work. The saw, gummed with pitch, moved with heavy resistance, and the steady ooze of the turpentine increased in volume.

"You'd better get that can, Jim," said the older man, and the other dropped from his perch into the underbrush and started for the road.

"Jest as well try to saw through a stick of taffy candy as this kind of tree," explained the waiting logger. "He's gone for the water-can, and we'll see if we can get through this vein."

Jim came back presently, carrying a leaky oil can heavy with water. A wedge was driven into the tree well above the saw and the can hung upon the wedge, so that the water leaked down upon the saw as it worked in and out.

"What good does it do?" I asked incredulously.

"Don' know," returned Jim, laboring at the saw, "but it makes awful easy sawing."

"Sort o' freezes the pitch," said the other philosophically.

As a matter of fact, the saw did move more freely, drawing in a little cold water each time, and the "frozen" pitch mixed with water frothed out in a white foam. After a long time of heavy sawing, the teeth began to catch more firmly, and a few more moments' work brought the saw very near to the "under-cut."

No message of its coming fall has reached the far top, now that the body of the tree is nearly severed; the branches stir less than at the first blows of the axe. The fir stands beautifully erect. The loggers squint up its length and say oracularly which way it will fall; they move the axes and water-can out of harm's way, and spring back to their perches. We stand on a fallen tree a few yards behind the loggers, and wait expectantly. There is an irresistible sense of excitement; even these men to whom it is such an old story feel it. Who can say what sudden wind will snatch the tree and throw it suddenly backward upon us? The brooding silence of the forest is absolute, save for the steady grate of the saw in and out, like stertorous breathing. Erect and motionless the tree waits.

Three Bridges and Tunnel, on Green River.

The men nod to each other; the sawing ceases; one handle is slipped off, and the saw drawn all the way through and laid back of the tree; one man springs down and lifts his perch out, and hands a great mallet to the other, who still stands upon his springboard. The mallet is lifted, and a loud sonorous chant rings through the stillness: "All clear ahead! Timber!" Then the mallet falls once, twice, thrice, upon the heads of the wedges. There is a slight creaking, the logger flings the mallet aside and rushes backward, the cleft widens, the great green head stirs; then, with a rushing, thundering roar, mingled with the sound of the rending fibres of the trunk, the giant tears its mighty arc through the air; a cloud of blackness envelops the fall: the air is dark with dust and moss and flying fragments. The roar is superb as the tree crashes its way through the underbrush, louder than cannon, but with no harshness; more like some mighty breaker that has climbed ten thousand miles of sea to beat its heart out on a lonely shore.

Buckley (1,882 miles from St. Paul; population, 1,000) is an important lumbering town in the White River valley. There are a number of hop ranches near the town.

In the Puyallup Valley.—After leaving the Green river, the road crosses two divides, first to the White river and then to the Puyallup, a picturesque stream fed from the glaciers on the slopes of Mt. Tacoma. The important coal mines of Carbonado, South Prairie and Wilkeson are situated at the headwaters of this river. Its lower course is through the most productive hop region in the world, where the possession of a few acres in hops makes the farmer independent for life.

Puyallup (1901 miles from St. Paul; population 2,000)

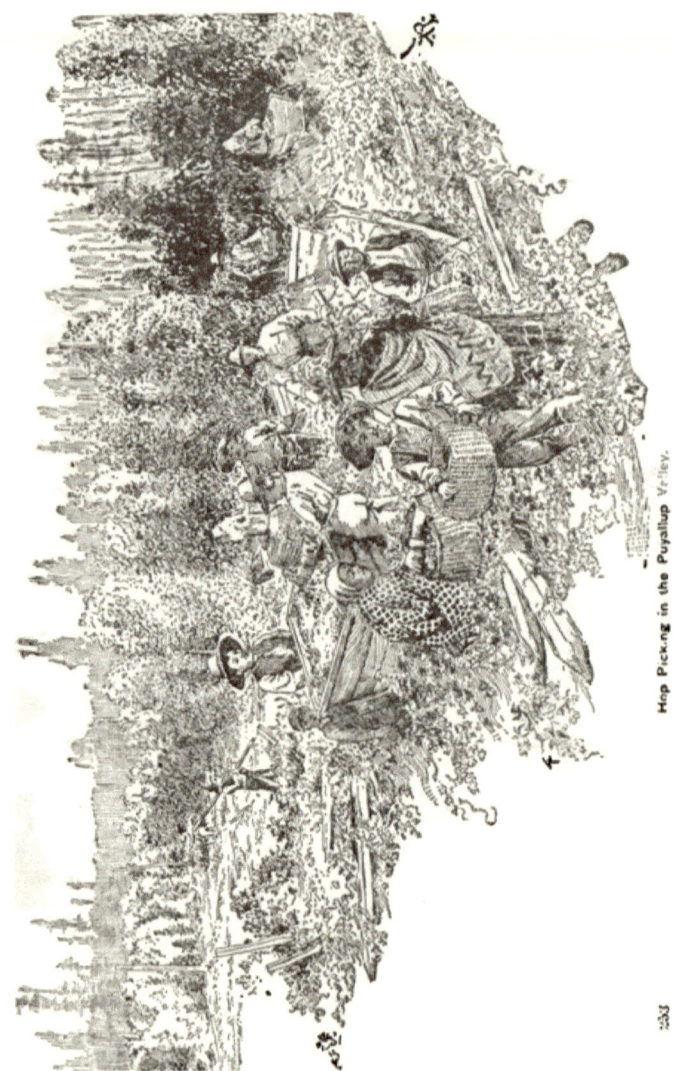

Hop Picking in the Puyallup Valley.

is essentially a hop town, being the trading point for all the hop-raising country in the valley of the Puyallup, Stuck and White rivers. The hop fields extend up to the very dooryards in the village, and the drying houses on the near hop farms are among the most conspicuous objects in the landscape. The tourist who has time to spare is advised to stop a day in Puyallup and investigate the very interesting industry which has created the town. The soil in this hop-growing valley seems to be inexhaustible. Wild land valuable for hop culture near Puyallup is worth from $75 to $100 per acre, and costs about $100 more per acre to clear. It is said that, taking an average of a period of years, every acre cultivated in hops will yield a net profit of at least $100. The price of hops varies widely from year to year, and is mainly dependent on the German crop. Some years it is claimed that there is no profit at all in hops raised in Washington, but in the long run the hop farmers all become comfortably well off. There are few forms of agricultural industry where so much money can be made from an acre of ground.

After leaving Puyallup the railroad traverses for about eight miles the Puyallup Indian reservation. These Indians own their land in severalty, and are, as a rule, industrious farmers. Their children are educated in the agency school, and the good order of the reservation is enforced by a justice of the peace and constables elected by the Indians themselves.

Tacoma (1,912 miles from St. Paul; population, 50,000) is the official western terminus of the Northern Pacific railroad and the point where it meets the commerce of the Pacific ocean. The road extends 100 miles further west, however, by a branch line that reaches the Pacific ocean at Ocosta and Hoquiam, on Gray's harbor. It has

Loading an Ocean Sailing Vessel at Tacoma.

also a second ocean terminus at South Bend, on Willapa harbor. From Tacoma the main line runs southward to Portland, and a branch turns northward to Seattle, where it connects with other lines controlled by the Northern Pacific that run as far as far as Vancouver, in British Columbia.

Tacoma is situated upon the tide water of the Pacific near the head of Puget sound, and occupies a commanding position both as a seaport and a railroad center. The arm of the sound upon which the city fronts is called Commencement bay, and furnishes an excellent harbor, where tha largest sailing vessels and ocean steamers lie at anchor or receive their cargoes of coal, lumber, wheat and other products of the region, at the spacious wharves, coal bunkers and warehouses.

Tacoma has had an extraordinarily rapid growth. When selected in 1872 as the Pacific coast terminus of the Northern Pacific railroad, the site was covered with a dense forest. The population in 1875 was only 300, in 1880 it was 760, in 1886 it was 6,907, in 1887 9,000, in 1888, 15,000, in 1889 25,000, in 1890, 30,000, and in 1898, about 50,000. The city is built upon a succession of benches or plateaus beginning at the head of Commencement bay, and sloping gradually upward to an elevation of about 300 feet, at the point where the bay joins the broader water of Puget sound. The landscapes and water views are superb. The Cascade range can be seen for nearly a hundred miles from north to south, and Mt. Rainier, one of the loftiest snow peaks in the United States, rises to a height of 14,532 feet, 10,000 feet of which are covered with snow fields and glaciers. This superb mountain, which has no rival in the world for beauty and grandeur, is in plain view from all the terraces of the new city. Tacoma is, next to San Francisco, the most impor-

Mount Tacoma From Commencement Bay.

tant wheat-shipping port on the Pacific coast. It also ships more lumber and more coal than any other port on that coast. The wheat goes around Cape Horn to Liverpool. The lumber goes to Calfornia, Mexico, South America, China, and Australia, and the coal is chiefly consumed in San Francisco. Lumber is manfactured at three large mills, one of which is the largest on Puget sound. The coal is brought in by rail from mines about thirty miles distant in the foot hills of the Cascade mountains. The principal mining towns are Carbonado, Wilkeson and Spring Prairie. It is also brought from Bucoda, south of Tacoma, on the Pacific division of the N. P. R. R. Wheat is received from all parts of the great wheat-producing region east of the Cascade mountains, and is stored and handled in enormous warehouses. Tacoma is the distributing point for emigration coming from the East and from California, and destined to all parts of Washington. It is also an attractive point for tourists.

It has one of the largest and best equipped hotels on the Pacific coast north of San Francisco, "The Tacoma," which stands on a high plateau overlooking Commencement bay, and a full view of the enormous snow peak of Mount Rainier. There are several handsome public school buildings, two colleges, and an Episcopal seminary for girls, called the "Anna Wright" seminary, in honor of the deceased daughter of Charles B. Wright of Philadelphia, ex-president of the Northern Pacific railroad, who has liberally endowed the institution. The Episcopal church is a beautiful stone structure, erected by Mr. Wright as a monument to the memory of his wife. Tacoma is the headquarters of the Western division of the Northern Pacific railroad, and has extensive car and repair shops. Pacific avenue, the principal business street, is a broad thorough-

Glaciers of Mount Tacoma.

fare, with numerous large and handsome buildings, and an extensive wholesale trade is done here. The city has water-works and gas-works, is well drained, and is remarkably healthy. Cable and electric roads furnish local transit. The manufacturing concerns include flouring and saw mills, a large smelter for smelting gold, silver, copper and lead ores, tile and brick works, furniture factories and a brewery. There are daily steamboats to Seattle, Port Townsend, Victoria, Olympia, and other places on the Sound. There is also regular weekly connection with San Francisco and with Alaska by ocean steamships.

A line of steamships under the British flag, but controlled by the Northern Pacific Railroad company, runs to Japan and China. The passage to Yokohama is made in about two weeks.

Tacoma and Seattle Line (from Tacoma to Seattle, 40 miles).—Tourists visiting Seattle from Tacoma should make the trip in one direction by rail and in the other by boat. The rail route runs through a series of highly fertile valleys, which are thickly settled with market gardeners, hop-raisers and fruit raisers and dairymen and which support a number of pretty and thriving towns. The trains run eastward on the main line for ten miles to Meeker Junction, passing through the hop metropolis of Puyallup, described elsewhere in this volume. From Meeker they turn north along the valleys of the Stuck, the White, the Black and the Dwamish rivers, and skirting the western shore of Elliot bay run into the heart of the city of Seattle. Frequent trains are run to accommodate the large travel between Seattle and Tacoma.

Sumner is a hop-growing village with about 500 inhabitants. The hop gardens come up almost to the doors of the pretty cottages. There is an academy for the higher

Glaciers of Mount Tacoma.

education of both sexes. Auburn, formerly called Slaughter, is a smart town of 1,000 inhabitants in a rich valley mainly devoted to hop culture and the small fruits and vegetables. Kent has 1,500 people and is the chief town on the line. With ten acres of land in this highly productive alluvial valley a farmer is looked upon as well-off. Kent is a well-built town in the midst of orchards, gardens and hop fields.

On Puget Sound.—All tourists visiting the Pacific coast should make a voyage on Puget sound, at least to the extent of taking the trip from Tacoma to Victoria and return. This is one of the most delightful and impressive excursions by water in the world. Nowhere else, save in Alaska and in Japan, can gigantic snow peaks be seen rising almost from the sea level to heights far above the clouds. The whole of the Cascade range from Mount Rainier to Mount Baker, its two white monarchs, is seen on the eastern horizon, and on the nearer western horizon rise the frowning rocky, snow-flecked walls of the Olympic mountains. All the shores are densely clad with evergreen forests. The waters of the sound are a clear sea-green and are enlivened by flocks of waterfowl. Seagulls follow the steamer and swoop down with clamorous cries for refuse from the tables thrown overboard by the stewards or for crackers tossed out by the passengers, who find much amusement in watching the movements of these tireless birds. Now and then a school of porpoises may be seen leaping out of the water in sportive, curving bounds.

The steamers on this route are large and handsomely equipped. A boat leaves Tacoma every morning, arriving in Victoria late in the afternoon and arriving in Tacoma on the return trip early next morning. Travelers should,

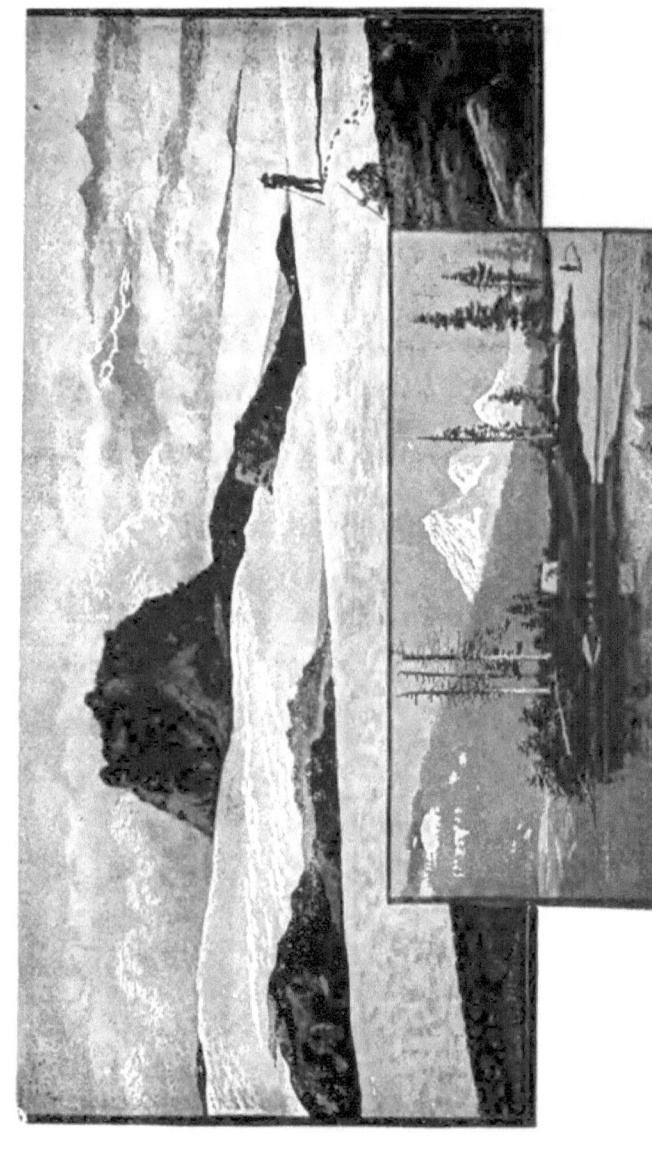

MOUNT TACOMA, AS SEEN IN AUGUST.
1. Looking westward, from an elevation of 10,000 feet, over a perpetual snow-field and the Carbon River Glacier.
2. Looking eastward, toward the summit, from Crater Lake.

however, arrange to spend a day in Victoria. The Sound is divided in its lower length by the large island of Whidby, which is thirty miles long. The Victoria boats take the western side of this island and call at Port Townsend. Another line of boats run east of the island as far as New Whatcom, calling at Everett, Anacortes and Fairhaven. Both lines touch at Seattle, which is the emporium of the middle Sound.

Seattle (41 miles from Tacoma by rail, and 27 miles by water, and 1,933 miles from St. Paul via the Cascade division; population, 80,000). This handsome and prosperous city is one of the oldest places on Puget sound, and was an important center of trade before Tacoma was founded. Its steady growth has not been checked by the rapid rise of the new city on Commencement bay. It is charmingly situated on a succession of high terraces which rise from the shores of Elliot bay. The city is laid out for a distance of three miles from the bay to the shores of Lake Washington, a fine body of fresh water, twenty miles long by about three miles wide. A similar lake, called Lake Union, connects with Lake Washington, and also with the Sound, and the suburbs of the city in a northeast direction advance to its shores. Seattle is the center of a remarkably complete system of steam navigation, which embraces all the towns and lumbering camps on the Sound, and also the navigable rivers of the region. A fleet of twenty-five steamboats is engaged in the local trade of the Sound, running to Tacoma, Olympia, Hood's Canal, Port Townsend, La Conner, Whatcom, and many minor points, and also up the White, Snohomish, Skagit, and Snoqualmie rivers. Ocean steamers run regularly to San Francisco, and the Alaska and Japan steamers touch here.

Educational facilities are provided by the State univer-

Snoqualmie Falls, on the Seattle, Lake Shore & Eastern Line.

sity, by the public schools, which occupy large and costly buildings, the Yesler college, an institution for boys, an academy for young ladies, a business college, and several private and denominational schools. There are 100 or more manufacturing concerns in the city, most of which are engaged in industries connected with the lumber trade.

There is an excellent system of electric and cable roads. An excursion that can be heartily recommended to visitors is to take a cable car to Lake Washington, where there are attractive lakeside resorts with facilities for yachting and rowing. Another pleasant cable trip is to the northern suburb of Queen Anne town, on the shore of Elliot bay. From the highest ground in the city, crossed by the lines of cable road running to Lake Washington, there is a superb view of the great mountain which is called Rainier in Seattle, and Tacoma in Tacoma.

In the summer of 1889, the entire business district of Seattle was totally destroyed by fire, including most of the wharves. The rebuilding of the city went on with a rapidity that was phenomenal and the new structures were all of brick and stone and far surpassed the old ones in their style and cost. The disaster resulted in making Seattle one of the handsomest and most solid cities in its architecture to be found anywhere in the country. All travelers are impressed by the beauty of the place and by the energy and progressive spirit of its people. The neighboring coal fields are one of the chief elements which contribute to the prosperity of Seattle. The mines now worked are chiefly in the vicinity of Renton and Newcastle, and are reached by a narrow-gauge railroad, twenty miles long. There are extensive coal fields, which have been explored, and are being developed, lying on the Green and Cedar rivers, near the base of the Cascade mountains. Coal is brought to the wharves in Seattle, and shipped by a line of steam colliers to San Francisco. Both the mining and shipping operations, as well as narrow-gauge railroad, are in the hands of the Oregon Improvement company. There is considerable agricultural land tributary to Seattle in the valleys of White, Green and Snoqualmie rivers.

Port Townsend is sometimes called the "Gate City of the Sound." It is situated at the entrance of Admiralty Inlet, on the Strait of Juan de Fuca, and is the port of entry for the entire Sound district. It has about 3,000 inhabitants, and its principal trade is in supplying the ships which enter and clear at its custom house. An iron furnace in the vicinity manufactures pig iron from hematite ore. There is a military post about three miles distant. The harbor at Port Townsend is an excellent one, being well sheltered from the north and west winds. The town is built upon two benches, the stores almost on a level with the water and the residences on a plateau about 100 feet high. Vehicles ascend by a gentle grade and pedestrians take a short cut by way of a long flight of stairs. The most conspicuous building is the United States custom house.

Victoria (117 miles from Tacoma) has a population of about 24,000, and is the seat of government for the Province of British Columbia. It is situated on the southern extremity of Vancouver's Island, on a small, landlocked bay which puts in from the waters of the broad strait of Juan de Fuca. Esquimault bay, three miles distant, is a station for the British navy, and has a large and extensive dry dock, constructed by the British government. The climate of Victoria is mild in winter and cold in summer, and the place is a **favorite** resort for tourists. Excellent roads lead into the country in every direction, and the scenery, especially along the shores of the strait, from whence the lofty and rugged range of the Olympian mountains is seen, is strikingly picturesque. Steamers leaving Tacoma in the evening arrive at Victoria the next morning. From Victoria, there is a steamboat connection with San Francisco, and also with Sitka, Alaska, and steamboats run across the Gulf of Georgia to Vancouver and New Westminster, on the main land.

The principal hotel is the Driard. The Parliament buildings are worth visiting. The two best drives are that to Esquimault and one which leads through the park out along the shore of the strait to the residence of the Lieutenant-Governor, who is the chief executive and representative of the Queen in the Province.

The following towns are on the eastern route, taken by the Sound steamboats that ply between Tacoma and Seattle and Whatcom.

Everett.—At the mouth of the Snohomish river, 30 miles from Seattle, is a new manufacturing town of 3,000 people, facing on both the river and the Sound and occupying the peninsula between the salt water and the deep, navigable stream. Here are located the ship-yards of the Pacific Coast Steel Barge company, which builds and repairs vessels of the new "whaleback" type. One of the largest paper mills in the world is also located at Everett, and a third important industry is the manufacture of steel wire nails. Lumbering, logging and farming on the tide

Castle Rock on the Columbia River.

flats are additional industries. The shore line of the Great Northern road is joined at Everett by the main line eastward across the mountains. There is also a connection with the Northern Pacific system by rail to Snohomish, six miles distant, by way of the Everett and Monte Cristo railroad, which runs to the Monte Cristo mining district at the base of the Cascade mountains.

Anacortes is a sea-port on Fidalgo island, facing Ship harbor. It has a fine land-locked harbor, to which ships can sail directly up the strait of Juan de Fuca from the Pacific ocean. Population, 1,500. River connection is had with the Great Northern and Northern Pacific systems by a road owned by the Oregon Improvement company.

Fairhaven is a town of about 3,000 people on a beautiful bay. It is on one of the lines of the Great Northern. On the north it touches elbows with the larger town,—

New Whatcom, population 6,000, formed by a consolidation of the old towns of Whatcom and Sehome. This place is built on the crescent shaped shore of Bellingham bay. Its industries are lumber and coal, and it has a large farming country back of it up the valley of the Nooksack river. Its railroads are the Great Northern and the Canadian Pacific, the latter running through sleepers to St. Paul. The voyage from New Whatcom to Tacoma occupies about twelve hours and is of constant scenic interest.

From Tacoma to Portland.—The distance from Tacoma to Portland is 144 miles and the latter city is the furtherest point from St. Paul to which the unbroken through trains of the Northern Pacific run. The road changes its direction at Tacoma, and runs nearly due south to the Columbia river, crossing first a number of

Salmon Leaping up Falls at the Da'les of the Columbia River.

gravelly prairies and several small streams flowing to Puget sound, following for a few miles the valley of the Chehalis, which flows into Gray's harbor, and then striking into the valley of the Cowlitz, a glacier-fed river of considerable size, which it follows down to the Columbia. The Cowlitz is navigable for about fifty miles for small steamboats. A good deal of fine farming, grazing and fruit country is seen on this journey in the valleys of the Chehalis and the Cowlitz. The train is ferried across the Columbia on an enormous transfer boat which takes engines and cars over at a single trip. At the crossing point the river is nearly two miles wide. Once on the southern bank the train runs up the river, keeping close to the shore, to the mouth of the Willamette, and then follows that stream to Portland. The attention of tourists is called to the superb views of Mount St. Helens and Mount Hood, which may be seen from the car windows, and to the beauties of the river scenery.

There are two lines for a part of the way between Tacoma and the Columbia. They diverge at Lake View and come together at Centralia. One of the through passenger trains follows one line and one the other. The route of most interest to tourists is that by way of Olympia, the capital of Washington.

Olympia (1,944 miles from St. Paul, population 4,000) is the capital of Washington, and is the oldest town in the country west of the Cascade mountains. It is beautifully situated at the head of the crescent-shaped body of water which was originally named Puget sound by an English explorer named Vancouver. The name is now generally applied to the whole body of water from the straits of Juan de Fuca to Olympia. Vancouver called the main body Admiralty inlet, and gave separate names to the smaller inlets, bays and channels. Olympia is an attractive place, with broad and well-shaded streets, and an abundance of fruit trees and flowers.

The court house is a remarkably handsome structure built of native sandstone. A State capitol costing $1,000,-000 is to be constructed. A good hotel, with broad piazzas, commands fine views of the town and Sound. Oyster fishing is an important industry. Electric cars run to Tumwater, three miles distant, where there is a water power that is used by several mills. Steamboats run daily to Tacoma and Seattle. There is also steamboat connection with the saw mill towns and lumbering camps on Hood's canal.

Puget Sound Clams.—An old settler writes thus to the *Olympian-Tribune* relative to the Olympia clams: "These mammoth clams, that live only in deep water and are only obtainable at the lowest tides, have a large, round opening at one end of the shell, through which they expand themselves, and I have seen them draw out through this opening, each one reaching the full diameter of an ordinary wash tub; and as to the "steaks" that may be cut from the neck of one big clam, dipped in egg and crumbs and fried, they would make a delicious breakfast for a family of four or five, equal to chicken's breast so served. In fact, these clams used to be called Puget sound chickens. We have not so many Indians hereabouts in these days to gather the big clams and bring them to our doors, but probably in the neighborhood of Butler's Cove they may still be found at lowest tide."

Centralia (1,961 miles from St. Paul; population 2,500) is an active trading town, doing business with the farmers in the Chehalis country. The neighboring valley lands produce large crops of all the small grains, Indian corn and potatoes. Apples, plums and pears, and the smaller fruits flourish. Several saw-mills are engaged in manufacturing cedar, spruce and pine lumber, and there are a number of shingle mills making cedar shingles. A branch of the Northern Pacific runs eastward down the valley of the Chehalis to Montesano and Aberdeen on that river, and ends at Oscosta, on Gray's harbor. A local railroad used mainly for logging runs eastward towards the Cascade mountains.

Chehalis (1,965 miles from St. Paul; population 2,500). This is a thriving town, supported by the fine agricultural country of the Chehalis valley. It is the county seat of Lewis county, and the seat of the State reform school. A Northern Pacific branch, described elsewhere, runs from Chehalis eastward to South Bend, a Pacific seaport town, on Willapa harbor. Chehalis makes furniture, lumber, shingles and flour.

Winlock, Castle Rock and Kelso are prosperous small towns in the Cowlitz valley, engaged in lumber manufacturing and in trade with the farmers in the valley. Old orchards show that this region has been settled many years. In fact, the pioneers went in from Portland before the State of Washington was set off from Oregon.

Kalama (2,016 miles from St. Paul and 40 miles from Portland), on the north bank of the river, is the county seat of Cowlitz county, and has 300 inhabitants. At one time this place had the ambition to become the commercial metropolis of the Columbia valley, and town lots were sold in the forests at high prices. Steamboats plying between Portland and Astoria call at Kalama.

After the train leaves the huge transfer boat on the south bank of the Columbia river it runs through a timbered country nearly all the way to Portland, with occasional clearings and farm settlements. In clear weather supurb views may be enjoyed from the train windows of Mount St. Helens and Mount Hood. St. Helens has a form like a sugar loaf and is about 9,000 feet high. Hood, more distant, has a sharp pyramidal peak and an elevation of about 11,000 feet. These gigantic mountains are covered with snow during the entire year.

By way of Tenino—In case the traveler goes from Tacoma to Portland by the other or westernmost line of the railroad, he will enjoy at Yelm Prairie, twenty-five miles from Tacoma, a revelation of unsurpassed grandeur, provided the sky be cloudless, in the view of Mount Tacoma, the loftiest of all the snow mountains. As the train rushes onward, occasional breaks in the forest allow the sight of this snow-clad peak to a great advantage. It is about forty miles distant, although its vast bulk is so distinct that it seems much nearer than that.

A view from Mount Adams, away to the eastward on the further side of the Cascade range, is to be obtained at several points as the train goes southward. It is seen across the wooded valley of the Nisqually, its white mass in bold relief against the sky, its sides seamed in summer with outcropping rock ridges, the hollows being filled with never-melting snow.

Tenino (1,950 miles from **St. Paul**).—The Olympia & Chehalis Valley railroad, a narrow-gauge line fifteen miles long, owned by an independent corporation, connects Olympia, the capital of Washington and the county seat of Thurston county, with the track of the Northern Pacific railroad at Tenino. Here are quarries of excellent gray sandstone.

Bocoda (1,954 miles from St. Paul) is a coal mining

town with a population of about 500. The coal is bituminous and is used for locomotive and domestic fuel.

Portland (2,056 miles from St. Paul; population, 90,000) is the oldest commercial metropolis and railroad center of the Northern Pacific, and is the largest city of the Pacific Coast next to San Francisco. It is a beautiful city, well built in both its business and residence districts, and standing upon a gentle slope stretching from the bank of the Willamette river westward, for a distance of about two miles, to a range of steep, wooded hills. The city extends for about the same distance up and down the river. Its residence streets are shaded with maples and ash, elms, horse-chestnuts and other shade trees, and most of the houses front upon lawns and flower gardens. Indeed, Portland is a city of flowers and foliage, the mildness of the climate and moisture of the atmosphere causing vegetation to flourish. The winter climate is so mild that roses usually bloom until the first of January.

The situation of Portland was determined by the fact that the Willamette valley was the first settled portion of Oregon, and the commercial city of the state naturally sprang up at the point nearest to the wheat fields of Willamette valley to which sea-going ships could get access. This point was not on the Columbia river, but as far up the Willamette as vessels of deep draught could go. Two lines of railroad belonging to the Southern Pacific system terminating here penetrate the Willamette valley, draining the country on both sides of the Willamette. One of these lines extend southward to the California boundary and thence to San Francisco A system of narrow-gauge railroad devised to furnish transportation facilities to portions of the valley not reached by the other roads, also terminates in Portland. The main line of the Oregon Rail-

Cape Horn, on the Columbia River.

road and Navigation Company extends eastward via the Union Pacific to Omaha, and by means of numerous branches reaches nearly all the productive country of Eastern Oregon, and a large portion of Eastern Washington. Westward from Portland the Northern Pacific main line reaches down the Columbia forty miles, and thence northward to Puget sound. Ocean steamships ply regularly between Portland and San Francisco, and river steamboats run on the Columbia and Willamette. Portland is thus a focus of the transportation system of the Pacific Northwest. It is also an important post for ocean commerce, and a large part of the wheat surplus of Oregon and Washington goes from the wharves of Portland by sailing vessels to Liverpool and other European ports.

Portland has many handsome business blocks which would be creditable to any city in the East. It exports about nineteen million bushels of wheat annually. Portland has a good electric and cable street-car system, water, gas and electric light works, a public library, daily newspapers, great wharves and warehouses, numerous handsome churches, and many spacious public school edifices, the largest of which, the High School building, is the handsomest public school structure on the Pacific coast. The exhibition building is a conspicuous structure.

The principal hotel is "The Portland," which occupies an entire city block and is built in the form of a letter H so that every room looks out on a street. It is unsurpassed in its appointments by any hotel on the Pacific coast. A fine view of the city can be had from the tower of the *Oregonian* building. Tourists are recommended to take the cable road to Portland Heights. It ascends an inclined plane of rather alarming steepness to a lofty residence suburb from which a landscape of wonderful extent and beauty can be seen, embracing both the Willamette and Columbia rivers and the snow peaks of Mount Hood and Mount St. Helens. Tourists will find much of interest in the life of the Chinese quarter and should visit the Chinese stores, the Joss house and the theatre. There are about 20,000 Chinese in Portland. An agreeable excursion can be made by electric car across the Willamette to Albina. The following is from a recent description of Portland in *The Northwest Magazine:*

"There is always a natural capital to every geographical division of the country to which each feature points with index finger, and in which is typified the supporting territory. The commercial and social center of these fertile valleys of the Cascade mountains is Portland, a city as marked in its appearance as is the country itself. It lies along the crescent of the river, nestles upon the sides of the encircling hills and spreads over the tableland on the opposite banks. Its business streets, its wharves, its residences all tell, in a language which any thinker may read, its past, its present and its future. To the traveler from the East whose eyes have been dimmed by the heat radiating from sandy mesas on which the sparse sage-brush serves only to emphasize the dreariness and desolation, the valleys leading to Portland seem like the vales of Tempe and the city appears at first sight like some municipality transported intact from New England. Closer investigation shows that this similarity has many exceptions, and, with all fairness, the differences are in favor of this young giant of the Cascades. There is more coloring in the Western city, more of the picturesque while nothing is lacking in the staunch qualities for which the Atlantic coast cities are famous. Life is brighter, fresher and more vigorous on the Western coast, and this fact is everywhere apparent. The somber blocks of residences are here noticeable by their absence. Each residence has about it an individuality which is as surprising as delightful. In the dooryards are rosebushes whose blooms would shame the choicest flowers of Eastern hot-houses. Vines clamber over gates and hide the fronts or sides of many homes in a veil of dark ivy or of the lighter Virginia creeper. Verandas tell the story of an atmosphere like velvet, whose caressing touch is sought in outdoor hours. Bright colored awnings add their variety to the scene and hammocks are found everywhere. Now and then palms are discovered with their great fronds lending a tropical trait to the picture which is well nigh deceptive unless reflection comes to the rescue. The great hills back of the city, with their rugged fronts and coatings of rough fir, bring back the imagination and emphasize the fact that here the natural surroundings act as a tonic and a comfort, not as a narcotic. The miles of wharves and warehouses, above which tower the slender masts of ocean vessels, the great elevators, the shipyard, the noise of heavy laden trucks, the screeching of switch engines, the rumble of trains, all corroborate the same impression.

The site of a city is as susceptible of analysis as is the camp of an army. The battalions of trade may make a temporary bivouac anywhere, but when they form a permanent base of supplies they do so for strategic reasons, whether consciously or unconsciously acknowledged. Generals have made mistakes and so have pioneers, but Portland is not one of them. Whether its location was an accident or a judgment, its prestige is certain and its future can be read in its surroundings.

Ages ago the elements began to carve out the future location and territory of Portland from the earth itself,

Cascades of the Columbia River.

Within the arms of the Blue mountains was a great sea. As the waters sought an outlet to the greater ocean, they burst through the hemming barrier in a mighty stream, which even to-day is famous for its size—the Columbia. From all the arms of that sea, reaching into what are now magnificent valleys, came other streams which cut through the silted strata of the old sea bed and joined the outlet. Thus by the hand of nature were the different territories connected, pointing clearly to a common center. As if the invention of man had been foreseen and provided for, the coming of the railroads did not affect geographical values. Engineers found that erosion had done more for them than thousands of navies could have accomplished in scores of years and they wisely followed the construction forces of ages past. The iron bound track crept through the passes of the mountains along the banks of the river, and the conditions which pointed to Portland as a commercial center were only doubled in strength, and nature and science have riveted to the city the wonderfully fertile districts of the mountains by furnishing natural and artificial highways to her marts.

The origin of Portland is in the main prosaic. In the earlier days when vessels depended more upon chance and barter, a venturesome captain turned inquisitively up the broad Columbia to dispose of his goods. The ocean-traveling hull found ample welcome in the river which it traversed until it reached its practical level of navigation. Here it reached its great tributary, the Willamette, which it followed until a trading station was begun, the stock being the cargo which had thus been brought nearer the consumer. This point naturally became the center of distribution for the country. Vessels came in greater numbers with each succeeding year. Wagon roads were built

Multnomah Falls, Columbia River.

to make the post accessible, and steamer lines were established. Trade increased, population multiplied, and additional buildings were erected until the little commercial sapling showed many concentric rings of growth and the trading station had become a city thoroughly metropolitan in character.

Subsequent events proved the wisdom of a choice of site which is so advantageous it might well be characterized as inspired. The Columbia rushes seaward with a velocity of twelve to fifteen miles an hour, and the heavy stream would nearly sweep vessels from their fastening at wharves along its banks. In spring, too, ice would hurt the refuge and would be a source of infinite trouble to shipping. All such annoyance is avoided by turning into the broad avenue of the Willamette. Here is depth, a gentler flow, and, in times of high water, the river instead of becoming a torrent is transformed into a great lake as far as the falls at Oregon City above Portland. Thus is Portland located on a navigable *cul de sac* connected by a magnificent watery highway with the Pacific.

River Excursions from Portland.—A number of very attractive steamboat excursions may be made from Portland. One is up the Willamette to the falls at Oregon City. Here the river makes a perpendicular leap of about fifty feet, forming one of the most magnificent cataracts in the world. The Government has constructed a canal around the falls, with locks cut in the solid rock. A very curious sight may be seen when the salmon are running up the river. Thousands of these brilliant-scaled fish attempt to jump up the falls at points where there are projections of rock. A few succeed but many fall back wounded into the whirlpools below.

Another interesting trip is to go down the Willamette and

Pillars of Hercules and Rooster Rock, on the Columbia River.

up the Columbia as far as the Cascades, where the Government has been engaged for nearly a lifetime in slowly excavating a ship canal in the rocky south bank of the river. A stretch of the grandest scenery of the Columbia is passed. On the south, mountain summits stand like a wall, grouped at times like an amphitheatre, at other times assuming romantic shapes, and frequently affording views of falling waters that are very beautiful. Here is Oneonta Fall, 800 feet of sheet silver, a ribbon of mist waving in the wind. Multnomah Fall is double. The water plunges several hundred feet, gathers itself together, and plunges again, about 800 feet in all. There are several other cascades of less note that never fail, and in early spring the face of the cliffs is threaded with them. A few miles westward are the Pillars of Hercules, two columns of rock several hundred feet in height, between which the train passes, as through a colossal portal, to the more open lands beyond. Near by is Rooster rock, rising out of the river, and pointing upward like a mighty index finger.

The Cascades are in about the center of the Cascade mountain range. The river, that has flowed placidly all the way from The Dalles, has become wider, and spreads out in unbroken stillness, no motion being apparent. It is gathering itself for the plunge over the Cascades. In a moment it changes from a placid lake to swift rapids, and soon becomes a foaming torrent as the fall increases and the waters encounter boulders in the stream.

Immediately at the Cascades the scenery is very fine. The mountains are grand, standing on the south like walls of adamant, and lifted to towering heights, their sides cleft open at intervals by deep ravines, the rock ledges of which are hidden by firs. Some of the rocky pinnacles and turrets along the heights are of strange, stern architecture.

Mount Hood, from the Head of the Dalles, Columbia River, Oregon.

On the north the mountains recede, and pyramidal forms contrast with tremendous frowning outlines, that stand like some Titanic fortress. There is a fine view of the Cascades from the train, and of the mountains on the north. At railroad speed the Lower Cascades are soon passed, and Bonneville, the point at which the steamboats on the lower river make their landing, is reached.

Near the Upper Cascades on the Washington side of the river, on a point of land that juts out so as to make a good defensive position, there is still standing an old block house, built forty years ago, when the Indians were more numerous than peaceable. War broke out all along the coast, from British Columbia to California, in 1855. The Indians had some sort of a unison, and outbreaks were almost simultaneous for that distance of 800 miles, though some of the more powerful tribes refused to join the alliance, and gave notice of danger. At that time the Cascades were already important as the portage where all things bound up the river had to make a transit. Suddenly the outbreak came. The blockhouse became the refuge of all settlers, who were defended by the male population, and by a handful of soldiers, stationed there at the time under command of a young lieutenant named Sheridan. So the legend of the Indian and the wonders of nature are supplemented by a bit of history that has for its heroic character the famous Gen. Phil. Sheridan, who afterward became one of the most conspicuous figures in the great civil war.

The Indians have a tradition that once the great snow mountains, Hood and Adams, stood close to the river at the Cascades, with a natural arch of stone bridging one to the other. The mountains quarreled, threw out stones, ashes and fire, and, in their anger with each other, demolished the arch. Before that time, the Indians say, their fathers had passed up and down beneath the arch in their canoes, and the stream was navigable; but when the arch fell it choked the river, and created the rapids that now exist. The legend goes on to say that the " Sahullah Tyhee," or Great Spirit, was so angry with the contending mountains that he hurled them north and south, where they stand to-day.

This legend has some foundation, judging from the present conditions. It is evident, from the state of the shores and the submersion of forests, that some great convulsion has occurred and thrown down the rocky walls adjoining the river. Just above the Cascades the view includes beautiful islands, not far from the brink of the rapids; and between the islands and the rapids some ancient forest has been submerged, with the tree trunks still standing beneath the waves. It is commonly known to river men and steamboat men that this submerged forest stands there, and it is often pointed out to travelers. How long since it grew on the shore, no one knows. Indian legends are never accurate, and we can only surmise that it was long centuries before the white man came.

In connection with this legend, there are scientific data to establish the fact that some great convulsion has taken place and blocked the stream. When the rock walls fell and choked the channel, the effect was to raise the waters and deaden the flow for eight miles above. The work of engineers who have built and superintended the railways constructed around the Cascades for twenty years back, has demonstrated that, for a distance of three miles on the south, a great spur of the mountains is moving toward the river. The engineers who made the examinations connected with the canal and locks the Government is now constructing around the Cascades, have determined that the impending mountain of basalt rests on a bed of conglomerate,

with a substratum of sandstone, pitching toward the river.
As the river wears away under the basalt, the rock masses
move toward it. It is very possible that at some remote
period, when the river had worn out a gorge, and precipices
lined the shore, the waters undermined this wall and aided
its descent on the incline of sandstone and conglomerate,
so as to produce the effect which is seen, and confined to a
short distance the fall that previously covered fifteen miles.

Still another enjoyable river trip is to Astoria, at the
mouth of the Columbia, a distance of a little less than a
hundred miles from Portland. The Columbia, on its lower
course, is a mighty flood, widening as it nears the ocean.
Its banks are covered with sombre fir forests and rise abruptly to low mountain ridges. Astoria is the principal center of
the salmon fisheries and is also an important lumber manufacturing place. The level ground at the foot of the
steep hills that border the river is of such scanty width that
the business streets are mainly built over the water on
piles, the roadways being of stout plank. Under the
streets and buildings may be heard the swash of the rising
and falling tide. Many of the fishermen save the cost of
building sites by living in house-boats which they moor on
vacant water lots. Sea-going ships, carrying wheat, often
take a part of their cargo here from lighters, in order to
have a less draft coming down the river from Portland
than they require when fully loaded. The canning of salmon is carried on at numerous establishments along the
river front. Fishing is done out on the bar in small boats
manned by men from almost every maritime nation of the
world. Astoria has a population of about 8,000. The forts
at the mouth of the river and the enormous jetty three
miles long, built out into the ocean to deepen the entrance,
are well worth visiting.

LAKE SUPERIOR DIVISION.

ASHLAND, WIS., TO STAPLES, MINN., 206 MILES—CONNECTING AT STAPLES WITH MAIN LINE TRAINS.

This line runs through a pine forest country for its entire length. It skirts the shore of Lake Superior from Ashland to Duluth, 76 miles, then follows the course of the St. Louis river for about 20 miles, and afterwards runs across the plateau of Northern Minnesota. At Aitkin it strikes the Mississippi river, and at Brainerd it crosses that stream.

Ashland, Wis., (population 15,000) is the county seat of Ashland county. Ashland is also the extreme eastern terminus of the Northern Pacific railroad system. It is an important shipping and manufacturing point. This prosperous town has a beautiful location on the picturesque Bay of Chequamegon, facing the Apostle islands. It has an excellent harbor and considerable lake commerce. It is the northern terminus of the Wisconsin Central railroad, running to Milwaukee and to many important towns in the center of the State. The Milwaukee, Lake Shore & Western line of the Chicago & Northwestern system also terminates here. The Chicago, St. Paul, Minneapolis & Omaha system has a line extending from St. Paul to Washburn, a few miles distant, across the bay, with a branch to Ashland. Ashland is the largest shipping port of iron ore in the United States. The ore is brought from the mines on the Gogebic range, about 30 miles distant, by two lines of railroad, the Wisconsin Central, and the Milwaukee, Lake Shore & Western; and is shipped by steam and sailing vessels from three immense ore docks, one of which belongs to the former railroad company, and two to the latter. These docks handle over 1,000,000 tons of ore annually, affording cargoes to nearly 800 vessels, the greater part of which are bound for Cleveland, O. The docks and approaches are over 3,000 feet long, and the docks proper are 1,405 feet long. On each side are 117 pockets holding 120 tons each. The capacity of each dock is 28,000 tons, and each required over 5,000,000 feet of timber for its construction. Ashland manufactures a great deal of lumber and makes charcoal, and iron and steel from the ore of the Gogebic range. A blast furnace makes charcoal iron. Ashland has a great reputation as a summer resort. It has a number of hotels; the Chequamegon house is one of the best summer hotels in the country, and is filled with guests during the warm season. The cool breezes from Lake Superior make the summer climate always agreeable and the opportunities for yachting, rowing and fishing upon the beautiful water, and for drives through the pine forests, render Ashland a delightful place in which to spend the summer months. Steamers, with excellent passenger accommodations run to Duluth and to all lower lake ports as far as Buffalo.

Trout Streams.—Between Ashland and Superior the Northern Pacific road runs through a picturesque forest region, traversed by many small trout streams which flow into Lake Superior. The most frequented trout stream on this road is Brule river, which is much visited during the fishing season by sportsmen from St. Paul and Minneapolis.

Iron Ore Docks at Ashland, Wisconsin.

A St. Paul club has erected a rude, but comfortable, log house for the use of its members. Boats and Indian guides can be procured there.

Superior, Wis. (Population 30,000.)—The present city of Superior was formed a few years ago by the consolidation of two municipalities—Superior, commonly called Old Superior, which dates back to the fifties and occupied the plateau facing the entrance to the Bay of Superior, and West Superior, a new town started in 1884 on the Bay of St. Louis facing Duluth. These two places grew together, and having common interests naturally united their local governments. The consolidated city occupies a harbor frontage on the three bays of Allouez, Superior and St. Louis, of over ten miles in length, and has become one of the most important commercial, milling and manufacturing points in the Northwest. In some respects Duluth and Superior form a single city. The wheat stored in the elevators of one is bought and sold in the grain exchange of the other. Vessels may take part of their cargo at one place and the rest at the other. The great coal companies which furnish from Ohio and Pennsylvania mines the fuel of the entire Northwest have docks on both sides of the harbor. There is a constant flow of people back and forth between the two towns, bent on errands of business or pleasure. Yet no future union is possible by reason of the barrier of the State boundary line, and each place seeks earnestly its own growth and advantage and is jealous of the success of its neighbor across the water. Duluth has at present about 50,000 inhabitants and Superior about 30,000. Each has grown with marvelous rapidity, but the conversion of Superior from a dead village into a city did not begin until after Duluth had secured its docks, its elevators, its railroads

Coal Docks at Superior, Wis.

and its shipping movement; and when it did begin it took hold of a tract of forest and changed it in a few years to a well-built town, with handsome streets, big factories, towering elevators and enormous docks.

The site of Superior is remarkably favorable for city building, and this fact has been a strong factor in its growth. It is a plateau sloping just enough to the water for good drainage, and traversed here and there by shallow ravines or coulees which serve as aids to the drainage system. On two sides of the broad triangle of land which the city occupies there is deep navigable water, and reaching nearly a mile inland is a long arm or inlet known as Howard's Pocket, on which is located the great steel barge plant. A shorter inlet called Tower Slip affords water frontage for the new flouring mills at the West End. Along the Bay of St. Louis are the five grain elevators, the huge coal docks, the oil docks and the merchandise docks, and there is ample room for the further march of commerce along the shore line up the bay towards the steel works. The sawmills and lumber yards occupy both the water fronts of Conner's Point. On the Bay of Superior side of the city there is a great deal of unoccupied water front for future docks and factories between the Point and the new flouring mills at the East End. The level ground of the plateau gives the numerous railways ample space for their tracks, yards and freight warehouses, and their spur tracks run out upon the docks and alongside the mills and factories. The great, notable and unique advantage of the site of Superior for the development of manufacturing and commercial movement lies in the fact that every sort of concern requiring good shipping facilities can build its plant where the lake steamers can load and unload on one side and the freight cars on the

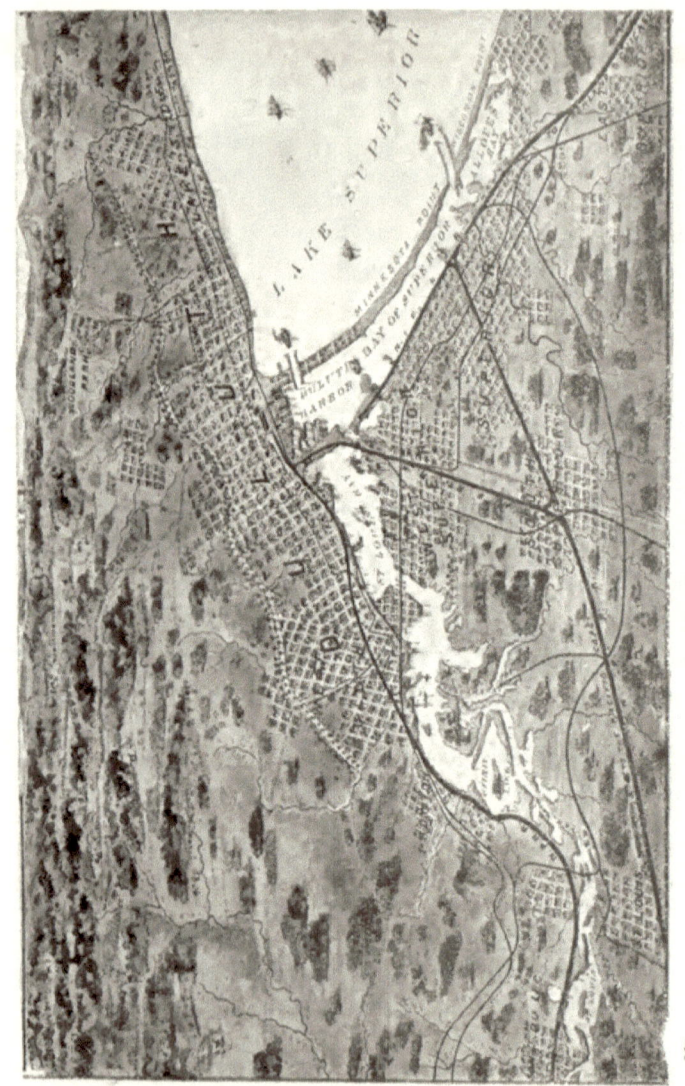

Duluth and the Superiors.

other. It is this fact, supplemented by liberal and energetic management of town site interests, that has produced the surprising growth of the past few years.

Two manufacturing plants of very great importance were located in West Superior at an early date in the history of the place. The first was Capt. McDougall's shipyard for the building of his peculiar craft known as the whaleback, and the second was the steel plant where the ribs, beams and plates of these vessels are made. These concerns alone employ workmen enough to make, with their families, a considerable town. The grain elevators, the coal docks and the saw mills came about the same time to employ another army of people, so that the new town sprang as if by miracle, under the magic touch of enterprise, into vigorous life. As an economical carrier the whaleback has made for itself a place in the face of all conservative scepticism and opposition. It is capacious, fast and seaworthy. Ugly in appearance and devoid of all attempts at ornament and beauty, it represents in marine architecture the materialistic spirit of modern times. It is, in fact, a huge, cigar-like steel tank, with machinery in its stern, and cabins perched above for the housing of its crew. Its shape offers the least possible resistance to winds and waves. No opposing force of air or water strikes it at a right angle. Everywhere there is a curved surface presented to ward off the blows. All the whalebacks are exclusive freight boats except the Christopher Columbus, which has a cabin for passengers extending over its whole length and supported on steel turrets. This craft found its first use in carrying passengers back and forth between Chicago and the World's Fair grounds. Both the building and running of these novel craft are under the personal supervision of their inventor, Capt. McDougall.

A new industry came to Superior in 1891 and 1892, the future influence of which in promoting the growth of the city can hardly be foretold. A general conviction that the head of Lake Superior is the best point for flour milling in the United States has been gaining ground in milling circles for some years, and all at once it ripened into action. The success of the big Imperial mill at Duluth confirmed the theory. During the years named, three large, first-class mills were erected or started at West Superior and three more at the East End. The new West End mills are the Freeman, the Grand Republic and the Minkota, with a combined grinding capacity of 5,300 barrels daily. At the East End the new mills are the Lake Superior, the Listman and the Anchor, whose combined capacity is 6,500 barrels. Add the old Gill & Wright mill at the West End, capacity 600 barrels, and we have a grinding capacity of the new milling center of 12,400 barrels a day. Add to this the capacity of the two mills at Duluth, 6,500 barrels, and it appears that the head of the lake now has a capacity of 18,500 barrels a day, or very nearly half the capacity of the mills of Minneapolis, which are rated at 40,000 barrels. This is a surprising development. Yet it is a natural and inevitable result of the settlement of the great wheat belt of the Northwest and the building of railroads to the point where the deep-water navigation of the great lakes penetrate farthest into the continent.

Superior is an important railroad center, and ranks among the leading shipping ports on the upper lakes. It has twelve large grain elevators with an aggregate capacity of 15,000,000 bushels, seven immense coal docks, and a merchandise dock. As a manufacturing town, it is already one of the foremost in the Northwest. An iron and steel plant was erected in 1888 with a capital of two millions of dollars.

There are two large lumber mills which make an annual cut of about 75,000,000 feet. An extensive wagon factory is located at South Superior and there are several barrel factories. The coal receipts are over a million tons a year. Coke ovens, owned by the Lehigh company, make coke from Pennsylvania and Ohio coal. A handsome hotel, of large dimensions, called "The West Superior," was completed in 1889. The railway terminal facilities are very extensive, and are used by the Northern Pacific, the St. Paul & Duluth, the Eastern Minnesota, the Chicago, St. Paul, Minneapolis & Omaha, and the Duluth, South Shore & Atlantic roads. Communication is had with Duluth by two lines of railway and by steam ferries. A recent commercial development of much importance was the building of an enormous iron ore dock on the Bay of Allouez for the shipment of ore from the Mesaba range and the building of a railroad from Superior to the range.

Duluth, Minn. (population 60,000), is the third city in Minnesota, and is one of the most important wheat markets and wheat shipping points in the world. The city is built upon high ground overlooking Lake Superior and the bays of Superior and St. Louis, and is over seven miles long from the extreme eastern suburbs on the shore of the lake to its western limits on the Bay of St. Louis. Its harbor is capacious and entirely landlocked, being entered by an artificial channel, cut across a long, narrow sandy peninsula, known as "Minnesota Point." The grain elevators, which are the most conspicuous structures in the commercial district, have an aggregate capacity of about 21,000,000 bushels. The neighboring elevators in West Superior are operated in close connection with the Duluth elevators, and the wheat stored and handled in both places is represented in the operations of the Duluth Board of

Trade. The grain is shipped in steam and sailing vessels of heavy tonnage; a steam propeller usually taking two or three sailing craft in tow. Most of the wheat shipments are to New York by way of Buffalo and the Erie canal. A large grain steamer, with a capacity of 90,000 bushels, equivalent to 180 car loads, can be loaded at Duluth in half a day. It has often happened that such a steamer, arriving at the elevators at 7 o'clock in the morning, has been outside of the harbor with her cargo aboard before noon of the same day. Duluth has become in recent years a more important wheat-shipping port than Chicago, and in the volume of grain annually dispatched to the East it now leads all Western cities. Next to wheat, the most important article of commerce is coal, the receipts of which are nearly 2,000,000 tons annually. Iron ore is shipped from the Mesaba range. The manufactures of the city consist of lumber, flour, iron and steel, and railway cars. The railways centering in the place are the Northern Pacific, the St. Paul & Duluth, the Chicago, St. Paul, Minneapolis & Omaha, the Eastern Minnesota, the Duluth, South Shore & Atlantic, the Duluth, Missabe & Northern, the Duluth & Winnipeg, and the Duluth & Iron Range. The latter road runs northward to the great iron mines in the Vermillion range. The fisheries of Duluth are an important industry. White fish and trout are caught in large quantities and shipped to St. Paul and Minneapolis, and to all the towns in Minnesota, the Dakotas and Montana. Duluth has a large, first-class hotel, "The Spaulding," and a number of smaller establishments.

The city with its suburbs is of ribbon-like shape, extending for over ten miles along the shore of Lake Superior, of the Bay of Superior, the Bay of St. Louis and the St. Louis river, and having but a narrow width between the water and the precipitous hillsides. Electric and steam roads afford rapid transit from end to end of the place and an inclined plane road runs up the high bluffs from the heart of the business district. A boulevard drive along the side of the bluffs affords admirable views of the lake and bays and of all the commercial activities of the city. Tourists should visit the Board of Trade, where the wheat trade is carried on. The Government fish hatchery, at the eastern end of the city, is well worth seeing.

A voyage on Lake Superior on one of the large passenger steamers which leave Duluth daily during the season of navigation for the Saulte Ste. Marie and for all ports on the lower lakes is one of the most healthful and agreeable journeys imaginable. There is rarely any rough weather to produce sea sickness. The air is singularly pure and exhilarating. The steamers following the south shore route call at Ashland, Bayfield, the copper-mining towns of Houghton and Hancock and the iron-shipping port of Marquette, and at the "Soo" are locked through the great canal. The north shore boats call at the Canadian city of Port Arthur.

The upper part of Lake Superior is one of the most interesting points to the geologist on the North American continent. It is on good grounds considered the oldest region in the world. The theory is that the formation of the lake is due to some great volcanic action, long prior to the ice period; perhaps that the lake itself was the mouth of a great volcano. Duluth is built on the rim of this lake basin, upon foundations of trap and conglomerates of every conceivable description, with seams of quartz and veins of iron, copper and silver often cropping out at the surface. The ancient lake bed extends some twenty miles above Duluth, over Grassy Point, Spirit Lake, and the bed of the St. Louis river, as far as Fond du Lac, around which the lake rim curves, inclosing a region of striking beauty. The chain of hills is here cut through by the St. Louis river, causing that wonderful series of rapids which, in a distance of twelve miles, have a fall of 500 feet through masses of slate, trap, granite and sandstone, and are celebrated as the picturesque regions of the Dalles of the St. Louis.

The mean temperature of Duluth, during the summer, is as follows: June, $57° 9'$; July, $61° 9'$; August, $63° 6'$; September, $58° 5'$. Summer visitors find here every convenience for fishing, hunting and sailing parties. Tourists and scientists usually have an abundance of time at their disposal, and are able at leisure to find out the most desirable localities. But there are many who come by lake, and have only a day to spare, or the brief period that a boat is waiting. To the latter class a trip to the Dalles of the St. Louis, via the Northern Pacific railroad, is one of the most profitable ways of spending the time.

The Gooseberry river is considered the best trout stream on the north shore, then Split Rock, and Stewart and Knife rivers, in the order named. Among the fine bays and islands most popular with tourists are Knife island and Stony Point, Agate, Burlington and Flood bays. Agate Bay, especially, is visited, and the name is very appropriate. Its shores are lined with agates, among an endless variety of other variegated and curiously colored conglomerates, all specimen chips from the neighboring rocks and hills, but worn more or less smooth by the perpetual friction and grinding of the wave-washed beach. The north shore is very precipitous, and abounds in fine scenery. Cascades and rapids are to be found on nearly all the streams.

Carlton (23 miles from Duluth and 131 miles from St. Paul; population, 1,000).—This is the junction of the St. Paul & Duluth and the Northern Pacific railroads, and a branch of the St. Paul & Duluth railroad, known as the Knife Falls branch, which runs six miles north to Knife Falls and Cloquet, where large quantities of lumber are manufactured.

Aitkin (87 miles west of Duluth; population, 1,000).— This is a lumbering town on the Mississippi river, which is navigable for about 100 miles above the place to Grand Rapids. Small steamboats carry supplies to lumbering camps along the river. Red Cedar Lake, with its fifty miles of shore, and five other lakes of good size, situated four miles west of Aitkin, are excellent places for hunting and fishing. Crystal Lake is distant two and a half miles south. Lake Mille Lac, twelve miles in the same direction, is noted for its beauty; and all are well worth a visit.

The country around the lakes is surpassed by none in point of attractiveness to the eye, being undulating and park-like. The glades and meadows are spangled with wild flowers in great variety, and the pebbly shores of the lakes, and azure, transparent waters, present a scene which impresses the beholder by its rare beauty. The hunting here is excellent. Elk may be found within seventy-five to one hundred miles north of this point, and in the immediate vicinity of Aitkin are deer, bear, geese, ducks, pheasants, grouse and woodcock.

Visitors to this portion of Minnesota desiring to see the red man in his wild way of living, may have their wishes gratified by driving out to the great and beautiful Mille Lac lake and Chippeway Indian reservation, about twelve miles from Aitkin. **Cedar Lake**, 92 miles west of Duluth, is only a side track.

Deerwood (97 miles west of Duluth; population, 50) is a favorite retreat for the hunter, and one of the wildest, least known and most beautiful points on the Northern Pacific railroad. An unbounded forest stretches in every direction, in which deer and bear tempt the adventurous sportsman to share with the Indians the excitement of the hunt. The small streams, and clear lakes of unknown depth, invite the lover of the rod to make his camp here. The invalid who craves repose, yet does not care to be too far away from the post-office or telegrams, finds here his Mecca. A small hotel has been built, and accommodation may also be found among the farmers at this point; or, if camping out is preferred, it is easy to obtain milk, eggs, ice, fresh vegetables and berries from the same source.

In a radius of three miles, there are over twenty known lakes, whose waters fairly teem with muscalonge, pike, black bass, whitefish, pickerel, croppies, wall-eyed pike, sunfish, rock bass, catfish, bullheads and suckers. It is not uncommon to take pike weighing upward of twenty pounds, and black bass six pounds, with a trolling spoon, while at the mouths of streams bass weighing from half a pound to two and a half pounds can be caught with the fly. The lakes vary in size from little gems a few hundred feet across to larger ones of several miles in diameter, many containing islands. Some of them have high, rocky shores, pebbly beaches, and deep blue waters; others, fringed with a growth of wild rice, are the feeding and hatching grounds of numbers of wild fowl. The more distant lakes can be reached by pony and buckboard, or by birch canoes, the latter carried over portages.

Brainerd (138 miles from St. Paul, and 114 miles from Duluth; population, 7,000).—Brainerd, City of the Pines, is situated on the east bank of the Mississippi river, on the main line of the Northern Pacific railroad, at an elevation of 1,600 feet above the sea. It is one of the most important, picturesque and attractive towns on the line of the railroad, north of Minneapolis and west of the great lakes, in Minnesota. Approaching the town from the south and east, the eye is attracted by the lofty smoke-stack (110 feet high) of the railroad company's shops, which here cover an area of about twenty acres, and consist of a round-house, containing forty-four stalls; machine shop, with capacity for handling twenty-two locomotives at once; boiler shop, copper shop, blacksmith forges, foundry and numerous other accessories of the headquarters of the motive power of a great railroad. Passing by this busy hive of industry, going west, the traveler is at once ushered into the business portion of the city, which stretches along parallel to the track on the south side for a distance of nearly half a mile. On the north side of the track are obtained glimpses, through the timber, of picturesque residences, churches, Gregory park, inclosing ten acres of stately pines, and the court house and jail. A strong dam was built across the Mississippi river about two miles above the business centre of the city in 1888 by a water-power company, which furnishes power for mills and factories. The dam created a back-water lake, which is one of the most capacious storage reservoirs for logs to be found on the Mississippi river. The principal manufacturing industries of Brainerd are making lumber and brick. The railroad company has, on the western bank of the river, a large and handsome sanitarium which is supported by a small monthly contribution from all the employes of the company engaged upon the eastern divisions of the road. These employes have the right to surgical and medical treatment and board, free of charge, when sick or injured. The hospital stands in the midst of a grove of pines, and has an excellent record for successful work.

Brainerd is the gateway to the vast lumber region north and east to the sources of the Mississippi. A hundred lakes, at varying distances of three to twenty-five miles from Brainerd, and of easy access, are stocked with black bass, wall-eyed pike, pickerel, muscalonge and other varieties of fish, all of exquisite flavor; numerous rice lakes afford breeding places for myriads of water fowl, while the forest is full of game and fur-bearing animals. Red deer and pheasants may be taken by the sportsman, within easy strolling distance of the town; and a black bear, wolf or wolverine often adds piquancy to the hunter's quest. There is a hotel at Gull lake, twelve miles distant northwest, with accommodations for twenty guests, and at Serpent lake, sixteen miles northeast, there are accommodations for perhaps an equal number. Mille Lac lake, twenty-two miles southeast, is the second largest and perhaps the most charming, of all the Minnesota lakes. Embowered in a magnificent forest of butternut, ash, sugar maple and other hard woods, its solitude has rarely been disturbed by the sound of the woodman's axe. It has an area of nearly 400 square miles, and a gravelly beach skirts its shores for nearly 100 miles. This lake is the source of the Rum river; its waters teem with fish, many of which are of marvelous size; black bass of ten and twelve pounds each are often hooked. Its shores abound with game, attracted hither in the fall by the immense crops of mast in the forest and wild rice in the thousand lakes. Openings in the forest, bits of prairie and meadow, produce wild strawberries, blueberries, raspberries and cranberries, hundreds of bushels of which are annually shipped from this station; the undergrowth is rich with ferns and flowers and flowering shrubs of exquisite beauty.

Gull River (121 miles from Duluth and 143 miles from St. Paul; population, 500).—Gull River, so called from the river which runs through the town, is a lumbering point from which great quantities of lumber are shipped for building purposes. One of the largest saw-mills in the State is situated here; also a sash and door factory, and a planing mill. Gull lake lies four miles north of the town. This is another of Minnesota's beautiful lakes, abounding with fish of all kinds. There is a steamboat on its waters which carries the tourist from eighty to one hundred miles around its shores. Two miles west of Gull River is

Sylvan Lake, also a very pleasant resort in summer. There are a great many deer, and some moose, in the neighborhood of these lakes. A moose was recently killed that weighed, when dressed, 800 pounds. Wolves and bears are also to be found. In the spring and autumn the rivers and lakes are alive with ducks and other water fowl. Years ago, one of the greatest battles between the Chippeway and Sioux Indians was fought here. "Hole-in-the-day," one of the Chippeway chiefs, was shot in this vicinity. "Bad Boy," so called by the Indians because he saved many of the white settlers' lives at the time of the Indian massacre in 1862, lives here.

Staples (143 miles from Duluth and 167 from St. Paul) is the junction point of the Lake Superior line of the Northern Pacific with the main line from St. Paul to the west.

LITTLE FALLS AND DAKOTA BRANCH.

Little Falls to Morris, Minn., 88 Miles.

This branch runs in a course slightly south of west, traversing first the wooded country which skirts the western bank of the Mississippi and then coming out into a fine rolling prairie country, dotted with numerous lakes. Owing to the diversified character of the country, the ride is an exceedingly interesting one from Little Falls to Morris, and it gives the traveler possibly a better idea of Minnesota's varied landscape than any other trip of equal length.

Grey Eagle is the first point of importance. It has a population of about 300, and is something of a summer resort, as it is delightfully situated in the midst of four noted lakes, which are visited every year by many fishermen from the cities. There is a hotel at Birch lake, built some years ago for their accommodation.

Sauk Centre, 37 miles from Little Falls, is the largest town on this branch, having a population of 2,200. It is a thrifty-looking, prosperous place, located on Sauk river, at the outlet of Sauk Lake, which is twelve miles long. It forms the natural geographical and business centre and outlet of an extensive area of rich agricultural country, well supplied with timber and water, and finely adapted to raising grain and stock, as well as to dairy purposes.

There are two large flouring mills, machine shops and manufactories, a fine waterpower, banks, newspapers, etc. The St. Paul and St. Vincent line of the Great Northern passes through here, and a short branch of that road runs north from this point. There is excellent hunting and fishing in the neighborhood, thousands of ducks and geese inhabiting the marshes west of the town at certain seasons.

Villard, sixteen miles west, is pleasantly situated near a chain of four lakes, between two of which the railroad track runs. The locality is famous for its fishing and hunting.

Glenwood, sixty miles west of Little Falls, is a picturesque town, situated in a circular valley at the east end of Lake Minnewaska, a most beautful body of water ten miles in length, occasional glimpses of which may be had from the train, 200 feet above. It is two to three miles wide and is surrounded by rolling country, well adapted to stock ranches. A number of springs of varied chemical analyses gush from the hill slopes on the north shore near the town, that are highly recommended for their medicinal qualities. A group of these are used to supply the town by means of pipes, and afford ample fire protection. The Northwestern Institute of the Y. M. C. associations of the Northwest is located on a twenty-acre tract bordering the lake, donated by the town, and here they take their summer outing. Glenwood is also a favorite summer resort for hundreds of others who come out from the cities of Minnesota and other States to the south and east. It is the county seat of Pope county. Population, 1,000.

Morris, the western terminus of the L. F. & D. branch, is the county seat of Stevens county, and has a population of about 2,000. It is the market for an extensive area of stock-raising and farming country, and is on the St. Paul and Fargo line of the Great Northern railway. Wheat, barley and corn are the principal farm products. There are numerous small lakes in the vicinity, where game and fish abound.

LITTLE FALLS TO BRAINERD, 30 MILES.

Belle Prairie (112 miles from St. Paul; population 800). —This town, in Morrison county, four and a half miles north of Little Falls, on the east bank of the Mississippi, derives its name from the beautiful, level strip of prairie, about twelve miles long, and varying from two to four miles in width, upon the edge of which it is situated. The soil of Belle Prairie is a rich, black sand, and well adapted to all kinds of agricultural products, especially wheat, potatoes and garden vegetables. The population of the country contributary to Belle Prairie is 1,000, the majority being French Canadians, who are mostly engaged in agricultural pursuits and lumbering. This town is one of the oldest settlements of Northern Minnesota. Mr. Frederick Ayer, the missionary, settled here in 1848, and erected a commodious school-house for the education of Indian children.

Fort Ripley (121 miles from St. Paul; population, 500).—This station derives its name from the now unoccupied fort, distant one mile, on the west bank of the Mississippi river, which, in the time when Minnesota was occupied in a great part by the Sioux Indians, was an important frontier military station. The old block house and barracks are still standing.

NORTHERN PACIFIC, FERGUS & BLACK HILLS BRANCH.

WADENA, MINN., TO MILNOR, N. D., 119 MILES.

This branch of the Northern Pacific system runs in a general southwesterly direction from Wadena to Fergus Falls, thence nearly due west, crossing both branches of the Red river, the Otter Tail and Bois de Sioux, at Wahpeton, and terminating at Milnor, 119 miles from Wadena. The country traversed between Wadena and Fergus Falls belongs to the beautiful and picturesque lake and park region, which is a combination of prairie and wooded knolls, interspersed with numerous lakes. West of Fergus Falls the road descends into the level valley of the Red river, which it traverses for the remainder of its length.

At Henning, 18 miles southwest of Wadena, the Mississippi river and the Red river of the North almost interlock. Forty rods east of the village site runs Leaf river, which empties into the Mississippi, and the same distance west the streams flow into the Red river of the North. Two miles south of the village are the Leaf mountains, or Painted hills, rising about 200 feet above the plains, making an elevation of about 1,700 feet above the level of the ocean. From these eminences a beautiful view is presented of the surrounding country. The town occupies a central location to three of the finest lakes in the park-like region; viz., Inman lake, on the east, with its crystal waters and heavily wooded shores; East Battle lake, on the west, with its islands, bays, rocks and headlands, embowered amid the shades of the primeval forest; and Leaf lake, on the north, with its deep, clear waters, and its shore line of twenty-five or thirty miles bordered by thick woods. There are several other charming lakes, such as Round lake, and its white, gravelly beaches; McDonald, Buchanan and Otter Tail lakes, the latter the largest of all, being ten miles long by three miles wide. These lakes all abound in many kinds of excellent fish, such as whitefish, pickerel, pike, catfish, and black and rock bass. This region has always been the resort and breeding ground of large numbers of water fowl, and no less than seventy varieties of birds have been found here.

Clitherall (29 miles from Wadena) is situated near three of the finest and largest lakes in the Minnesota park region—Clitherall lake and the two noted Battle lakes, west and east, respectively. Clitherall lake is a beautiful sheet of water, somewhat in the shape of the capital letter Y, extending from northeast to southwest, about four miles in length, with an average depth of 60 feet. It teems with every species of fish known to the Western lakes, from the monstrous buffalo of forty and fifty pounds advoirdupois, or the shy pickerel of twenty pounds, down to the beautiful perch of a couple of ounces. The lake is also haunted by water fowl in great numbers, from the pelican and goose to every species of duck. On its shores there is a small Mormon settlement, the oldest in Otter Tail county, the people having made their homes here as early as 1865. They are followers of Joseph Smith, and bitter denouncers of polygamy and their cousins at Salt Lake. Their settlement is one mile and a half from the station, and is finely situated in a beautiful grove of oaks on the north shore of the lake. They have about five hundred acres under cultivation, and the railroad runs through their fields in sight of the settlement.

South of Clitherall, for ten miles, stretches a grand prairie, and he must indeed be a poor shot who cannot here bag as many grouse as he wants. The Leaf mountains are the favorite haunts of deer, which are killed by hunters in great numbers every autumn. The Indians say that these mountains have been visited every year by them, in pursuit of deer, as far back as their oldest people can remember. Not even the presence of the white man and the railroad can drive the Indian from his "hunting grounds." Even now, at all seasons of the year, the tourist can see here and there a wigwam on the north shore of the lake, and the eyes of a shy pappoose peeping at him from behind a bush.

Battle Lake.—Ere beautiful Lake Clitherall is lost to view, as the train speeds along through pleasant groves and picturesque scenery, it rounds a high bluff, and another picturesque sheet of water is seen, covering an area of four by nine miles. This is the well-known Battle lake The town of Battle lake lies at the west end of the lake, and a large amount of wheat is marketed here. A lookout has been erected by the Northern Pacific railroad, the view from which is magnificent. Seventeen beautiful lakes can be seen within a radius of five miles, all of which are well stocked with fish. Besides these there are many ponds where, during spring, summer and autumn, aquatic fowl are abundant. There are two Battle lakes, West Battle lake and East Battle lake. West Battle lake, the queen of Otter Tail county lakes, lies one mile north of the station, and is the largest of the three lakes named. It is a favorite resort for fishing parties, and the finny tribe seems inexhaustible. This lake has an average depth of seventy-five feet. A steamer, sail-boats and numbers of row-boats ply its waters. East Battle lake is hidden among the islands and woodland hills, and is renowned for its romantic scenery. The lake is quite irregular in form, its shores being broken by grottoes, dells, lovely little coves and bays. It is about four miles long and from half a mile to two miles wide, containing three large islands. Wild ducks congregate here in the spring and autumn in countless numbers.

The Battle lakes take their name from the famous and bloody conflict which was fought on the neck of land that divides their waters, between the Chippeway and Sioux Indians, in which the former won a dearly bought victory, killing every one of their enemies, but losing 500 of their own warriors. The battle ground is only a mile and a half from Clitherall, where the fortifications, breastworks, rifle-pits, and even the mounds over the graves, still remain as a record of the bloody and fatal strife between the savages for the possession of this most coveted hunting ground. On the north side of the lakes is still another earth fortification, where at some time another terrible battle was fought between the Indians. A breastwork, in circular form, incloses about an acre of ground, and inside the circle are a number of rifle-pits. Arrow-heads, shells and other relics have been found in this place.

Fergus Falls has a population of over 4,000, and is the county seat of Otter Tail county, the largest well-settled county in Minnesota. The city is three miles square, and is built up more or less for nearly two miles up and down the Red river, and over a mile in breadth north and south.

To the north, overlooking and protecting the valley, are groves of timber, through which stretch narrow strips of prairie. South of the river the land is for the most part prairie, on which are several planted groves of rapidly growing trees. The principal street, Lincoln avenue, is built up compactly on both sides for half a mile, and business overflows thence up and down the cross streets. Within an area of two miles north and south, by three miles east and west, are six distinct water-powers, with over eighty feet fall. The red river at this point leaves a high upland region, and descends a distance of over 200 feet in a few miles to the level of the Red river plain, furnishing 10,000 horse-power, which is used for milling and manufacturing purposes. The favorable situation of Fergus Falls at the southern end of the celebrated Red river valley, surrounded by a rich, well-developed agricultural and stock-raising country, and in the midst of the famed park region of Minnesota, gives the place a front rank among the thriving towns of the Golden Northwest.

Fergus Falls is on one of the main lines of the Great Northern railway, and a branch line of the same road runs northward to Pelican Rapids, twenty-two miles distant. One of the three insane asylums of the State is here.

Breckenridge, 77 miles from Wadena, has a population of 900, is the county seat of Wilkin county, Minn., and is situated on the eastern bank of the Red river, at its junction with the Bois de Sioux river. It is one of the oldest settlements in Northern Minnesota, and was an Indian trading post as long ago as 1857. The town was burned during the great Sioux Indian outbreak in 1862, and eight of its inhabitants were killed. A battle was subsequently fought between eighty soldiers fortified in a stockade and a large force of Indians. The savages were finally driven off after two days' futile effort to capture the stockade. Breckenridge was not rebuilt until ten years later. In 1873 the St. Paul & Pacific railroad, now the Great Northern, was completed to the place, and the surrounding country began to be occupied by farmers. Just across the river, one mile distant in North Dakota, is

Wahpeton, with a population of 2,000. This town, situated on the Bois de Sioux, just above its confluence with the Red or Otter Tail, is the county seat of Richland county, one of the best agricultural counties in North Dakota. It is forty-six miles south of Fargo, and at the head of navigation of the Red river of the North. Wahpeton has a water-power, formed by the Otter Tail, with a fall of sixteen feet, furnishing a steady and reliable volume of water. In 1869 the first claim hut was put up on what is now the town site. In 1873 a trading house was established, and traffic was carried on with the Indians, who occupied nearly the entire country from Big Stone Lake to the British dominion for miles on both sides of the river. The town is now in the midst of an agricultural country of superior fertility, and ranks, as a commercial center, among the first in North Dakota.

The **Dwight Farm**, which comprises some 7,000 acres and has the reputation of being one of the most scientifically managed large farms in the Northwest, lies immediately north of Farmington, the first station west of Wahpeton.

Milnor, the present terminus of the road, is 120 miles from Wadena. It was founded in 1883, and rapidly became an important business point. The surrounding country consists of rolling prairie, and is all fertile to a high degree, there being scarcely any waste land. Milnor is the county seat of Sargent county, and has 500 inhabitants. Fort Sisseton Indian agency is thirty miles south.

THE MANITOBA DIVISION.

WINNIPEG JUNCTION, MINN., TO PORTAGE LA PRAIRIE, MANITOBA, 306 MILES.

This division includes the Duluth & Manitoba, which extends to the Canadian boundary line at Pembina, 189 miles, 94 miles of which is through one of the most productive wheat regions in Minnesota. Crossing the Red river at East Grand Forks into North Dakota, the road runs almost due north for 70 miles, through the lower Red river valley, a region scarcely surpassed anywhere on the globe for natural fertility, and now producing a larger average yield of wheat per acre than any section in the United States with the exception of the Pacific coast.

At the international boundary, two miles north of Pembina, the Duluth & Manitoba connects with the Northern Pacific & Manitoba railroad, which runs down the Red river valley to the city of Winnipeg. A branch of this latter road runs from Morris, thirty miles north of Pembina, into Southwestern Manitoba, and another line, owned by the same corporation, runs from Winnipeg to Portage la Prairie. The Northern Pacific & Manitoba road was originally chartered by the Manitoba Provincial government to build a system of roads in the Province to compete with the Canadian Pacific. The charter was subsequently confirmed by the Dominion government.

Fertile (45 miles from Winnipeg Junction) is the first point reached of any importance. It has a population of about 500, and is an important local trading point. A branch continues due north from here to Red Lake Falls, thence to a junction with the main line again at a point a few miles east of the Red river.

Red Lake Falls, the only place of any consequence on that branch, is a manufacturing and milling town at the junction of the Clearwater and Red Lake rivers, with a population of 1,000. There are no less than thirteen valuable waterpowers on these two rivers, in and near the town, and just below the junction of the rivers is a very large power which has been improved by a stock company. Red Lake Falls has two flouring mills and two saw-mills.

Crookston, the county seat of Polk, the largest county in Western Minnesota, is an interesting, pleasant-looking town of 5,000 people that has been steadily gaining in population and wealth the past few years. There are now fine, large business blocks, elegant modern residences, and everything else that indicates advanced social conditions and commercial thrift. Nature has favored Crookston. There are two splendid water-powers, one of which is developed and furnishes 75,000 horse-power, and is used to run the flouring mills, pump water for the city for fire and domestic purposes, and run the machinery which furnishes the electric light with which the streets, business houses and residences are lighted. There is a decided lack of capital for manufacturing and larger mercantile enterprises. The water-power that is in use demonstrates what might be done with a strong financial backing. The valley of the Red Lake river extends seventy-five miles to the north and east of Crookston. It is all fertile, and a well watered agricultural region with a rich, deep, black loam, the valley being from five to fifteen miles wide. There is no waste land. Beyond this valley is the heavy timber of the reservation. On the river is a saw-mill that cut in one season 21,000,000 feet of lumber and many thousands of lath and shingles. Crookston is most advantageously situated for the manufacturing of lumber from the Red Lake reservation, being near, and a good distributing point.

Polk county has seventy-five townships, an assessed valuation of $7,000,000, over a million and a half acres, of which 250,000 are under cultivation, and a population of 33,000. The Northern Pacific and Great Northern operate six lines of railroad in the county, reaching into the best portions and helping the development in the most effective way. A large per cent of the population is made up of Norwegians, who have used the lands to the best advantage. There are many French Canadians, also, a few of the townships being populated almost wholly by them. Here and there are Germans and Bohemians. The wheat yield of the county in 1891 was estimated at from six to seven million bushels.

The Red Lake Reservation is a large tract of land in Northern Minnesota, nearly a parallelogram in form, running northeast and southwest, with an extreme length of about 150 miles and a nearly constant breadth of about eighty miles. The soil and timber vary greatly in the different portions. The northern half, which is low and often swampy, is covered by immense tracts of white cedar of excellent quality, tamarack and arbor vitae.

The southern half of the reservation is much the more fertile, consisting of rolling land with innumerable little lakes and streams, and contains nearly all the pine timber. In its midst is Red' lake, the largest in the State, consisting really of two lakes united by a narrow, shallow strait, altogether making a body in shape something like a gigantic dumb-bell. The greatest length of the two lakes is about sixty miles and the breadth twenty-five miles.

Along the southern edge the shore is bordered with high bluffs, generally covered with hardwood timber, extending also up the eastern coast. Numerous streams cut through these highlands and empty in the lakes. White Earth reservation, on which are nearly 100,000 acres of pine land, is mentioned elsewhere in this book, with some interesting features of its aboriginal inhabitants. These lands are well situated in a compact body, but do not abut on any considerable stream, so that they will depend on future railroad facilities for development.

The *Northern Minnesota Wilderness* is so-called from the fact that it a vast area of undeveloped country, the chief resources of which are pine and hardwood and iron ore—an almost unbroken forest from its eastern boundary on Lake Superior to the Red river. It is not, by any means, uninhabited. Indians, lumbermen, fishermen, and miners give it a population that is much scattered, but sufficient to relieve it of the term "wilderness." Its southern border might in a rough way be located by a line drawn from Duluth to a point 50 miles east of Crookston, at the southwest corner of the Red lake reservation. The great Mesaba iron range, the Rainy lake mining region, on the northern boundary, and the vast forests of pine are being brought into touch with the world by the railroads.

East Grand Forks, 105 miles from Winnipeg Junction, has a population of 1,200, and is situated on the Minnesota side of the Red river of the North. The railroad shops are located here, and there are two grain elevators and a number of stores. It is one of the liveliest towns in Western Minnesota, and is connected by both railroad and highway bridges with

Grand Forks, North Dakota, which is claimed by its enterprising people and many Western travelers to be the handsomest town of its size and age in the Northwest. It certainly has good grounds on which to claim this distinction. It has a population of about 8,500, half of which has been acquired since 1890. A well-known magazine writer says:

The striking feature about Grand Forks, which is sure to impress the stranger most at first view and to occasion interest and inquiry, is the number of tall, solid, city-like buildings on the main business street. These structures, four and five stories in height, are of the latest styles of architecture, and are finished in the costly and tasteful way now popular in the cities. They have passenger elevators, tiled hall-ways, polished hardwood interior work and are prodigal in the use of ornamental iron and brass. There are no such buildings in any other North Dakota town, and none, so far as I am aware, in any town in the West of the population of Grand Forks. They represent the accumulated wealth of less than twenty years' occupancy of this fertile Red River country. The question will be asked at the outset, I imagine, why Grand Forks is able to make such an exceptionally fine showing of stately business blocks? The answer will be evident to any one who will take a half-hour's stroll from end to end of the town, following the course of the river. Grand Forks does not depend wholly on handling grain and on the trade that comes from selling goods and machinery to a farming country. It has another important resource— that of manufacturing, and it is this, added to the business of trading with a highly productive agricultural district, that has given it an altogether exceptional degree of prosperity. Manufacturing enterprise was not forced at the start for the purpose of town booming, but came about naturally from the situation of the place at the junction of the Red Lake river with the Red. The former river is the outlet of Red lake, the largest body of water lying wholly in the State of Minnesota, and with its tributary, the Clearwater, it drains the best pineries in that State. Logs are floated down to Grand Forks, and the railroads centering here and running out across the prairies north, south and west made this an excellent point for the manufacture and distribution of lumber. The mill owned by T. B. Walker saws 15,000,000 feet a year and it is all wanted for local consumption in North Dakota.

Grand Forks is the headquarters of the North Dakota Milling Association, controlling the output of a dozen first-class flouring mills in various parts of the State, which is about 5,000 barrels daily. There are several splendidly equipped, well-managed hotels here that entertain travelers of luxurious tastes in a manner that has given the town a great reputation. The Great Northern railway has two lines here—one reaching to the Pacific coast and the other to Manitoba.

Grafton, with a population of 3,000, is county seat of Walsh county, one of the great wheat-producing counties of North Dakota. The land in this county, as in all the lower Red Lake valley on the Dakota side, is rolling prairie, with occasional strips of timber following the course of the streams which run into the Red river of the North. The yield of hard spring wheat has seldom fallen below twenty bushels, and often averages as high as thirty bushels. The North Dakota and Manitoba line of the Great Northern passes through Grafton, making it an important shipping point. It is a thrifty, progressive town made up of Americans, Germans and Scandinavians. A small colony of Icelanders are settled just beyond the eastern corporate limits. They also are thrifty in their way, but mix very little with other nationalities. The Northern Pacific runs for a dozen miles to the northeast, touching the Red river again at the pretty little town of

Drayton, in the extreme southeast corner of Pembina county, whose northern line is the international boundary. The town has about 700 people, representing the best type of those enterprising Canadians who settled on choice spots along our northern border in the days when the Red River country was "frontier." Drayton is said to be the wealthiest town, in proportion to its population, in the Northwest. It draws trade from the broad prairies to the west and from an extensive area of country across the river, in Minnesota.

Pembina, the seat of the county of that name, is two miles south of the Canadian line, and has a population of 1,000. It is 189 miles from Winnipeg Junction, 414 from St. Paul, and 68 from Winnipeg. Pembina is the oldest town in the West, having been settled by the Earl of Selkirk's colonists as long ago as 1801. Pembina has a beautiful situation at the junction of the Pembina river with the Red river of the North. It was for many years one of the posts of the Hudson Bay company. From a fur-trading post, frequented by Indians and half-breeds, its character has been changed in recent years to that of a prosperous market-town for a rich farming country. About a mile above the town stands Fort Pembina. Just across the Red river of the North, in Minnesota, is the town of St. Vincent, and immediately north of the international boundary line is the important town of Emerson, with a population of 2,000. Pembina and St. Vincent are connected by ferry across the Red river. Pembina county is largely settled by Canadians, French-Canadians, and Icelanders, with a considerable native American element. A trip to Pembina can be highly recommended to the tourist who wishes to see something of the rich wheat country of the lower Red River valley, and at the same time to visit a town which has an interesting frontier history, reaching back to the beginning of the present century.

West Lynne, Manitoba, is the first town on British territory. It is a suburb of the large town of Emerson, which is situated on the opposite side of the river. The two places are connected by a fine iron bridge. Emerson has many substantial brick blocks, and is a place of considerable trade.

Morris is the junctional point whence runs west a branch 146 miles to Brandon, a prosperous wheat-shipping station and a centre for considerable country trade. Near Morris is a large colony of Mennonites, who speak the German language, although they, or their ancestors, migrated from Russia. They live in small villages, and are an exceedingly plain and thrifty people in their habits of life. They are industrious, and have a reputation for strict honesty in their business transactions. Many curious articles of domestic furniture, brought from Russia, can be seen in their houses. The most conspicuous features of these dwellings is always an enormous stove or furnace, constructed of bricks or stone, which occupies the center of the living room.

THE MORRIS AND BRANDON LINE.

From Morris to Brandon, Manitoba, 146 Miles.

This branch of the Northern Pacific & Manitoba system leaves the main line at Morris, in the Red River valley, and running in a general course a little north of west ends at the flourishing town of Brandon, the second place in population in the province. It traverses a fine prairie country for its entire distance, well occupied by farmers. This is the best wheat region of Manitoba. The average yield is high, and nearly the whole crop grades " number 1 hard." At Wawanessa the Souris river is crossed, and at Brandon the road enters the valley of the Assiniboine. The country is level for about twenty miles west of Morris, and further on it becomes more and more rolling. There are occasional groves of timber.

Brandon is in point of population (about 4,000) and importance only second to Winnipeg, the capital of the Province of Manitoba. Situated on the south bank of the Assiniboine river, it enjoys many natural beauties and attractions as well as solid advantages. Its elevation affords a pleasing variety when compared with the average prairie city, while the hygienic conditions with which it is favored can scarcely be surpassed. Twelve years ago its present site was chosen and in that length of time a beautiful and well-built city has been erected that gives every assurance of increased prosperity and influence.

Brandon has three railroads: The Canadian Pacific main line; the Great North-West Central, reaching into the extensive stock region of North-West Territory, across Assiniboia, and the Morris and Brandon branch of the Northern Pacific. The Canadian Pacific has a branch running southwesterly from a point a few miles west of Brandon to the Souris coal fields, thus furnishing this city a good quality of coal at a reasonable price.

There is, however, nothing that so distinguishes Brandon and at the same time the country surrounding it as the number of elevators it possesses. No fewer than eight elevators and a fine large roller-process flouring mill are found requisite to meet the demands of the grain trade at this point. The title, "Wheat City," by which she is frequently known, is apparently most appropriate. Brandon claims to have been the largest primary wheat market in the world.

A marked characteristic with Manitobans is their conspicuous regard for the education of their children. Brandon is foremost in this matter, having primary, intermediate and high schools of importance. They have already completed the erection of a large and very commodious building for the central school and it will not be doubted that her present high rank will be maintained and ample provisions will be made for her future needs in this most important department. The Dominion government has a fine building here which is used for post-office, customs office and Dominion land office, and the Provincial government has a reformatory for boys, near here.

Winnipeg is 482 miles from St. Paul. It is the capital of Manitoba, a province of the Dominion of Canada, and has 40,000 inhabitants. The city is built upon a plain where the Assiniboine and Red rivers unite, and has a

suburb south of the Assiniboine called Fort Rouge, and a
more important suburb across the Red river called St.
Boniface. Winnipeg is a well built and prosperous city,
with trade relations extending throughout the Canadian
Northwest. It was originally a Hudson Bay company
trading post, protected by the military garrison at Fort
Garry, and was first settled by fur traders in the early
part of the present century. A long and interesting frontier
history is associated with the place. Nothing now remains
of old Fort Garry but its stone portal. The Hudson Bay
company is still the most important mercantile concern
in the city, conducting large wholesale and retail stores
and a depot for furs. All the operations which this vener-
able corporation carries on in Manitoba, Assiniboia-
Alberta, and the unorganized territories of the Canadian
northwest are directed by a chief commissioner in Winnipeg. Among the points of interest to tourists in the city
may be mentioned the old Episcopal church, built by the
Hudson Bay company, on the walls of which are many
mural tablets in memory of the deceased officers of the
company and the members of their families; the Parliament House, which is the capitol of the Province; the
residence of the Lieutenant-Governor; the Royal Infantry
school and barracks; the cathedral and schools of St.
Boniface; the Carleton, St. Johns and Manitoba colleges;
and the stores of the Hudson Bay company. The main
street of the city is of unusual width, and is substantially
built up for a greater part of its length of two miles with
handsome buildings of yellow and red brick. One of the
finest edifices in the city is the Dominion post-office
building. Another is the "The Manitoba," a magnificent
American hotel and depot built in 1890 by the Northern
Pacific Railroad Co. The City Hall is also a very beauti-

ful building, in front of which is a tall, graceful monument dedicated to the soldiers who were slain in the Riel rebellion. Winnipeg is on the main line of the Canadian Pacific railroad, and three branches of that road center there. It manufactures flour, lumber, beer, furniture, machinery and many other articles, and has an extensive jobbing trade. It is a genuine social, commercial and political capital, and keeps pace in its growth with the development of the Canadian Northwest.

An enthusiastic writer in describing the city, says: "What does Winnipeg possess? Well, among other things worth mentioning, she has branches of all the leading Canadian banks, branches of all the great Canadian and English loan and land companies, agencies of leading Canadian, British and American life and fire insurance companies; an active Board of Trade, and grain and produce exchanges; ably-edited daily and weekly newspapers; excellent telephone, telegraph and messenger service. Two electric light and one gas company; street car lines on all principal thoroughfares; many miles of water mains; an excellent sewerage and drainage system; a splendid police force and fire brigade, and unexcelled fire-alarm system; eighty-three miles of graded streets, ten miles of paved streets and 150 miles of plank sidewalks; five colleges, normal school, fifteen public school buildings and twenty-one churches. Besides this, it has a world-wide fame, its name being familiar all over the civilized globe; it has a prosperous present and a bright future, never so bright as at the present; it has a continually increasing population, a gradually-growing commercial importance; it has energetic, public-spirited citizens, who are contented with their present lot and hopeful for the future."

Portage la Prairie, the northern terminus of the Northern Pacific & Manitoba railroad, is situated in the very centre of Manitoba, near the Assiniboine river on the Canadian Pacific's main line, 49 miles west of the city of Winnipeg, 531 miles from St. Paul, and has a population of 3,000. It is also the southeastern terminus of the Manitoba & Northwestern railway, which runs northwesterly through a fertile region of Manitoba and Northwest Territory a distance of about 225 miles, its object being to reach Prince Albert, a growing town on the Saskatchewan river 500 miles distant, and its ultimate destination being probably a terminus on the Pacific ocean, thereby forming the most northern route across the Rockies. Another railway—the Lake Manitoba canal and railway—has been charted by the Government of Canada, and has a land grant of 6,400 acres of Government land per mile. It is projected to run northerly from Portage la Prairie to the southwestern shore of Lake Manitoba, thence northerly about 100 miles to the newly opened Lake Dauphin region, in which there are thousands of the choicest homesteads to be found anywhere in the Northwest, and which are being rapidly taken up by settlers.

Portage la Prairie is situated in one of the oldest settlements in Manitoba. Settlers as early as 1860 began to come in and settle on the beautiful prairies to the north, east and west of it. These prairies, called the " Portage Plains," soon became known far and wide as the very garden of Manitoba, whose fertility and freedom from drought, flooding and frost made it a farmer's Eden. As a result of these beneficent qualities of soil and climate, no portion of Manitoba is so thickly settled as the Portage Plains.

The Central school building is a large, fine, solid two-story brick structure, capable of accommodating 800 children. The Home for Incurables is a recently erected Government institution, and is the most beautiful building in the place. It is of solid brick, with a double tier of verandas, and presents a fine appearance as seen from the windows of passing railway trains.

FARGO & SOUTHWESTERN BRANCH.

Fargo to Edgeley, North Dakota.—109 Miles.

This important branch of the Northern Pacific runs through one of the finest agricultural regions in N. Dakota. The road extends to Edgeley, twenty-one miles west of the James river. The country traversed is for the first forty miles level prairie, then becomes slightly rolling, and the uneven character of the ground increases after the Sheyenne river is crossed at Lisbon. Between Lisbon and La Moure the drainage for the most part is into numerous small lakes and ponds. The whole country is of almost uniform fertility. The settlement has been rapid all along the line since it was opened a few years ago, and several thrifty, substantial towns show that the country has been prosperous.

Sheldon is an important trading and wheat-shipping point, there being five elevators in the place. It is a thrifty community of some five hundred people, forty-one miles from Fargo. Sheldon has a reputation for fine draft horses, which are raised near here and shipped East.

Lisbon and Ransom County.—Among all the North Dakota counties there is none that possesses more natural beauty than Ransom, and very few that can equal its record of steady progress and unbroken prosperity. Its special beauty comes chiefly from the Sheyenne river, which, entering the county in its most northwestern township, flows southwest until it touches one of the townships of the southern tier. Everywhere the Sheyenne forms an exceedingly picturesque valley, wooded for the most part with a fine growth of sturdy oaks and graceful cottonwoods. There are a few small lakes and ponds in the neighborhood of Ransom, but the river is the great landscape feature. On both sides of the bluffs that buttress the narrow and winding valley, the surface of the country spreads out in vast stretches of gently-undulating and highly fertile prairie.

Lisbon, the county seat, is the commercial centre of a wide scope of farming country, and in many respects a handsome town. It has about 1,500 inhabitants. The North Dakota Soldiers' Home and a Baptist educational institution are located here. The "Soo" line passes a few miles to the northwest.

La Moure, 88 miles from Fargo, has a population of 1,000. It is the county seat of La Moure county and is located at the crossing of the Fargo & Southwestern branch and the James River Valley railroad; is situated on the James river, from 1,400 to 1,500 feet above the sea-level, with a gradual slope to the river, affording fine drainage, the surrounding country being chiefly a beautiful, slightly undulating prairie. La Moure has a handsome brick hotel costing $25,000. The town was first established in 1883, and has had a steady, substantial growth. The railroad will finally be extended to some point on the Missouri. The James River Valley railroad, following the course of the James river, was opened from Jamestown, forty-nine miles north of La Moure, to La Moure in 1885. It has since been extended southward to Oakes, on the Chicago & Northwestern and the "Soo" lines.

Farming in the Vicinity of La Moure.—The soil of

the middle James River valley, of which La Moure is the commercial center, is peculiarly suitable for the growth of all cereal and root crops. The No. 1 hard wheat grown here has made itself famous in the markets of the world, and has been shown, by the official analysis of the Agricultural Department in Washington, to surpass all the wheats grown in any other part of the United States in weight, nutritive qualities, etc.

Edgeley, 109 miles from Fargo, is the present terminus of the Fargo & Southwestern railroad, and is the northern terminus of one of the Dakota divisions of the Chicago, Milwaukee & St. Paul road. It was established in 1887, and has a population of about 500. The surrounding country is well settled with a thrifty population of farmers engaged in the raising of grain and stock. Stages run from Edgeley to Napoleon, the county seat of Logan county, about forty miles west.

SANBORN COOPERSTOWN & TURTLE MOUNTAIN BRANCH.

SANBORN TO COOPERSTOWN, NORTH DAKOTA, 36 MILES.

This branch is completed to Cooperstown, 36 miles north of Sanborn. It traverses a remarkably rich prairie country for its entire length. The surface grows more and more rolling as the train advances northward, until in the vicinity of Cooperstown it is diversified with numerous ridges of hills. The soil on these hills, except on their crests, where it is somewhat stony, is as valuable for farming as the level stretches between them.

Cooperstown, with a population of 500, is the county seat of Griggs county. The town was established in the spring of 1883, and in the fall of the same year the railroad from Sanborn was completed, making it a terminal point and an important centre of trade. Cooperstown has a court house built of red brick at a cost of $30,000, which is one of the most substantial and imposing public edifices in North Dakota.

Griggs county is one of the best parts of North Dakota for mixed farming. A large part of its surface is admirably adapted for wheat culture, and there are numerous lakes and ponds, bordered by meadowed lands and excellent pasturage tracts, which give good facilities for stock-raising. The Sheyenne river runs through the eastern part of the county, affording several good mill powers, and having on its banks numerous groves of timber, which are of great value in giving the farmers cheap fuel. The lands of the Cooper Brothers, who are among the largest land-owners in North Dakota, are mostly all in Griggs county.

JAMES RIVER VALLEY RAILROAD.

JAMESTOWN TO OAKES, NORTH DAKOTA, 69 MILES.

This line begins at Jamestown, and following the course of the James river, runs southward to Oakes, where it connects with one of the lines of the Chicago & Northwestern system, and also with a line of the Minneapolis, St. Paul & Sault Ste. Marie Ry. It furnishes the connecting link between the railroad system of North and South Dakota. The road traverses a good agricultural country. The valley proper of the James river is a narrow one, the bottom lands having a width of from one to three miles between the rolling uplands on either side. Occasional groves of cottonwood are found near the stream. The valley has a light black-loam soil, and for general fertility and adaptability to both small and large farming is unsurpassed.

Grand Rapids, 41 miles from Jamestown, has a population of about 300, and is situated in the midst of fine farming country.

La Moure, the next and larger town, is mentioned in the Fargo & Southwestern description, which branch extends to Edgeley, twenty-one miles west.

At Glover, the second station below La Moure, is the big farm of Samuel Glover, containing several thousand acres, finely equipped and well managed, on 2,700 acres

In the Lower James River Valley.

of which, in 1891, he grew over 60,000 bushels of high-grade wheat.

Oakes, terminus of the James River Valley branch, has upwards of 700 people. It is an important railroad point, having a principal line of the Minneapolis, St. Paul & Sault Ste. Marie Ry., and a feeder of the main line in South Dakota of the Chicago & Northwestern. This gives Oakes a strong commercial advantage in an extensive area of wheat and stock country. It has had a steady growth.

JAMESTOWN AND NORTHERN RAILROAD.

JAMESTOWN TO LEEDS, N. DAKOTA, 108 MILES.

This important branch of the Northern Pacific system, leaving the main line at Jamestown, follows the valley of the Pipestone river for a distance of about thirty miles, the general direction being northwest; then turning north, crosses the James and Sheyenne rivers, and terminates at Leeds, on the Great Northern's main line, northwest of Devil's Lake. With the exception of a range of gravelly hills between the James and the Sheyenne, the whole region traversed by the road is a rich prairie, more or less rolling, and taking a leading rank among the best agricultural sections of North Dakota.

Carrington (43 miles from Jamestown; population, 500) was established in 1883, by the Carrington & Casey Land company, a corporation owning large tracts of land in the vicinity of the place. It has two hotels, two newspapers, two elevators and numerous stores and shops, and is an important grain-shipping point. It is the county seat of Foster county, settled largely by Americans who came here from Eastern States with little else than energy and a practical knowledge of farming. They met with many reverses, but one or two good crops placed them on a firm footing, and they are fixtures in the country. These stout hearted pioneers now live more at ease, and work more with their heads than with their hands. It is the history of Eastern and Middle States repeated. At Carrington is the junction of the

Mouse River Branch, which leaves the Jamestown & Northern R. R. and runs due west to Sykeston, a distance of thirteen miles. From Sykeston it will be continued in a northwestern direction to some point in the valley of the Mouse river, a further distance of about seventy-five miles, traversing for its entire length a rolling prairie country having the general characteristics, as to fertility, of the country between Jamestown and Carrington.

Sykeston (thirteen miles from Carrington and fifty-six miles from Jamestown, population 300) is the county seat of Wells county, and is situated near the source of the Pipestone river, and a short distance from the bold elevation known as the "Hawk's Nest," which is a sort of abutment of the coteaus, and is a conspicuous object in the landscape for many miles around. Sykeston is a town created by the real estate and farming operations of the English company of Sykes & Hughes. This company owns and farms large tracts of land in the vicinity, and makes active efforts to attract American emigrants to this portion of the Northern Pacific. The town has a newspaper, two elevators, a school, and a number of stores and shops.

New Rockford (fifty-nine miles from Jamestown; population, 700) is the county seat of Eddy county, and is situated on a prairie sloping to the west of the James river. It has two elevators, two newspapers, and numerous mercantile establishments, and is surrounded on all sides by stretches of fertile prairie, extending as far as the eye can reach. The railroad here crosses the James river, a small stream at this point. The source of the James is about thirty miles west of New Rockford. At Sheyenne (seventy miles from Jamestown) the Sheyenne river is crossed. It has a volume of water at this point not greater than that of the James, but becomes on its lower course an important river.

Fort Totten.—This military post is situated on the southern shore of Devil's lake, about midway between its eastern and western extremities and ten miles from the Northern Pacific. The buildings are substantial brick structures, and the fort has a more permanent appearance than is usual with frontier military stations. There are two small hotels at the fort which accommodate tourists and sportsmen. A steamboat runs to Minnewaukan, and also to Devil's Lake, a town of about 2,000 inhabitants at the head of a deep bay on the northern shore of the lake.

Minnewaukan (90 miles from Jamestown) was established in 1884. It is the county seat of Benson county and has a population of about 500. It is a favorite summer resort for tourists who wish to enjoy the scenery of Devil's lake and its facilities for fishing and shooting. Minnewaukan is the trade center for a large extent of country. It has a newspaper, a bank, a grain elevator, a flour mill and numerous mercantile establishments. A steamboat runs during the season of navigation between Minnewaukan and Fort Totten and Devil's Lake.

Devil's Lake.—This remarkable body of water is about 50 miles in length, and has a width varying from one to five miles. It has no outlet, and its waters are strongly saline. It receives no important streams, and in consequence appears to be slowly diminishing in volume by evaporation. Well-marked former beaches show that the level of its waters was at one time about twenty feet higher than at present. A considerable portion of the shore line of the lake is heavily timbered with large oak trees. These forests add greatly to the attractiveness of the lake in an open prairie country like North Dakota. The waters of the lake are of a beautiful sea-green color, and are said to have possessed valuable curative properties. The lake abounds in pickerel, and is the resort of myriads of wild fowl; geese, brant, and different species of wild ducks frequent its waters, and make it a favorite resort for sportsmen.

The Indian name is Minnewaukan, which means "spirit waters." The lake was believed by the Indians to be haunted; and there is a legend which relates that a party of Sioux Indians once attempted to cross it in boats, in spite of the warnings of the medicine men, and that their canoes were seized in the middle of the lake by some mysterious power and dragged to the bottom, so that neither boats nor voyagers were ever seen again. Since that time the Indians never ventured upon the lake in any sort of craft.

A large portion of the southern side of the lake is occupied by the reservation of the Cut-head Sioux Indians, who number about 2,000 souls, and are peaceable and tolerably industrious, cultivating small spots of grain and potatoes, and keeping cattle and horses. They are mainly Catholics in religion, and there is a mission for the reservation under the management of the "Gray Nuns," where the Indian children are educated.

Leeds is a station on the main line of the Great Northern railroad, and the terminus of the Jamestown and Northern branch of the Northern Pacific. Besides enjoying the benefits of railroad competition, Leeds lies in the centre of a fine country.

ROCKY FORK AND COOKE CITY RAILROAD.

LAUREL TO RED LODGE, MONTANA, 50 MILES.

This road was built in 1888 and 1889 for the purpose of reaching the remarkable coal deposits on the Rocky Fork, south of the Yellowstone, and also, by a future extension from that place, to afford railroad transportation to the silver mining camp of Cooke City, near the eastern borders of the National Park. The road was open for traffic in the spring of 1889 as far as the new town of Red Lodge, created by the coal mining operations. It crosses the Yellowstone runs through a picturesque grazing country, reaching its present terminus by gradients of from 26 to 110 feet per mile.

THE ROCKY FORK COAL.—This coal is bituminous in its character and is so rich in combustible matter that pieces of it can be lighted with a match. The veins are from six to thirty feet in thickness and the out-croppings are on the sides of the hills, situated so that they can be economically worked by means of levels. The coal is mined in large quantities for railway consumption and is shipped for domestic fuel to all the Montana towns.

Red Lodge (50 miles from Laurel, population 1,000.) —This active mining town was laid out in March, 1889, and developed with a rapidity rarely seen except in the mining camps where placer gold is found. The resources of the place, in its inexhaustible coal mines, its abundant and easily utilized water-power, and in the grazing and farming regions surrounding it, make it one of the most important towns in Montana. It has considerable trade with mines and cattle ranches as far south as Wyoming.

Palisades of the Yellowstone.

ROCKY MOUNTAIN RAILROAD OF MONTANA—YELLOWSTONE PARK LINE.

LIVINGSTON TO CINNABAR, MONTANA, 51 MILES.

This branch of the Northern Pacific system was built for the purpose of facilitating tourist travel to the National Park. After leaving Livingston it runs through the lower canyon of the Yellowstone, and then through a narrow but fertile valley, and terminates at Cinnabar, just north of the northern boundary of the park. The scenery along the road is among the most picturesque and beautiful to be found in the entire Rocky Mountain region. The mountain peaks on the eastern side of the valley are singularly bold and impressive. Their summits are crowned with beetling crags of massive rock and are covered with snow the greater part of the year.

Horr, two miles from the terminus of this branch, is a lively coal-mining village, where thirty-six coke ovens are in operation, making coke equal in quality to the famous product of Connellsville, Pennsylvania.

Cinnabar, the terminus of the Park branch, derives its importance from its railway business, and from the teaming to the Cooke City silver mining district. Stages leave Cinnabar, connecting with each arriving train, for the Mammoth Hot Springs hotel, which is the rendezvous and distributing point for all the tourist travel in the National Park.

NORTHERN PACIFIC AND MONTANA BRANCH.

LOGAN TO GARRISON, MONT., BY WAY OF BUTTE, 123 MILES.

Trains on the road are made up at Bozeman and follow the mail line twenty-four miles before diverging at Logan. The road runs up the valley of the Jefferson river, one of the three forks of the Missouri, and through the Jefferson canyon, a savage gorge in one of the outlying ranges of the Rockies. The scenery is bold and fantastic. The Main Divide of the Rockies is crossed at Pipestone Pass at an altitude of about 6,000 feet, the road winding like a serpent along the flanks of the range and gaining over one hundred feet of elevation in every mile. Numerous high trestle bridges spanning ravines are crossed. There is a small tunnel at the summit. On the western side the road descends rapidly to the valley of Silver Bow creek. Here the mountain views are particularly impressive. Suddenly the smoky city of Butte lies in front of the train as the line makes a curve, its whole bulk of closely built streets of smelters, reduction works and mines being distinctly visible on the near slope of a mountain side.

Butte City, 1,232 miles from St Paul, population, 50,000, is situated near the head of Silver Bow Valley, and about fifteen miles west of the Pipestone Pass of the main range of the Rocky mountains, on ground sloping to the south. Its altitude is 5,701 feet. It is the county seat of

Silver Bow county, and is famous for its quartz mines, which are so largely developed as to make Butte the most important mining center in the world.

In 1875 the first mill was constructed for working the silver ores of the camp, and the population did not exceed 200. To-day Butte counts its inhabitants by the thousands. The veins are true fissures, yielding largely of copper and silver, and assaying well. It is estimated that there are over 300 miles of veins in the district, varying in width from thirty to fifty feet, and developed to a depth of from 400 to 1,500 feet. Butte has daily newspapers, an opera house, a handsome court house, built of brick and stone, a street railroad system, electric, steam motor and cable, gas and electric light, and is, in short, a brisk and busy city. The great silver mines and mills are on the immediate outskirts of the city, and each is the center of a populous village of workmen and their families. Railway facilities are furnished by the Northern Pacific, the Union Pacific and the Butte, Anaconda and Pacific, the latter being a line to Anaconda. The following description of Butte appeared in the *Northwest Magazine*.

There is only one Butte. This city of mines, perched on the backbone of the continent, is unique. There is no place like it on the face of the globe. True, it has resemblances with Virginia City and Leadville, as those places were in their palmy days, but Butte, with all the picturesque phases of mining life which they exhibited, has a dignity and solidity that comes from the possession of great and permanent wealth. Besides, Butte flourishes all the time. She has no ups and downs. The fluctuations in the price of silver only make her more or less rich in her steady increase, but she is never poor—never depressed. Within a radius of two miles from her court house ores of silver and copper of the enormous aggregate value of twenty-five millions of dollars are annually dug out of the earth. Nowhere else on the surface of the globe does so small an area of territory yield from the storehouse of nature such a vast sum of wealth. A very large share of this great annual revenue which Butte extracts from the rocks goes to labor. It follows that labor is nowhere more independent or better paid. Being a wealthy place Butte is naturally luxurious, but luxury here does not take the form of handsome houses and stately business blocks, or of costly public improvements. All these will come in time, but thus far the traditions of a mining camp are dominant. The richest man in Butte died lately, leaving an estate of seven millions. His home was a one-story brick cottage of five or six rooms. Two-story dwellings are common in the newer points of the city, but they are noticeable exceptions to the rule of the little cottage of wood or brick. You can't judge of a man's means by the exterior of the house he lives in. A friend took me to see the "little three-room cottage" he was building. It had, in fact, but three rooms and a kitchen, but the rooms were large and furnished in fine woods, and the "cottage" will cost him seven or eight thousand dollars. I have sought for a solid explanation of this predilection of Butte people for living on the ground floor. One old resident accounted for it in this way : "You see, the miners first lived in tents ; then they built shanties, and when they were rich enough to build houses they didn't put in any stairs or upper stories, because they were not used to such things." Another man said that the women did not like to climb stairs in the thin atmosphere of this high altitude.

The same fondness for hugging the ground from which the wealth of the city comes is shown in the business structures. Until very recently there was not a three-story structure on the main street. Many of the wealthiest merchants carry on their trade in one-story buildings. The banks are very rich—one of them ranks third in the United States—but they are housed in insignificant edifices. How, then, is Butte luxurious? In daily expenditures for living. The city is an enormous consumer for her population of 50,000. Nothing is too good to eat, or to drink or to wear. The finest of California fruits are brought in by the car-load; fish come from the Atlantic, from Lake Superior, from the Pacific and from the trout streams of the mountains, and early vegetables from Salt Lake City; beef comes 1,500 miles from Kansas City and Omaha; beer by the train load from Milwaukee and St. Louis; more champagne is drank than in any Eastern city of a hundred thousand inhabitants. There is also marked extravagance in clothing, in jewelry and in furniture. In the little one-story cottages you will often find rich furnishings, silverware, porcelain and costly pictures. In amusements, too, there is much lavish use of money. The best actors and singers come to the opera-house. Lavish expenditure is shown in the support of innumerable bar-rooms and other resorts, which are always conspicuous in mining towns, in the many hack carriages to be seen on the streets at all hours of the twenty-four, in the charges for small things and small services—the barber charges a quarter for a shave and the boot-black from fifteen cents to a quarter for a shine. In the dry-goods houses you will find the costliest fabrics and latest fancies of Eastern fashion; in the jewelry stores diamonds that can scarcely be matched for cost this side of Chicago; in the grocery stores every

Silver Mine and Mill at Butte

delicacy to tempt the palate that a world's commerce affords. The daily newspapers contain full telegraphic news, dispatches which only a liberal patronage could enable them to take. For street conveyance there is a cable road, a steam motor road and an electric road. If the visitor is diposed to criticise the lack of noticeable business blocks and the streets of one-story cottages, he should reflect that the costly construction work of Butte is underground—in shafts piercing the mountain side to a depth in some places of 1,400 feet and in miles and miles of galleries, cut out of the solid rock and the hard ores. Millions of money have gone into these subterranean streets and chambers, and many more millions have been taken out. A network of ore veins enwraps and underlies the city. A map of Butte showing by diverse colors the various mining claims looks like a crazy quilt.

Let me now resume in a paragraph or two a few leading facts concerning the situation and appearance of Butte. The city begins in the valley of Silver Bow creek, where are the railway yards and the Parrot smelter, and climbs by a grade not steep for a mountain town one of the foothills of the Rockies. On the crest of the hill the shaft houses, concentrators and rock piles of the chief mines—the Anaconda, the Mountain View, the Parrot, the Lexington, the Moulton and the Alice stand out boldly against the sky-line. Main street runs from the valley to the hilltop and thence on to the suburb of Walkerville, and is an exceedingly lively and picturesque thoroughfare. A very good way to get a comprehension of the physical geography of Butte is to take the cable road on this street to its terminus and return by the same route. On the down trip you enjoy a view of remarkable interest and grandeur. The city is right at your feet, densely built and teeming with activity; beyond are the black smelters in the brown valley flaunting their banners of smoke and steam in the frosty air. Yonder is a long ore train on its way to Anaconda, and around to the left a passenger train that has come all the way from Puget sound is climbing the grade on the pine-clad slope of the Main Divide, on its way to St. Paul and Chicago. To the right, and close to the town, rises the bare, cone-shaped butte, which gave a name to the early placer diggings near its base, and later to the quartz camp that became a village, and from a village developed into the richest mining city in the world. Beyond the valley are piled range on range and peak on peak of the Rockies, forming a superb amphitheatre of black and white—black with the pine forests and white with snow—walling the far horizon on every side.

About midway up the hill slope are four parallel business streets, crossing Main street, each with peculiarities of its own. First comes Mercury street, the favorite resort of the nether world, rather dull by day, but very lively by night—a noisy, jolly, irresponsible street, always shown to strangers as a curiosity. Next comes Park street, the chief avenue for small retail commerce and for the merchandise trades; further up is Broadway, on which stand the leading hotels and the opera house and then, on the upper confines of the business district, is Granite street, with its stately court house and with office buildings occupied by lawyers and real estate agents. The best sites for business buildings on ground not already occupied are on Broadway and Granite and these two streets are plainly destined to rapid improvement. The best residence district is west of Main street, running out for half a mile on nearly level ground, then dipping down into a gulch and rising on a sightly hill-side where there is ample room for expansion.

An electric road runs from the railway stations across town to the verge of the new residence suburb and a steam motor line goes from the business center through South Butte to Meaderville, three miles distant.

The Mines of Butte.—Butte City is to-day the largest and most prosperous mining camp on the face of the earth, its title to the honor being undisputed by any mining man who has ever set foot within its confines and examined the wonderful mineral resources with which it is surrounded. The first mining done about Butte was along the bed-rock of Silver Bow creek, which flows from east to west not more than three hundred yards south of the city limits. This was late in the fall of 1863, when placer-mining for gold was being carried on so successfully in Alder Gulch and other parts of Montana. At that time Silver Bow creek was worked for the gold it contained, but after the coarser metal had been washed from the gravel many of the miners began to cast about for the source from which the gold came, while others drifted off in search of other diggings. During the early spring of 1864, those who stuck to the diggings erected crude cabins on the present townsite, and christened the place Butte, after a large bald hill that stands just west of the city limits. As near as can be learned the first quartz location was made north of the city on August 14, 1864, since which time the number of locations has increased to about 4,000. During the early days of Butte little value was placed on the quartz properties, because there were no facilities at hand for treating the ores and no immediate prospects of such a desirable state of affairs being brought about on account of the isolated condition of the camp. Valuable prospects sold for a mere song, the Lexington, which is now one of the greatest gold and silver producers in the camp, being purchased by the late millionaire, A. J. Davis, for a twenty-dollar horse and afterwards sold by him to a French company for $1,000,000. This sale is a sample of many others made in those days. The claims were undeveloped, and no one then knew or suspected that only a few feet below the surface large and rich bodies of gold, silver and copper ore awaited the arrival of capital and backbone to be uncovered, reduced and added to the world's metal. As time progressed hundreds of claims that cannot now be purchased for millions of dollars passed from the possession of the original locators to the hands of others, because of the yearly assessment work not being performed thereon by the former owners. This is the history of every mining camp where the native metal does not protrude from the ores as an incentive for the proprietor to hold on, do his assessment work and sell his property for what it is worth. During the last fifteen years mining men with capital to back them have bought up many of these properties and developed them to an extent that their value is now estimated in the millions of dollars. Smelters for the treatment of base ores, found all the way from a depth of from 100 to 1,000 feet in depth, have been erected, while mills for crushing the oxidized or free-milling ores, found from the surface to the depth of 500 feet, have also been put up.

Down a Butte Mine.—Mr. Hall first conducted us over the smelter which is built on the slope of the mountain, writes a correspondent of the St. Paul *Pioneer Press*. At the top are great heaps of ore brought from below, and others of rock salt dumped there by the railroad. The latter is added, ten per cent. to the ore, and both are shoveled into great hoppers which break the ore into small chunks. These pass down into the "dryer," which has a great fire at the end. The mass then goes under the "stamps," which weigh 1,000 pounds each. That's what sixty-stamp smelter means, for instance, that it has a capacity of that number of great hammers. These crush the ore into powder. Fourth, it goes lower into the roasting cylinders, where the heat changes the sulphide into chloride by means of the afore-mentioned salt. Sulphur is the miner's great enemy, you know. It and the arsenic now go off in smoke. Fifth, this black flour-like earth is cooled for half a day, and then it is mixed with 300 pounds of quicksilver to 4,000 pounds of pulp and goes to the amalgamating pans, then to the "settlers," lastly to the "retorts," furthest down the mountain, and lastly we saw the great bars of bullion ready to ship.

All this was very interesting. Machines always seem to me like people. Some of them worked with an intelligence of their own, though controlled by the master spirit; others, like the stamps, doggedly worked along like great stolid, stupid laborers of muscle, not even rejoicing in their power; but the propelling engine, gleaming, intricate, nervous, was like the man of brain whose mind impels and compels such others. We went into the changing room where miners' clothes hung about a fire to dry, and, before descending the shaft, went into the great engine room where sat a man, his eye fixed upon an indicator, his ear strained to going signals, the mistaking of which might in an instant flick out the life-flames of dozens of men. He it is who brings up and lowers "the cage" in the shaft. "He's a cool fellow," said Mr. Hall, "the best we've ever had. Men simply won't run this machine. The terrible and continued responsibility unmans them. We have put good, tried engineers here, and after half an hour they would have to be removed. They'd be drenched with sweat and fairly crying under the strain." While talking Mr. Hall had fitted me out for my trip in gossamer, rubbers, and an old cap, and we all stepped into the cage, a sort of fenced-in freight elevator, while the miners gathered around to see if we were frightened. To balance the weight of the rods and shaft are four "bobs" containing fourteen tons of scrap iron.

Going down a mine is like being shot from a catapult down a well. One hasn't much time to realize what the sensation is for his progress is 1,000 feet in eighteen seconds. My remembrance is that it was exciting, cool, black, upside down and exulting. We staggered out at the 1,300-foot level, each lighted a candle—some of the mines are lighted by electricity, but not the "Alice"—and began our subterranean walk. At every hundred feet long passages lead off under the town. These galleries are roofed in with timbers to prevent caving in, though there's no such danger with this granite ore as there is in coal mines. These passages are pitchy, damp, and sometimes cellary to foulness, though usually ventillated from a great shaft. There are twenty-eight miles of them in the "Alice." We walked about four.

Two hundred men work below here; only a short time at once, though. At the end of every lead you will see two men, their candles stuck into the rock only intensifying their weirdness and the surrounding darkness, directing a power drill which is worked by the compressed air machine above the mountain. This drill makes a hideous noise in the quiet gallery. When it has bored a sufficient hole a charge of dynamite is put into it, and the miners decamp. Every minute or so we could hear the sullen roar of this somewhere. This ore is afterward loaded into iron carts, and run over tracks to the shaft and elevated in the cages. There is only one thing of beauty in a mine, the wonderfully beautiful fungus growth that drapes the galleries everywhere, in some places so that one must brush an entrance. It hangs like huge powder-puffs by a tiny thread, and feels like damp swansdown. It is like the description of an angel's raiment, shining and white. It is like the purer and unselfish deed of a criminal, but as evanescent, for it shrivels into an odious, malodorious, yellowish leathery mass as soon as it comes into the daylight above.

I enjoyed the experience, but was glad to come up into the sun and bustle of the over-world, and while bathing my face in distilled water, like the Princess of Wales in-so-far, to hear Mr. Hall tell about their "Alice hospital and reading room" for miners, of which association he is president, the fire brigade, and the great smelters at Anaconda.

Silver Bow (7 miles from Butte) is the junction point of the Montana Union with the Utah Northern branch of the Union Pacific which runs south to Ogden, Utah, and has a population of about 1000, chiefly engaged in railroad work.

Anaconda (population 10,000; 26 miles from Butte on a short spur leaving the road at Stuart).—The town is picturesquely situated at the head of a small mountain valley in the midst of magnificent scenery. It is well built, having a number of brick blocks. The great smelting and reduction works of the Anaconda company are the life of the place. These works were established at this point on account of convenience for procuring fuel, the slight expense for which ores could be run down grade from the mines in Butte, the abundance of pure water, and the excellent location for a town. The annual output of copper matte is greater than at any other point in the world. Two groups of enormous structures about two miles apart constitute the works that employ about 300 men. The fuel used is coke, coal and pine wood, the wood being brought from the mountain gulches down a long flume into which a stream has been diverted, the flowing water performing the work of transporting the sticks of wood.

Warm Springs is principally important as the site of the Montana Insane asylum, which occupies a number of buildings surrounding the copious spring of warm sulphur water. The mineral water is used beneficially in the treatment of insane patients. The valley narrows in a short distance above Warm Springs. The debris of old placer mining can be seen at many places along the river.

Deer Lodge (1,272 miles from St. Paul and forty miles from Butte; population 1,500) derived its name from the abundance of deer that roamed over its broad open prairie, and from a mound which, on a winter's morning, bore a resemblance to an Indian lodge when the steam issued from the hot spring on its summit. Deer Lodge is the seat of Deer Lodge county, and appears quite attractive, nestled midway in the valley, 4,546 feet above the sea. The town is well laid out, and, with its public square, large public buildings, court house, jail, churches and educational establishments, makes a good impression. There is a Presbyterian college of Montana for both sexes located here. There is also a Catholic school for the education of girls, conducted by the Sisters of Charity; and a hospital, under the charge of the same sisterhood. The Montana penitentiary, located at Deer Lodge, is constructed with two wings, containing eighty-four cells.

The town is a general supply and distributing point for several fertile valleys and the surrounding mining districts. Deer Lodge valley extends fifty miles southward, and is composed of farming and grazing lands. The latter rest on the foot-hills and mountains, while the former are lower down, adjacent to the mouths of the streams. There are remarkable boiling springs in the valley. Many bright mountain trout streams course through its broad expanse, some having their sources eastward in the Gold Creek mountains, and others coming from the west through the low, rolling, open country between the Deer Lodge and Flint Creek valleys. Deer Lodge county is noted for the number, extent and richness of its placer mines, and for years it has led the production in placer gold. Among the surrounding mountains, Powell's Peak, twenty miles west of Deer Lodge City, and 10,000 feet in height, is prominent. There are many small lakes in the mountains, which are full of trout, and large game also abounds.

HELENA & JEFFERSON COUNTY, AND HELENA, BOULDER VALLEY & BUTTE RAILROADS.

From Helena to Elkhorn, Mont., 58 Miles, with a Branch from Jefferson to Wickes, 5 Miles.

This branch leaves the main line at Prickly Pear Junction, five miles south of Helena, and extends twenty miles in a western direction, along the valley of the Prickly Pear creek, up into the heart of the Rocky mountains. It crosses a mountain spur by a high-grade line, showing some very bold and successful engineering work. It then descends into the Boulder valley to the town of

Boulder (37 miles from Helena), the county seat of Jefferson county, which has a population of about 1,200. It is situated in a fine agricultural valley and is the central trading town for a number of productive silver mines. Four miles distant are the Boulder Hot Springs, where there is a good hotel and a bathing establishment, with a large plunge bath. Good accommodations for tourists and invalids. The waters are much used in cases of rheumatism.

Elkhorn (58 miles from Helena; population, 500).—The road leaves the valley of the Boulder and climbs a mountain by a three per cent grade to the mining camp of Elkhorn, where there is ore of the richest and most successful quartz mines in Montana.

Wickes (25 miles from Helena, population, 800).—At Jefferson a branch diverges and keeps on up Prickly Pear creek, five miles to the smelting town of Wickes, where ores are roasted, chloridized and converted into ingots. The ingots are shipped to separating works in Baltimore, Md., where the gold and silver are separated from such lead and copper as they may be combined with.

HELENA & RED MOUNTAIN AND HELENA & NORTHERN RAILROADS.

Helena to Rimini, Mont., 17 Miles.

This branch of the Northern Pacific system is a mining road, which leaves the main line at Helena, and terminates at Rimini, on the eastern slope of the main divide of the Rocky mountains. Rimini is a central transportation point for the ores of the important group of mines.

Helena to Marysville, Mont., 20 Miles.

This line runs in a northerly direction from Helena at the base of the Rocky mountains, and ascends to the mining village of Marysville, population 1,100. There are many important mines near Marysville, the most productive of which is the famous Drum Lummon, which in 1887 yielded over $2,000,000 of gold and silver.

DRUMMOND & PHILIPSBURG RAIL-
ROAD.

DRUMMOND TO RUMSEY, MONT.—31.4 MILES.

This branch of the Northern Pacific system was constructed in 1887 to afford an outlet for the productive mining district of Philipsburg and Granite mountain. It follows the valley of Flint creek to Philipsburg, and then by higher grades reaches the terminal station of Rumsey, in the immediate vicinity of the Granite Mountain and other mines.

Philipsburg (25 miles from Drummond; population, 1,000) is one of the oldest mining towns in Montana. The first silver mill in Montana was established at this place in 1866. The mill and mine are still owned by the original company, called "The Hope Silver Mining Company," and is still in successful operation. Beside the trade of the surrounding mines there is considerable ranch country tributary to the town.

Granite Mountain (population, 500; near Rumsey station, 31 miles from Drummond).—This is a mining village created by the prosperous activity of the great Granite Mountain mine, and of several other mines in the immediate vicinity. It is reached by a good but steep road from Philipsburg at the foot of the mountain, and is a unique little town, built among the huge granite boulders and rocks on the mountain side, partly hiding in the crevices, partly clinging to the precipitous wall where there is only room for one side of a street. Most of the inhabitants work under ground in the mines, or in the huge silver mill near by. The scenery is superb. The savage peaks of the main divide of the Rocky mountains with their snowy summits look almost as grand as the famous Swiss Alps, and the bright green valleys below make a pleasing contrast with the rugged slopes of the mountains. The Granite Mountain mine is the most valuable silver mine in the world. It was discovered in 1872, but was first profitably developed in 1883. It has since paid to its stockholders over $3,500,000 in dividends. The ore is base, containing silver, antimony, arsenic, zinc, and copper as sulphides, and native silver in considerable quantity. The average assay value of the ore is 145 ounces of silver to the ton.

BITTER ROOT VALLEY RAILROAD.

MISSOULA TO GRANTSDALE, MONT., 50 MILES.

This branch was built in 1887, from Missoula, on the Northern Pacific main line, up the picturesque and fertile valley of the Bitter Root river, as far as the new town of Grantsdale, 36 miles. The Bitter Root is in some respects the best agricultural valley in Montana. It is lower by nearly 1,000 feet than the valleys near Helena, and has a much warmer climate. Apples and small fruits are successfully grown. There are some valuable mining properties in the mountain range on the western side of the valley. The streams abound in trout, and the mountains in large game, such as Rocky mountain goats, elk and bear.

Tyler (28 miles from Missoula) is the station for Stevensville on the opposite side of the river, a prosperous agricultural town, with a population of 300. Close to the town is the St. Mary's Mission, the oldest of the Jesuit missions in Montana. It was established by Italian priests nearly twenty years before there were any white settlers in the region. The old church, mill, and mission house are still standing.

Victor (36 miles from Missoula) is a new town created by the railroad, and has a population of 500. Silver mines and a fine agricultural country promise to make of it an important place.

Grantsdale (50 miles from Missoula) is a new town,

surrounded by a very attractive country of irrigated farms and stock ranges. Numerous mineral locations have been made on the slopes of the neighboring mountains, which promise an important mining development. This is a fine region for hunting and fishing. The mountain streams abound in trout, and mountain goat, mountain sheep, elk and bear may be shot on the Bitter Root range, which bounds the valley on the west.

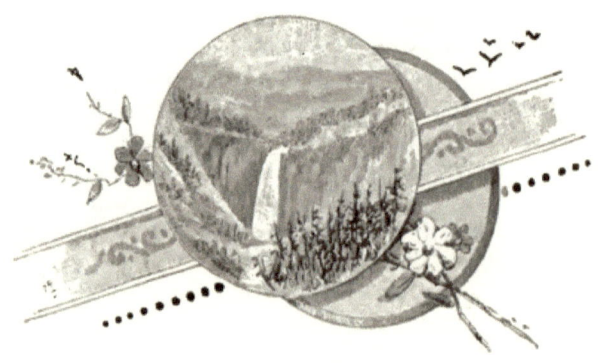

DeSMET AND CŒUR D'ALENE BRANCH.

FROM MISSOULA, MONT., TO MISSION, IDAHO, 159 MILES, CONNECTING AT MISSION WITH STEAMERS FOR CŒUR D'ALENE CITY, FROM WHENCE THERE IS RAIL CONNECTION FOR SPOKANE.

The trains on this road start from Missoula and keep on the main line six miles to DeSmet. There they diverge and run down the irrigated agricultural valley to the Missoula, past the old settlement of Frenchtown, a French Catholic community. After crossing the river the farming valley soon changes to a narrow mountain gorge, through which the road runs on benches high above the dark green waters of the stream. A number of mining camps are seen on the opposite side of the stream. At St. Regis the road turns up the narrow valley of the St. Regis de Borgia creek, following the route of the old Mullan wagon road, which was built by the army in 1861 and 1862, from Fort Benton to Walla Walla, to serve as a military route and to open the way for emigrants to reach Oregon. The Bitter Root mountains are climbed on grades too steep for the hauling of more than six loaded cars in one train, and the line descends into the valley of the South Fork of the Cœur d'Alene river, the great silver-mining district of Northern Idaho.

Mullan (128 miles from Missoula and 118 miles from

Spokane, population 500) is the town for the Hunter group of mines, of which the Morning mine is the best developed. The town has water works and electric lights.

Wallace (134 miles from Missoula and 112 miles from Spokane) is the busiest center of a number of mining gulches, and the point of division of the branch road which runs up a narrow valley to Burke, eight miles distant. It is a compactly built town with water works and electric lights. Stages run across two mountain ranges to Murray, the center of the gold placer district of Pritchard creek.

Murray is an active business town of 1,000 inhabitants, surrounded by huge gravel piles from the placer diggings. It is built on gold, literally as well as figuratively, for not only does it depend solely on the gold mining for existence, but the whole gulch where its buildings stand is valuable placer ground. Besides the placer diggings where the earth and gravel is washed in sluices to separate the nuggets and gold dust, there are three quartz mills for crushing and pulverizing the gold-bearing quartz. Murray is the county seat of Kootenai county. Placer gold was discovered in 1883 on Pritchard creek, a tributary of the Cœur d'Alene river. Early in 1884, there was a remarkable movement of miners, tradesmen and adventurers, to this hitherto wilderness region. What is called in mining camps a "stampede" took place. From two to three thousand people made their way through the depths of the forest during February and March to the valley of the Cœur d'Alene and its tributaries, dragging their supplies with them on toboggan sleds. A number of camps were speedily established, and the development of the region began; but, owing to the fact that the gold was found in soil from six to twelve feet deep, with gravel and boulders, the development was slow. Many of the first comers were forced to leave for want of means to open claims. The district has, however, made steady progress, and now yields a large and constantly increasing amount of gold.

Wardner is an important mining town of 1,000 inhabitants, situated in a narrow gulch shut in by high mountains, four miles from Wardner Junction, on the railroad, and 149 miles from Missoula. On the slopes of these mountains in the immediate vicinity of the town are several important silver mines. The most productive of these are the Sullivan and Bunker Hill. The ores from these mines are concentrated before shipment to Montana and Eastern reduction works. The town is picturesquely built in a narrow gulch, where there is only room for one street.

Mission (159 miles from Missoula, and ninety-seven from Spokane) is the point of transfer from the trains to steamboats, which run down the river and lake sixty miles to Cœur d'Alene City. The old Jesuit church at the Mission, built in 1847, is an interesting building to visit.

The trip by steamer on Lake Cœur d'Alene and the river is hardly equaled for beauty and natural scenery by any water journey of equal length in the United States, unless it be on the Hudson river.

Cœur d'Alene City (219 miles from Missoula and 32 miles from Spokane; population 500) is beautifully located in the pine forests at the foot of the lake of the same name, and in the immediate vicinity of Fort Sherman, one of the most attractive military posts in the United States. Lake Cœur d'Alene is one of the most beautiful mountain lakes to be found anywhere in the world. It is surrounded by the spurs and foot-hills of the Bitter Root and Cœur d'Alene mountains, and its shores are covered with open and park-like forests. Its length is about thirty miles, and it receives two navigable streams, the St. Joseph river and the Cœur d'Alene river.

From Cœur d'Alene to Spokane is a run of a little over an hour, the main line being reached at Hauser Junction. The only town on the way is Post Falls, on the Spokane river, a lumber manufacturing place of about 500 inhabitants, with an excellent water-power.

SPOKANE & PALOUSE RAILROAD.

From Spokane, Wash., to Juliaetta, Idaho, 121 Miles, with a Branch From Pullman to Genesee, 29 Miles.

The traveler who desires to form anything like an adequate conception of the agricultural wealth of the State of Washington, should not fail to leave the main line of the Northern Pacific at Spokane and make a journey over this branch through the wonderfully fertile Palouse country, which stretches at the foot of the mountains, in a belt about fifty miles wide, as far south as the Snake river. From the deep canyon of the Snake, a region of like fertility and general characteristics, generally known as the Walla Walla country, extends over 100 miles further, following the trend of the Bitter Root and Blue Mountain ranges. The Palouse country is upheaved in gentle grassy hills with rounded tops, and every acre is highly fertile, the summits of the hills being fully as valuable for grain fields as the slopes in the valleys which lie between. Wheat yields from twenty-five to fifty bushels to the acre, and oats, barley and rye do proportionately well. The whole country in its natural state is covered with a luxuriant growth of bunch grass, on which cattle and horses pasture the year round. The winters are mild and the snowfall light. The Spokane Falls and Palouse branch diverges from the main line at Marshall Junction, a small town 9 miles from Spokane.

Spangle (20 miles from Spokane) is an active trading point with a population of about 500.

Oakesdale (46 miles from Spokane; population, 1,200) is the crossing point of the Union Pacific line from Spokane to Portland.

From Belmont, 51 miles from Spokane, a short branch road runs to Farmington, an agricultural village with 400 inhabitants, near the Idaho line.

Garfield (58 miles from Spokane; population, 700) is the point where the Spokane and Palouse crosses the Farmington branch of the Union Pacific.

Palouse City (68 miles from Spokane Falls) is the oldest town in the Palouse country, and has a population of 1,500. Logs are floated down the Palouse river to this place from the slopes of the neighboring mountains. Considerable placer gold is mined on the waters of the Palouse. The country around Palouse City is exceedingly fertile and picturesque.

Pullman (84 miles from Spokane; population, 1,500) is the point where the Spokane & Palouse road crosses the Moscow branch of the Union Pacific, and is a well-built town, central to an extensive region of excellent farming country. The Washington Agricultural college is located here. Artesian wells supply the town with water.

Moscow, Idaho (population, 3,500, 94 miles from Spokane) is a handsome town situated in a rolling prairie country and surrounded by well improved farms. It is the trade center of a large part of the rich grain-growing country of Northern Idaho. The State Agricultural college occupies a commanding brick structure. There are excellent hotels and large department mercantile stores. Opals are mined at a point six miles north of the town, being found in the basaltic rock, which everywhere underlies the region.

East of Moscow the road strikes one of the tributaries of the Potlatch river and descends rapidly through forest-clad ravines to the deep, narrow valley of that stream. Kendrick and Juliaetta are the two towns of the Potlatch country, and each have a population of about 500. At Juliaetta there is an inclined plane railroad running from the valley near the town up a steep ascent to the level of the plateau, and used for getting wheat down and merchandise up.

The Potlatch Country is a high plain, deeply seamed by a number of gorges through which flow swift streams. The divisions made by these gorges are called ridges, and each has its local name. On the plateau the land is very rich and produces heavy crops of grain. Fruit thrives, and there is no better country for apples, prunes, plums, pears and berries west of the Rockies. The region is heavily grassed and is excellent for stock. Its climate is even milder than that of the neighboring Palouse country, a mountain spur shielding it from north winds.

The Genesee Country.—South of Pullman lies the Genesee country, which is an extension of the Palouse plains and reaches southward to the great canyon of the Snake river. The chief towns are Uniontown, Colton and Genesee, each a thriving center of farming trade, with a population of about 500. The farming country is everywhere attractive and raises great crops of wheat, oats and flax. Most of the farms have flourishing orchards.

Lewiston, Idaho (about 15 miles from Genesee) is an old and prosperous town, situated at the junction of the Snake and Clearwater rivers. The Spokane & Palouse road will eventually be extended to this place, following the Potlatch and Clearwater rivers down from Juliaetta. Lewiston has a population of 1,500, and has a large trade with the surrounding farming country, and with the mining districts of Northern Idaho. Steamboats run up the Snake river, and also, at high water, on the Clearwater river.

The drive from either Uniontown or Genesee to Lewiston is one of the most strikingly picturesque that can be found in the whole range of western travel, and tourists are strongly advised not to omit it. The road passes over a beautiful rolling and fertile country for the first five or six miles, and then comes suddenly out on the brink of an enormous and precipitous declivity overlooking the valleys of the Snake and Clearwater rivers, and a vast extent of hilly country stretching off to Craig's mountain on the south and Blue mountains on the southeast. Lewiston seems to be within rifle-shot distance at the foot of the precipice, but is only reached by a zig-zag drive of over five miles down the mountain side. The valley in which Lewiston is situated is fully half a mile in vertical distance below the general level of the rolling plains country north of it.

SOUTH OF SNAKE RIVER.

An extensive, fertile and beautiful agricultural country lies south of the Snake river in Washington and laps over on the west into Oregon. It extends from the Snake and the Clearwater southward to the Blue mountains, and has an average width of about fifty miles. Its length from the bend of the Snake river at Lewiston to its western limits is about 150 miles. It is one of the most productive grain-growing regions in the world. The average yield of wheat, taking one year with another, is about thirty bushels to the acre, and crops of forty to fifty bushels to the acre are by no means extraordinary. The region is rolling or hilly, and slopes southward up to the forest line on the Blue mountains. It is penetrated by the lines of the Washington & Columbia River railroad, which connects with the Northern Pacific at Pasco, and also by lines of the Union Pacific system. The aspect of the country improves gradually as the distance from the river increases, and before reaching Walla Walla the country has become very fertile. The Walla Walla river is a small stream that pours into the Columbia—merely a channel cut through sand and sage brush, although further up there is an occasional fringe of willows.

Whitman (5 miles from Walla Walla), is merely a side track. It, however, marks the scene of a deplorable tragedy. In 1836 Dr. Marcus Whitman, a physician, who was also a clergyman, was sent out from the East as a missionary to the Cayuse and Umatilla Indians. Even at that early day

Christian sympathy was drawn toward the aboriginal tribes of the upper Columbia, and to this instrumentality the preservation of the Northern Pacific country to the United States is mainly due. Dr. Whitman established his mission at Wai-lat-pu, now Whitman's station, where he faithfully labored among the red men. In 1847 he was making a professional visit to the Hudson Bay post at Wallula, from which his station was twenty-five miles inland, on the Walla Walla river, combining, in accordance with his usual custom, the practice of medicine with the preaching of the gospel. When at Wallula, Whitman saw the arrival of a Roman Catholic priest and his party, and heard the boast made that Oregon was certain to belong to the British, as Gov. Simpson, of the Hudson's Bay company, was in Washington making negotiations to that end. This news weighed so heavily on the missionary's mind that, though late in the autumn, he prepared for and undertook a midwinter journey across the continent, made representations to the Government as to the true value of the country, piloted the first wagon train through to the Columbia river the following spring, and so was greatly instrumental in preventing British ascendency in the Pacific Northwest. The year after Dr. Whitman returned to his mission, he, his wife and others were massacred. It seems that the measles broke out among the Indians with great fatality. The medicine men of the tribes charged Whitman with causing the disease, and one night the cruel savages murdered their benefactor with all his companions. The massacre occurred at the north end of the ridge, west of the railroad. There the victims were buried, and efforts are now making to raise a monument "to the memory of Dr. Marcus Whitman and his associate dead." This tragedy led to the Cayuse war of 1848.

Walla Walla (56 miles from Pasco) is beautifully situated upon an open plain that is watered by the divided flow of the Walla Walla river. Beyond it the Blue mountains stand like a wall, and among the foot-hills is the richest agricultural district known. The city has 6,000 inhabitants and a handsome business street, with substantial blocks of stores,—some very fine ones. Though no forest trees are native to the plain, the streets are lined with shade trees, usually poplar, and the gardens are filled with orchards and vineyards. The private residences are often beautiful. Near town is the military station of Fort Walla Walla, and the presence of troops adds something to the business as well as to the attractions of the city.

Walla Walla has ten churches, a public library, a remarkably handsome court-house, which is one of the finest public buildings in Washington; two opera houses and a city hall; St. Mary's Hospital, conducted by the Catholic order of the Sisters of Mercy. Whitman College is an institution for the higher education of both sexes, having complete classical and scientific courses. St. Paul's School for girls is an institution for boarding and day scholars. The Catholics have two schools. St. Vincent's Academy for girls occupies a large brick building in the midst of pleasant groves, and St. Patrick's School is a day school for boys.

The agricultural country tributary to Walla Walla along the slopes of the Blue mountains and the adjacent plains is of remarkable fertility, the soil being adapted in an especial degree to the production of wheat, and a yield of forty bushels to the acre is not at all unusual. This is also a fruit country, the apple, pear, plum and cherry, grapes and all the berries being raised in profusion and perfection. Fifteen miles beyond Walla Walla the railroad comes down from the hills into the valley of the Touchet river, and follows up that stream to Palouse Junction, whence the main line runs northward to Riparia, on the Snake river, and a branch continues up the Touchet, thirteen miles further, to Dayton. Prescott (51 miles from Wallula Junction, and 20 miles from Walla Walla) is a small town with a flouring mill. Bolles' Junction (56 miles from Wallula) is an unimportant station. The principal towns south of Snake river beside Walla Walla are the following:

Waitsburg (80 miles from Pasco; population 900.)—This is the oldest town in the Touchet valley, and was settled in 1870. It is a place of considerable business importance, as a milling and wheat-shipping point, and a country trade centre.

Dayton (90 miles from Pasco; population, 3,000) is, next to Walla Walla, the oldest town in Washington south of Snake river. It stands at the junction of the Touchet river and Petit creek, in the midst of a beautiful and exceedingly fertile and agricultural country. The Touchet furnishes good waterpower, which is utilized for several sawmills and factories. It is the county seat of Columbia county, and was named in honor of Jesse Day, the pioneer settler. The surrounding country is upheaved into high hills with rounded tops; the summits and slopes of these hills are as fertile as the bottom lands in the narrow valleys between them; in fact, the farmers prefer the hill tops for wheat fields.

Pomeroy, county seat of Garfield county, has a population of 1,500, and is the market town for a large and productive farming country. It is the terminus of a branch railroad.

Athena, Oregon, has a population of 650, and is an important wheat-shipping town.

Pendleton, Oregon (43 miles from Pasco) is situated near the base of the Blue mountains on the Umatilla river, and is the county seat of Umatilla county. It is a large, active, commercial town, with a population of 4,000. Its shipments are wheat, stock, wool, barley, rye, oats, fruits, etc. The country surrounding the town resembles in its appearance and general character that around Walla Walla, and is finely adapted to farming and stock raising.

Snake River flows deep down in an immense Canyon, whose cliffs are a thousand feet or more in height. Generally, the points are rock-ribbed; for the strata show on every bluff. To ascend these cliffs is impossible, except some ravine is followed to its source, or a roadway is graded carefully winding up the face of the acclivities. The shipment of grain would be attended with difficulty if the farmer had to haul his load down such tremendous hills, and spend hours returning to the plain above with his empty wagon. The evil is remedied by the construction of shutes leading for thousands of feet from the summit, down which the grain is poured to the warehouse on the river. There is communication between the various shipping points by means of a telephone, and the business is transacted with dispatch. The farmer simply delivers his wheat on the hill, and goes home rejoicing. The landing places are merely warehouses, with perhaps a store. The canyon of Snake river looks like an inferno;-but the traveler who judges the country by this river scenery is entirely out of his reckoning. For example, to climb the grade opposite Lewiston is two hours' hard work, over two miles of distance; but, when foot is placed on the surface of the rim rock, a rolling prairie region of excellent farming land is spread out as far as the eye can reach. This is the case generally on the Columbia and Snake rivers. The bars lying at the foot of the high bluffs along the river have proved to be especially favorable for peach culture, and the yield is large and the crop has never failed.

Medical Lake, Washington

CENTRAL WASHINGTON RAILROAD.

FROM CHENEY TO COULEE CITY, 108 MILES.

This road was built as a feeder to the Northern Pacific as far as Davenport in 1888, 1889, and 1890. It traverses, for the entire distance, a fertile rolling prairie country, diversified with occasional small groves of pine timber, and yielding large crops of all the small grains. This region is generally known as "The Big Bend Country," from the fact that it is surrounded on the north and east by the big bend in the Columbia river. It has a mild, agreeable climate, and is well adapted for general farming, the raising of cattle, horses and sheep, and also for fruit culture. The trains on this branch start from Spokane.

Medical Lake (26 miles from Spokane) is situated in the midst of a group of small lakes, three of which having great depth, are very strongly impregnated with alkaline salts, and their water has remarkable curative properties. One in particular attracts hundreds of invalids, especially persons affected by rheumatism, skin diseases, and nervous complaints. Many undoubted cures of a remarkable nature are recorded. This medical lake, *par excellence*, has a medium strength of salts, while another has a very strong impregnation, and the third is very weak. The region is delightful, and can be made a very pleasant resort. The country people come and pitch their tents and take their baths as they choose.

The early history of this lake is this. A Frenchman, named Lefevre, who was sorely afflicted with rheumatism, was tending sheep around the shores of the lake. He found that after washing the sheep in the lake water that his rheumatism was less painful, so he began to bathe his shrunken limbs, for one arm was wasted away and carried in a sling. The result was a perfect cure of the rheumatism, and restoration of the wasted arm to its natural size. Lefevre still lives at Medical Lake in perfect health, no longer a poor shepherd, for the increase in value of lands from the discovery of the medical properties of the water has made him independent.

The town of Medical Lake is situated on the eastern shore of this lake; it has three hotels, a soap-making establishment, which uses the waters of the lake, and an establishment for evaporating the waters and producing a salt which is sold for medical purposes. Medical Lake is much resorted to by invalids, and is a favorite camping ground and excursion place for the country people in the vicinity.

Deep Creek (315 miles from Spokane) is an active country trading town, surrounded by a well-settled farming district, and having a small but valuable water-power from the creek for which it is named.

Davenport (57 miles from Spokane; population, 600) is the central town of the Big Bend country, and was established in 1883, long before a railroad was projected through this region. It is the diverging point of numerous stage and mail routes. Fort Spokane, 25 miles north of Davenport, at the junction of the Spokane and Columbia rivers, is a United States military post, garrisoned by two companies of infantry. The soldiers are stationed at this point to keep an eye on the Indians on the neighboring reservations north of the Spokane and west of the Columbia rivers.

Wilbur (88 miles from Spokane) is a new town of about 500 inhabitants. The surrounding country is rolling prairie.

Almira (103 miles from Spokane) is a farming center with a population of 400.

Coulee City (124 miles from Spokane, population 500) is the terminus of this branch. The surrounding country is mainly used for stock raising. The town is situated at the middle crossing of the Grand Coulee, the most remarkable scenic feature of the Big Bend country. It is a profound volcanic crevice, extending across the country for a distance of seventy-five miles, and reaching the Columbia river at both extremities. Its walls are of basaltic rock, and of an average height of about 800 feet. The floor of this great chasm varies in width from a few hundred feet to half a mile, and contains many alkali ponds. At only two places are there natural crossing points for wagon roads. At these places, known as the "Middle" and "Upper" crossings, the walls of the canyon have been broken down by volcanic action. Stages run from Coulee City to the Okanogan mining towns.

NORTHERN PACIFIC AND CASCADE BRANCH.

This branch leaves the main line at Crocker, Washington, at the head of the Puyallup valley, and sends out spurs to the coal mining towns of Douty, Burnett, Wilkeson and Carbonado. Of these the largest is Carbonado, which has 1,000 inhabitants and is built on a mountain bench high above the brawling waters of the stream. Mining operations have been carried on here for many years. The mines are owned by the Southern Pacific railroad company, and the coal is shipped to San Francisco, by ocean vessels loading at the coal bunkers in Tacoma. At Wilkeson, Burnett and Douty are valuable mines which ship to all points along the Pacific coast and also supply the local market of Tacoma. The coal found in this field is of different qualities, but may all be classed as bituminous. One mine furnishes a coking coal, another a gas coal, and others coal particularly adapted for locomotive and steamship use.

UNITED RAILROADS OF WASHINGTON.

TACOMA AND OCOSTA LINE, FROM LAKE VIEW JUNCTION, 9 MILES FROM TACOMA, TO OCOSTA— 100 MILES.

This branch of the Northern Pacific is a direct line from Tacoma and Seattle to the lower Chehalis valley, and to the sea-port towns of Gray's harbor. It traverses much rich alluvial country, where farming is successfully carried on along the valleys of the Black river and the Chehalis, and gives access to the valleys of the streams flowing into Gray's harbor from the north, and into the Pacific from the western slopes of the Olympic mountains.

Gate City (52 miles from Tacoma) the junction point of the road from Centralia on the N. P. main line, is a new agricultural and lumbering town of 500 inhabitants.

Elma (63 miles from Tacoma) on the Chehalis, population 500, was an established town before the railroad was built and is supported by farming.

Montesano, (73 miles from Tacoma), county seat of Chehalis county, is a handsome town of 2,000 inhabitants, situated on the Chehalis at the head of regular navigation at all stages of water. It has saw-mills and a large country trade, and ocean steamers come up to its wharf from Portland and from San Francisco.

Cosmopolis (88 miles from Tacoma) is a saw-mill town of 500 people, eight miles down the river from Montesano.

Aberdeen (87 miles from Tacoma, population 2,500), is built on level ground on the Chehalis, at the mouth of the Wiskah, and is an active lumber manufacturing town. It has a salmon cannery and a shipyard where coasting vessels are built of the stout fir timber which abounds in this region.

Hoquiam, three miles below Aberdeen, stands on a delta where the Chehalis and the Hoquiam rivers join and the waters of both flow into the head of Gray's harbor. Population 1,500. The chief industry is lumber manufacturing. Hoquiam has an opera house and one of the largest hotels in the State, a handsome structure facing the salt water and surrounded by attractive grounds.

Ocosta (100 miles from Tacoma), terminus of the railroad, is a lumbering and shipping town of 500 people, situated at the lower end of Gray's harbor in a deep cove, sheltered from the winds and waves of the Pacific by Peterson's point.

Westport, on Peterson's point, is an attractive summer resort, with three hotels and some lumbering industry. The pine forests reach to the surf of the Pacific. Stages run along the hard beach to North Cove, on Willapa harbor, there connecting with steamboats for South Bend. This trip is exceedingly novel and picturesque. Tourists making it can return to the main line of the Northern Pacific by a branch from South Bend to Chehalis.

CHEHALIS-AND SOUTH BEND LINE, 56 MILES.

This line diverges from the Pacific division of the N. P. at Chehalis, and crossing the low range of wooded hills known as the Boisfort mountains, reaches the agricultural valley of the Willapa river, and follows that stream down to South Bend. The only town of importance before the terminus is reached is

Willapa City, a pretty village in the midst of orchards and grain fields, to which steam boats run from points on the bay and river.

South Bend, on the Willapa, five miles above its mouth in the bay of the same name, is on deep water and is reached by large steam and sailing vessels from the Pacific Ocean. Willapa bay is one of the best and most capacious harbors on the Pacific coast, having a deep and safe entrance and land locked waters spacious enough for hundreds of vessels to lie at anchor. South Bend has important lumber industries, and with the completion of the new railroad will soon become a wheat and coal shipping port. Salmon canning is an established business, and oysters are shipped from the flats on the bay to San Francisco and Portland, and to the Sound cities. Ocean steamers run to San Francisco and Portland. Steamboats run to Sealand, North Cove and Willapa City. Population of South Bend, 2,500.

SEATTLE, LAKE SHORE AND EASTERN RAILWAY.

From Seattle to Sumas, 125 Miles, with a Branch from Woodinville Junction to North Bend, 35 Miles.

The Seattle, Lake Shore & Eastern railroad was originally a local Seattle enterprise which started to build a line from that city across the Cascade mountains as far east as Spokane, where it was expected that it would head off the Great Northern and become the west end of that road. The road was built by the local company fifty-nine miles eastward from Seattle to the base of the mountains, and about forty miles were constructed westward from Spokane. A line was also built northward from Woodinville Junction, twenty-four miles out of Seattle, nearly due northward to Sumas, on the British Columbia boundary. Sumas is 125 miles from Seattle, and the primary object of this line was to give the Canadian Pacific entrance to Seattle. The company became involved in financial difficulties and a few years ago it sold out its lines to the Northern Pacific, turning over its stock on condition that its debts should be assumed by the purchasing corporation. Thus the S., L. S. & E. became a division of the Northern Pacific system. All plans of building across the mountains were abandoned before the transfer of ownership occurred, and the line to Sumas has become the main line, and that from Woodinville up to the coal mines at Gilman, to the superb cataract of the Snoqualmie river, and to the hop-fields of North Bend, is run as a branch. The Sumas line connects at that place with a branch of the Canadian Pacific, running to Mission, on the main line of that road, and also with the Bellingham Bay and British Columbia railroad, which runs to Whatcom, twenty-three miles from Sumas.

An independent line, built under a Canadian charter, runs from Sumas to Vancouver, by way of New Westminister, and is operated as an extension of the S., L. S. & E., forming a through line from Tacoma and Seattle to the two chief cities on the main land of British Columbia. The Lake Shore & Eastern, on the other hand, has penetrated a region that was for the most part a wilderness before it was constructed. It crosses the valleys of all the rivers that run into the Sound from the east, and crosses them at points about midway between the foothills of the mountains and the tidewater of the Sound. The road is interesting to intending settlers who may wish to make homes in the Puget Sound country by reason of the fact that it makes accessible a great deal of good land along the valleys of the Snohomish, the Stillaguamish, the Skagit and the Nooksack rivers, that when tilled can be made very productive of hops, oats, hay, fruits and vegetables, and that can be cleared at moderate expense. In the lower parts of all those valleys farmers have been established for many years, sending their products out on small steamboats. They prospered even before the era of railways and cities on the Sound.

Snoqualmie **Falls** (52 miles from Seattle) is one of the most superb cataracts in the world, and is not surpassed for beauty and grandeur by any of the famous waterfalls in Switzerland. It is reached by three hours' rail journey from Seattle, and the railroad runs to the brink of the chasm into which the Snoqualmie river plunges over a sheer precipice 300 feet high. The waters of the river are of a deep blue color, the walls of the gorge are covered with a luxuriant growth of trees, vines and shrubs, and the sunlight forms vivid rainbows on the mist clouds that rise from the depths of the chasm. The color effects of this wonderful scene are of a rare and surprising beauty. Tourists can leave Seattle in the morning, pass three hours at the falls and return in the afternoon. The following description of the falls is from the *Northwest Magazine:*

A river of like name begins life in the glaciers of Mount Si, one of the front rank peaks of the solid battle line of the giant Cascades. Peacefully and contentedly, yet with an occasional stir of harmless activity, this clear and shallow green river flows onward for several miles, apparently innocent of its own approaching tragedy. A few feet above the falls it plays around a group of stones, flashing now and then a spray of white as flint occasionally gives evidence of pent-up fire. The seeming mirth of rock and stream recall Browning's "Old Brown Earth," who

>—" sets his bones
>To bask i' the sun, and thrusts out knees and feet
> For the ripple to run over in its mirth
>Listening the while, where on the heap of stones
>The white breast of the sea lark twitters sweet."

A dull boulder audaciously obstructs the stream's happy course, perhaps to warn it of the peril that lies beyond. Heedless, the river flows on, and dividing, encompasses the stony obstacle. Immediately the crisis is at hand and with one bold leap the stream becomes a cataract, falling over the precipice nearly three hundred feet into a gloomy chasm. It leaps—it aches! Do streams, like "hearts, after leaps, ache?"

A moment ago the water was wont to go warbling so softly and well, and now its serenity has been interrupted; it is no longer a river but a boundless, turbulent and never-ceasing overflow; a liquid avalanche, a tragedy of water.

Were it not for the ugly rock that darkly protrudes itself at the top of the fall, much of the graceful movement, resulting from the division of the stream, would be lost. From below it falls the wavy white spray, and in fancy an unseen mermaid sits upon the rock, her long sea-hair blown outward to the sun.

The entire fall, as seen from above and opposite, does not drop directly, but rather assumes a graceful curve as it glides continuously through the air, downward yet onward, like some huge gull that delays and yet delays his descent to earth. An equally attractive view of the waterfall is seen from the bottom of the chasm, which is reached by descending a long flight of steps, nearly three hundred in number. At the foot of the cliff in the lower river, large logs which have been precipitated over the abrupt declivity are often seen tossing about in their wrath.

The chief characteristics of Snoqualmie falls are color, grace and volume. The water is a study in color, as beautiful and subdued in tone as a marine pastel. The river itself is a dark, cool green, but as it curves over the precipice the volume of water changes to a pure aqua marine tint. This fresh contrasting color is soon lost as the fall breaks forth into joyous foam, undefined and unconstrained. Changing again, its snowy substance turns to pearly smoke, and, moving, groups itself into hundreds of graceful points which resemble the last triumphal shoots of sky-rockets, that inverted point below to their own fate. The fairy pinions form ever and again, and as one waits expectantly for them to burst, they are lost in mist and spray, which rise like incense from the boiling cauldron where the river has been poured. These graceful formations give a feathery and floating appearance to the fall, and comprise its most beautiful feature. On a cloudy or rainy day snow white and sea green are the distinctive shades, softened by tints of pearl. A faint heliotrope rose hue enters, having no more definite location than the first dim hint of sunrise color that mysteriously steals into the gray of dawn. When the sun is out it plays all day with kaleidoscope brilliancy about the water, implanting in the spray a perfect rainbow, which rises higher and higher as the great golden charioteer draws darkness into light.

To a person devoid of the sense of hearing, a gigantic waterfall must seem as tame as its painting in oils, for in sound is its volume and force given full utterance. It is one of the grand orchestral climaxes of nature's music, whose sounds range from the first faint, sweet note of the spring time song-bird and the the soft undulating vibration of the running stream, to the majestic melody of the mountain's thunderous avalanches and the distant artillery of the opposing clouds. The noise of a fall holds as distinct a position in the world of sound as do the separate instruments of an orchestra that blend together in a harmonious whole. Analytically, however, the sounds of this mass of falling water are two-fold, and, strangely enough, their different sources are discoverable. From where the river dashes tumultuously to the foot of the precipice, comes the thunderous tone of distant canyon, deep, melodious and mighty. The continual thud falls upon the ear like a rich musical chord from a base viol. Outside, the softer yet more searching sound of the foamy spray arises, resembling, at a distance, the moans of forests sighing for sunshine and their lost birds. Together the two sounds comprise the one distinct noise of a great fall. Either alone could not compose its music which, like the tones of an organ, is two fold in its melody.

While standing on a little piazza slightly overhanging the canyon, it is impossible to avert the eyes from the magnetic sight. The beauty, volume and grace of the falls of the Snoqualmie fascinate and electrify until, like a "long draught of soul wine," they enter the spirit, bringing satisfaction and perfect rest. The fall is emblematic of eternity, for as long as sun shines and rain falls, the ceaseless activity of this masterpiece of nature must go on forever and forever.

The eye is turned away, and beyond and below lies a clear, shallow, green river, slowly winding its tranquil way through miles of forest to a homeless sea.

Snohomish (37 miles from Seattle), county seat of the county of the same name, is a pleasant place of orchards and flower gardens, of pretty homes, of busy business streets, of mills where fragrant cedar shingles are split out of sections of huge tree trunks, of railway activity and of steamboat wharves, whence little brown, puffing boats depart for Everett, at the mouth of the river, and for farms and villages up streams. The population is not far from 3,500. It is not a raw, new town, like so many in this new State, but can show in its central district evidences of a respectable age in the old warehouses that overhang the river, and in many-gabled structures that evidently date from another architectural epoch. In fact, the pioneer settler came to the place as long ago as 1860. The new Everett &

Monte Cristo road runs a number of local trains daily for passenger travel to and from Everett. This road makes use of the main line of the S., L. S. & E. road from Snohomish northward to Getchell, thirty miles, before turning eastward to reach the mines at the foot of the Cascade mountains. The main line of the Great Northern road, leaving the Sound at Everett, runs through Snohomish and follows the course of the Skykomish river up to the mountains at Stevens Pass. A large business is done in the manufacture of cedar shingles by five mills located in or near the town.

There are no large towns on this road north of Snohomish. Lumbering and the manufacture of cedar shingles are the chief industries of all the settlements, and all do some trade with farmers who cultivate the bottom lands along the rivers. Arlington and McMurray are smart villages with about 500 people each. Sedro and Woolley are practically one place, though under separate municipal governments. They are on the Skagit river, a broad and powerful stream, fed by mountain torrents. Here the Seattle & Northern road crosses, running west to Anacortes, on the Sound, and east to Hamilton, where there are coal and iron fields. The Fairhaven & Southern line, from Fairhaven, on the Sound, to coal mines six miles east, also crosses here. It belongs to the Great Northern company. Nooksack is an attractive place in the valley of the river of the same name.

Sumas (125 miles from Seattle, population 500) is an important railway junction point and does some business in lumber and shingle manufacturing. It is built close to the international boundary line, on a small prairie. Besides the Northern Pacific line to Seattle, Sumas has a local road to New Whatcom, a branch of the Canadian Pacific, and also the Burrard Inlet and Fraser Valley road westward to New Westminster and Vancouver.

New Westminster, B. C., is an old, handsome town of 8,000 inhabitants, dating back to 1853. It rises in terraces from the shore of a noble river, the Fraser. From the highest points you can look over the broad delta westward for sixteen miles to the river's mouth in the Gulf of Georgia. All the residence lots have a frontage of sixty-six feet, and four of them make an acre. Thus every household can have front trees, roses and lilacs, and a kitchen garden, and few houses are so situated as to be deprived of a share in the views up and down the Fraser. Sawing lumber and canning salmon are the chief industries, and there is a good deal of trade with farmers along the rich bottom-lands. A branch of the Canadian Pacific reaches the town, and a branch of the Great Northern comes to the opposite bank of the river and its passengers are ferried across. The Northern Pacific connecting line crosses the Fraser on a bridge which cost $250,000.

Vancouver, B. C., is the western terminus of the Canadian Pacific railway, since the completion of that road to the tidewater of the Pacific in 1886. Its population is about 15,000. It has a remarkably advantageous site on a peninsula between the deep waters of Burrard Inlet and the shallow tidal flow of False creek. The inlet is a miniature Puget Sound, deep, land-locked and mountain rimmed. It puts up into the land from the Gulf of Georgia for over twenty miles, and the largest ships that float can enter the narrow entrance, less than half a mile wide, and lie at anchor anywhere on this beautiful fiord, or can go up either of its two branches to lumber mills and camps in the heart of tremendous mountain fastnesses. False creek, too, has a commercial value, for rafts of logs are towed up to sawmills on its banks at high tide. Between the inlet and the creek the ground on which the city is built swells up

like a turtle's back, giving perfect drainage in one direction
or the other and offering no steep ascents to worry teams
and put pedestrians out of breath. The business district
runs along the back and the neck of the turtle, and on
what we might call its head there is a well built-district of
both residences and stores. Across False creek is a populous suburb connected with the city by three bridges.

The mountain panorama north of the inlet is so striking that it holds the eye for a time from any close inspection of the city at our feet. Gigantic peaks, dark, forbidding and cloud-swept, rise from the water's edge to
altitudes of five and six thousand feet. Only in a few
places do their frowning walls recede a little from the tide
to allow a little room for human occupancy—an Indian
village with its church spire opposite the town and a saw-
mill settlement further up. Gloomy defiles reach far back
into the heart of the mountains, and on the crests of the
tallest peaks are scarfs and hoods of snow, making the
dark foliage of the firs appear black by contrast. The
waters of the inlet, where tall ships ride at anchor and
sail boats glide about, look very peaceful and inviting
by contrast with these rugged giants of the Coast Range
that thrust their feet into the tide flowing in from the
Pacific Ocean. Now look seaward. Beyond the throat
of the inlet lies English bay, and in the far west gleam
the waters of the Gulf of Georgia, which separates
the British Columbia mainland from Vancouver Island.
Ships coming in from sea bound to Vancouver city sail up
the Strait of Fuca, round the south end of Vancouver Island
and turn north up the Gulf of Georgia to Burrard Inlet.
From the open sea beyond Cape Flattery to the inlet the
distance is about 150 miles.

Now let your eye follow the long expanse of the

young city. Note the handsome granite buildings of the Dominion post-office, and the banks, the many solid business blocks, the long stretch of Cordova street, where trade most concentrates, the parallel length of Hastings street and the cross street called Granville, up which trade is steadily marching from the water-side to the Hotel Vancouver and the pretty opera house, both owned by the Canadian Pacific railway. The volumes of smoke here and there along both water fronts come from mills engaged in sawing fir and cedar lumber for shipment by rail to the eastern provinces of Canada, and by sea to Australia and South America. That brick factory with the monumental chimney in the extreme eastern end of the town is a sugar refinery, getting its raw material from the Sandwich Islands, and the cluster of smoky buildings near by from a big foundry and machine shops where steamships, engines, and sawmill machinery are built and repaired. That cluster of masts belong to sailing ships that are taking on cargoes of lumber for foreign ports. If we are lucky enough in our day of observation we shall see one of the huge, white China steamers starting on her long voyage across the Pacific.

Chancel of the Greek Church, Sitka.

Sitka, Alaska

A Trip to Alaska.

Alaska extends from a point six hundred miles north of the dividing line between the United States proper and the British possessions to the shores of the Polar Sea, and as far west of San Francisco as the coast of Maine lies to the east.

There is so much of romance associated with the idea of a trip to this far and mysterious Northland, so much that appeals to the imagination of even the most phlegmatic and sober-minded among us, that could it be brought home to the American people, with the force and vividness of some great and sudden event in contemporary history, that it is possible to make comfortably and inexpensively, within the narrow compass of fourteen days, a voyage extending to within a few degrees of the Arctic circle and embracing many of the greatest wonders of that land of icebergs and glaciers, not all the ships that sail American waters would be adequate for the conveyance of the rush of travel that would at once ensue.

So erroneous, however, are the prevailing ideas with regard to our distant possession, and so liable to become the foundations of utterly wrong inferences are even those actual facts regarding the country, which have, by slow degrees, found entrance into the public mind, that such statements as that a temperature of zero is rarely ever known at Sitka, that often an entire winter will pass without ice being formed thicker than a knife blade, and that there is not a day in the year when vessels may not load and unload in the harbor of the capital city, are received with more or less incredulity, and regarded as utterly inconsistent with the fact that perpetual snow is found within three thousand feet of the sea-level, and that rivers of ice, 1,000 feet deep, run down to the sea from far in the interior of the country. Visions, too, are conjured up of cramped and greasy little whale boats, making tedious voyages, at irregular intervals, through rough seas that in so great a distance cannot fail to be tempestuous.

That large and well-appointed steamships are engaged in a regular service, and that the long voyage they make is never productive of more than a transient squeamishness, however susceptible be the traveler, are almost incredible pieces of news to those who hear them for the first time; and yet, while such erroneous notions as have been cited are current, one venturesome traveler after another, to the surprise, and not unfrequently against the advice and remonstrance of his friends, ventures forth to put the claims and pretensions of the railroad and steamship companies to the test, and return to be the hero of the social circle in which he moves. But if this is the condition of things to-day, it will be but a short time before the Alaska excursion will no longer be the subject of these various misconceptions, but will have taken the place to which it is entitled in popular estimation.

Tacoma is the starting point for the Alaska excursion, and it is there that our company, drawn from every part of the country and even from abroad, will gather in the spacious halls of its great hotel, within twenty-four hours of the advertised time of sailing. During the season of 1888, that hour was 4.00 A. M., and passengers went aboard the previous evening, to look out in the early morning through the windows of their staterooms upon the city of Seattle, beautifully situated on a series of terraces rising from the east shore of Elliott Bay.

Seattle is the oldest American city on the Sound, and has long been a place of considerable importance. The enterprise of its people and their unbounded faith in its future, even after Tacoma was selected as the western terminus of the great transcontinental line over which the traveler has journeyed, need no setting-forth in these pages; neither do the great and varied resources of the rich country tributary to it, for have they not been advertised through the length and breadth of the land? On the outward voyage, the tourist has to content himself with surveying the city from the deck of the steamer, deferring until his return that more careful inspection of which the city and its environs are so well worthy.

A delightful three hours' sail on the broad waters of the Sound, the Mediterranean of the Northwest, with its fir-lined shores, and the glorious, snow-crowned peaks of Tacoma and Baker looming up against the sky in regal majesty, and the steamer runs alongside the wharf at Port Townsend, the port of entry for the Puget Sound district. This town, not inaptly called the Gate City of the Sound, possesses an excellent harbor, with both good anchorage and adequate shelter. It takes but a short time for compliance with the requirements of the Customs as they affect an outward-bound steamer, and off we go again, this time right across the Strait to San Juan de Fuca, an outlet to the open sea. As the kingly form of Mount Tacoma recedes into the distance, that of Mount Baker increases in distinctness, while we have also a fine view of the Olympic Mountains on our left, and the lofty ranges of Vancouver Island, for whose beautiful capital we are now steering, right before us.

So exceedingly picturesque and generally attractive is the appearance presented by the City of Victoria to an approaching steamer, that it is with no little satisfaction that the traveler learns that a stop of several hours will be made in its harbor. While there is no lack of American cities that have attained, within a period corresponding to that of the growth of Victoria, far greater magnitude and commercial importance, the beautiful capital of British Columbia is fashioned after so very different a pattern, and presents, if not to old-world eyes, at least to most Americans, so quaint an appearance, with its ivy-covered houses, its admirable roads and its fortifications, that it is hard to believe that it is really the young city it is. It is, however, but little more than forty years since the United States ship *Vincennes*, entering the Sound through the Straits of Fuca, found what is now its site a most forbidding picture of savage life. It was the Caribou mining excitement of 1868, that first brought any considerable population—and that a mere transient one—around the post established here, a few years before, by the Hudson's Bay Company. In 1870, although it had in the meantime been made the capital of the Province, Victoria contained but 3,270 inhabitants. Its present population is about 15,000, and there is probably no more self-contained city of its size in the world, for it has its own orchards and pastures, forests and coal fields, while its manufactories are as varied as those of many cities ten times its size.

It is not, however, with these things that the transient visitor is chiefly concerned, nor even with the exceptionally fine climate it enjoys, except in so far as the clear skies and balmy air he is almost certain to find there may contribute to the sum total of his enjoyment. It is rather with its superb situation, with the sea on three sides, bordered by picturesque shores and grassy hills. These will assuredly delight him, as will also—and possibly still more—a drive through its glorious woods, with their lovely undergrowth of almost tropical luxuriance, to the neighboring village of Esquimalt, with its fine harbor, its immense dry dock, its naval arsenal, and the ships of

Thlinket War Canoe.

the British Naval Squadron of the Pacific, of which it is the rendezvous. Returning to the city, he may stroll into one of its old curiosity shops, filled with a tempting display of those various artistic products in which the native races of the northwest coast so greatly excel. On his way back to the steamer, he will not fail to admire the striking picture presented by the almost land-locked inner harbor with its shipping, its Indian canoes, its narrow rocky entrance, and its white lighthouse, standing out against the dark foliage of the adjacent woods; nor the glistening peaks of the Olympic Mountains, over in the State of Washington, nor yet the trim and tasteful, but unpretentious, government buildings overlooking James Bay.

While, among the thousands of tourists who visit this city annually, there may be one or two who will give it a bad name, because they have had to pay for some trifling article a few cents more than they had been accustomed to, or rushing into the post-office just as the mail was being made up were surprised to learn that postage stamps were obtainable only at the stationery stores, ninety-nine out of every hundred leave this beautiful and interesting little city with regret, and carry away with them only the pleasantest recollections of their brief visit.

When the steamer once more gets under way, we feel as though our voyage had at last begun in good earnest, and maps, guide books and glasses make their appearance, in numbers almost sufficient to start a bookseller and optician in business. One will have provided himself with "Alaska and its Resources," by Mr. W. H. Dall, of the Smithsonian Institution, a work which, although twenty years old or nearly, is still the only comprehensive and trustworthy description of the Territory, as a whole; another will have the Alaska volume of Mr. H. H. Bancroft's " History of the Pacific States ;"

while a third will produce from his baggage Dr. Sheldon Jackson on "Alaska and Missions," an excellent work founded on extensive observation during several years' residence, and dealing especially with the labors of the various Christian missionaries in this great field. Others, desirous of seeing the impression produced upon transient visitors like themselves, will be conning the pages of Miss Scidmore's "Journeys in Alaska," or those of "Our New Alaska," by Mr. Chas. Hallock; while probably some English tourist, with the love of mountain climbing and adventure characteristic of his race, will follow the wanderings of Mr. Whymper or Mr. Seton-Karr, in the respective works "Travels in Alaska" and "The Shores and Alps of Alaska."

Before reaching any broad expanse of open water, the steamer passes through a picturesque archipelago, which faintly foreshadows in beauty the island-studded waters through which will lie so large a part of our voyage. A momentary interest is here excited by our passing on the right the island of San Juan, the possession of which, as every reader will remember, was awarded to the United States, in 1872, by the Emperor of Germany, then King of Prussia, to whom had been referred the interpretation of a treaty of somewhat ambiguous phraseology.

Almost uniformly smooth as is the navigation of the Inland Passage, the arrival and departure of the steamer at or from particular points can not be predicted many hours in advance, so much depends upon the state of the tide. Even in this high latitude night comes at last, and the first question in the morning, from almost every passenger is, "Where are we now?" If, therefore, it were possible to relieve the ship's officers of the endless string of questions with which they are plied, as to the whereabouts of the steamer at particular times, it would be a grateful task to do so, but all that is practicable is to point out the principal landmarks and the chief points of interest, so that these more or less troublesome inquiries may be reduced to a minimum.

For fully a day and a half after leaving Victoria, we have on our left the great island of Vancouver, 300 miles in length, and by far the largest island on the Pacific Coast. Having passed through the archipelago, to which reference has already been made, and which occupies the extreme southern portion of the Strait, or Gulf, of Georgia, as it is variously designated, we come to the greatest expanse of water to be met with on our entire trip, save those occasional points where we are able, for a brief period, to look out upon the open sea. Before long, however, we have the large island of Taxada on our right. This island, which is largely in the hands of speculators, among whom is at least one American company, contains an immense deposit of iron ore, rendered especially valuable by its exceptionally low percentage of phosphorus.

Another unbroken expanse of water, and we enter the first of those wonderful river-like channels through whose picturesque sinuosities three-fourths of our voyage will lie. This is Discovery Passage. It lies between the western side of Valdes Island and the northeastern shore of Vancouver Island. The southern extremity of the former island, known as Cape Mudge, is a peculiar headland about 250 feet high, flat and wooded on its summit. As the steamer approaches this point, every passenger on deck expects it to continue on its course through the broad open waters to the right. Instead of that, however, it leaves the headland to the right, and enters the narrow passage, not more than a mile in breadth, lying to the west of it. For 23 miles it follows this picturesque waterway, overshadowed by noble mountains rising from both shores.

From an expansion of the Passage, caused by an indentation on the Vancouver shore, known as Menzies Bay, we pass into

Alaska's Thousand Islands, as seen from Sitka.

the famous Seymour Narrows, a gorge two miles in length, and less than one-half mile in breadth. Through this contracted channel, the tides rush with great velocity, sometimes running nine knots an hour. The steamer is usually timed to reach this point at low water, but it rarely happens that the waters are not seen in a state of tumult sufficient to constitute their passage a decidedly interesting feature of the voyage.

At Chatham Point, a low, rocky promontory on the Vancouver Island shore, we take the more westerly of two apparently practicable channels, and enter Johnstone Strait, 55 miles in length. For some distance, this channel is very similar to Discovery Passage, though it subsequently broadens out to a width of from one and one-half to three miles. The magnificent range that rises from the Vancouver Island shore is the Prince of Wales range, the highest point of which, Mount Albert Edward, rises 6,968 feet above the waterway that washes its base. It is never entirely free from snow, traces of which, indeed, extend down the dark sides of the mountain to within 2,000 or 3,000 feet of the sea level. A noble snow-covered peak is about this time a prominent object on the right, while nearer at hand many beautiful inlets engage the traveler's attention. For some miles northward from the entrance to Johnstone Strait, the land on the right is Thurlow Island. This is succeeded by Hardwick Island, from which it is separated by Chancellor Channel, connecting with the broad waterway which seemed to the traveler the more likely course for the steamer to take when, a few hours before, she entered the narrow Discovery Passage. Another channel intervening, and we have the mainland of British Columbia forming the eastern shore of the strait. It is much indented by bays and inlets, and many fine lofty peaks tower up beyond it, while on the opposite or Vancouver Island shore, Mount Palmerston presents an exceedingly fine appearance. The islands which have been mentioned are only those larger bodies of land separated from the mainland by narrow channels, and for the most part so mountainous that they would be mistaken for the mainland in the absence of any statement to the contrary. The thousands of islands, from mere rocky points, a few square feet in extent, to those larger summits of submerged mountains which may sometime become the sites of delightful summer homes, it is impossible to particularize; and it need only be said that in their multitude and variety—each having some beauty peculiar to itself—they form, with the bold shores of the strait and the distant snow-covered peaks, a series of pictures of which the traveler never wearies and which he can never forget.

The northern entrance to Johnstone Strait is occupied by a beautiful archipelago, the two largest islands of which are Hanson Island and Cormorant Island. On the latter, between which and Vancouver Island we continue our course northwest through Broughton Strait, is Alert Bay, with a large salmon cannery, an Indian village and a Mission. The remarkable conical peak long visible on Vancouver Island is Mount Holdsworth.

From Broughton Strait, fifteen miles in length, we suddenly emerge into the broad Queen Charlotte Sound, a magnificent expanse of water, twelve to eighteen miles from shore to shore. The extensive views here obtained present a striking contrast to the scenery of the narrow passage through which for some hours the steamer's course has lain. An interesting point on the west shore is Fort Rupert, a post of the Hudson's Bay Company, with a large Indian village adjoining it. Continuing on its course, within a short distance of the Vancouver Island shore, our good ship next enters Goletas Channel, where we have Galiano and Hope Islands, together with some hundreds of smaller islands, on our right, and picturesque mountains of considerable elevation on both right and left.

We have now to bid farewell to the great Vancouver Island, whose most northerly point, Cape Commerell, we leave to the left. Emerging from the channel, which affords us, at its western entrance, an exceedingly fine retrospective view in which Mount Lemon is a prominent object, we look westward over the broad expanse of the Pacific Ocean. Here, if anywhere on our entire voyage, we are sensible for a short time, of a gentle swell. Those, however, whom the mere mention of the open sea would be sufficient to drive to the seclusion of their cabins, may take comfort in the assurance that the steamer had scarcely begun to yield to its influence when it passes under the lee of the great Calvert Island, and enters the land-locked channel of Fitzhugh Sound. Here, again, we have superb scenery on either side, the mountains of Calvert Island culminating in an exceedingly sharp peak, known as Mount Buxton (3,430 feet), the retrospective view of which is very fine. The scenery on the mainland and the islands on our right is similar in character. The soundings here indicate very deep water, although there is excellent anchorage in many of those beautiful bays which are formed by the indented shores. As we approach the northern extremity of the Sound, where Burke Canal opens out on the right (opposite the great Hunter Islands, the most northerly of the three large islands which, with a number of smaller ones, form the west shore of the Sound), the scenery increases in grandeur, the lesser and nearer hills being clothed to their summits with coniferous trees, while the more distant ones, overtopping them, are covered with snow. Here a surprise awaits the traveler in the sudden turning-about of the steamer, whose helm is put hard-a-starboard with the result that, instead of continuing its course through the broad and exceedingly attractive Fisher Channel, it turns sharply to the left, through the narrow Lama Passage, which, midway between its two extremities, itself makes a sharp turn northward.

On the shore of Campbell Island, we pass the trim native village of Bella Bella, with its little church. On the opposite shore are a number of graves, some of them with totem poles, one of the domestic peculiarities of this region, of which more will be said in its proper place.

The northern entrance to Lama Passage, through which we emerge into the broad Seaforth Channel, with its multitude of picturesque islands, is extremely narrow, but entirely free from concealed dangers. Just before turning westward into Seaforth Channel, we have the finest scenery we have so far gazed upon, the grouping of the mountains being grand in the extreme. If it be afternoon, its exquisite beauty will be greatly enhanced by atmospheric effects utterly unlike anything that ninety-nine out of every hundred of our fellow passengers have ever before seen. The sunset, too, is almost certain to be of such indescribable grandeur that pen and brush will be thrown down by the despairing author and artist, who will alike resign themselves to the ravishing beauty and splendor of the scene.

Another turn in our remarkable devious course, and we are steaming northward through Milbank Sound, through whose broad entrance we look out to the open sea. Islands succeed islands, and mountains, mountains; and the traveler is almost as much impressed with the mere geographical features of this extraordinary region as with the beauty of its scenery. Here we see, for the first time, glacier paths on the mountain sides, the lofty pyramidal Stripe Mountain, so called from the white streak on the southern flank, being an especially prominent object. Leaving Point Jorkins, the southern extremity of the great Princess Royal Island, on our left, we continue our course almost directly northward through the long and narrow Finlayson Channel, some 24 miles long, with an average width of two miles. The bold shores of this fine channel are densely wooded to a height of 1,500 feet or more; precipitous peaks, rising to a height of nearly 3,000 feet, occurring at intervals, with still higher mountains, whose dark masses are relieved with patches of snow, rising behind them. Waterfalls of remarkable height here add a new element of beauty to the incomparable series of pictures revealed to us with the continued progress of the steamer. A contraction of the channel known, for twenty miles, by the name of Graham Reach, and, for the next ten miles, as Fraser Reach, brings us to the north point of Princess Royal Island, where we turn westward through McKay Reach into Wright Sound. There is nothing here calling for special notice, although it must not be understood that the scenery is, on that account, any the less picturesque. It is worth while studying these successive channels upon the charts of the United States "Pacific Coast Pilot," so singular is the appearance they present. Grenville Channel, which we enter from Wright Sound and which lies between Pitt Island and the mainland, is, for fully fifty miles, as straight as any canal in the world. Its scenery, on both sides, is exceptionally fine, the mountains grouping themselves with magnificent effect. Those near at hand are clothed with dark foliage, others more remote, assume a purple hue, while many are seen to be seamed with the paths of glaciers and avalanches, the higher peaks being in every case covered with snow. Many beautiful islands start up in mid-channel, uniformly covered with a dense growth of fir, to the very edge of the water. The channel, too, is, at places, exceedingly narrow, and the precipitous mountains which rise from its shores attain a height varying from 1,500 to 3,500 feet. From an expansion of this channel, we pass through a narrow strait known as Arthur Passage, which has Kennedy Island on the right, and the large Porcher Island, with many fine mountain peaks, on the left.

If the frequent recurrence of geographical designations

render this brief description of the Alaska trip less interesting to the general reader than it otherwise would be, there will be a counterbalancing advantage gained by the actual traveler, who will find none of the more entertaining works that have been written on the subject of any great value to him as practical guide books.

Continuing our actual course, we emerge from the channel last-named into the great Chatham Sound, a broad expanse of water from whose distant shores rise imposing mountains. The eastern shore is here formed by the remarkable Chim-sy-an Peninsula, which, though forty miles long and from five to fifteen miles in breadth, is connected with the mainland only by a narrow isthmus.

Continuing our course northward through the broad Chatham Sound, with Dundas Island on our left and a range of snowy mountains, presenting a magnificent appearance, on our right, (Mount McNeill, the highest of its peaks, rising 4,500 feet above the sea, and having the appearance of being much higher by reason of our seeing its entire height from the ocean level), we soon cross, in latitude 54° 40′, the boundary line between British Columbia and the United States Territory of Alaska. Here, we shall do well to acquaint ourselves with such facts relative to the extent, physical conditions, ethnological features and natural resources of the "district" (to give it the ill-chosen name by which it is known to the United States Government) as will, at least, give us a comprehensive and, in the main, correct idea of the great territory we are about to visit.

As to its history, little need be said, for its Russian occupation is of no practical concern to us, while on the other hand, every reader will remember the circumstances of its transfer to the United States Government in 1868, for the sum of $7,200,000. Its extent is probably not nearly so well known, or, if the numerals which represent it have been learned by heart, it is still doubtful whether they have created in the mind any adequate conception of the vast extent of the province. Availing ourselves, therefore, of the figures and comparisons that we find ready to our hand in the Reports of Governor Swineford and Dr. Sheldon Jackson, we may remark that its extreme breadth from north to south is 1,400 miles, or as far as from Maine to Florida, and that from its eastern boundary to the western end of the Aleutian Islands is 2,200 miles; so that the Governor, sitting in his office at Sitka, is very little farther from Eastport, Me., than from the extreme western limit of his own jurisdiction, measuring, of course, in a straight line. Its coast line of 18,211 miles is nearly twice as great as the combined Atlantic and Pacific coast lines of the United States proper, and its most westerly point extends beyond the most easterly point of Asia a distance of nearly 1,000 miles. In actual extent it is as large as all the New England and Middle States, together with Ohio, Indiana, Illinois, Wisconsin, Michigan, Kentucky and Tennessee combined, or as all that portion of the United States lying east of the Mississippi River and north of Georgia and the Carolinas. A country so vast as this must be a poor one indeed, if the paltry $7,200,000 paid for it does not turn out to bear little more than the same proportion to its value that was borne by the pepper-corn rent in so many old English legal conveyances to the valuable estates for whose holding it was the nominal annual consideration.

With regard to its physical conditions, it is sufficient for our present purpose to say that a large part of it is still passing through the glacial period; that it contains in Mount St. Elias the highest mountain on the North American Continent, and in Mount Cook, Mount Crillon and Mount Fairweather peaks exceeded in height only by Mount Popocatepetl and Mount Orizaba, in Mexico; that its great river, the Yukon, computed

FORT WRANGELL, ALASKA.

to be not less than 3,000 miles long, is navigable for a distance of 2,000 miles, is from one mile to five miles in breadth for no less than 1,000 miles of its course, and is seventy miles wide across its five mouths and the intervening deltas; and that, while the climate of the interior is Arctic in the severity of its winter and tropical in the heat of its summer, that of the immense southern coast, with its thousands of islands, is one of the most equable in the world, by reason of the Kuro-siwo, or Japan current, a thermal stream which renders the entire North Pacific Coast, even in this high latitude, warm and humid. Only four times in forty-five years has the temperature at Sitka fallen to zero, while only seven summers in that same period have been marked by a higher temperature than 80° Fah. The influence of moisture in regulating temperature is too well known to call for any further remarks under this head, and the facts above given are stated only that they may help to dispel from the non-scientific mind the erroneous notions relative to the climate of this great territory, that so largely prevail.

With the exception of the Tinneh, a tribe which has forced its way to the coast from the interior, the natives of Alaska are *not Indians*. Their traditions, manners, customs and other race characteristics prove them to belong to the Mongolian branch of the great human family. Between their racial and tribal designations, the visitor, who hears of Thlinkets, Hydahs, Chilkats, Auks, Sitkans and many others, is liable to get somewhat confused. It may, therefore, be not only interesting but otherwise of advantage to him to know beforehand that the native population of the Territory, estimated to number 31,240 at the United States census of 1880, is divided into five races: (1) the Innuit, or Esquimaux, numbering 17,617, who occupy almost the entire coast line of the mainland; (2) the Aleuts, numbering 2,145, inhabiting the Aleutian Islands; (3) the

Face of Muir Glacier, from the Top.

Tinneh, numbering 3,927, found chiefly in the Yukon district, on the Copper River and at Cook's Inlet, and the only race not supposed to be of common origin with the rest; (4) the Thlinkets, numbering 6,763, occupying almost exclusively that southeastern division which the tourist is on his way to visit; and (5) the Hydahs, 788 in number, on the southern half of Prince of Wales Island. The various tribes with which the traveler will come into contact are of the Thlinket race—described by Dr. Jackson as "a hardy, self-reliant, industrious, self-supporting, well-to-do, warlike, superstitious race, whose very name is a terror to the civilized Aleuts to the west, as well as to the savage Tinneh to the north of them."

Deferring statements as to their tribal peculiarities to a place at which they can be set forth with greater advantage, let us now glance at the resources of the country, so far, at least, as they have been brought to light. These comprise: (1) its world-renowned seal fisheries; (2) its salmon, cod, whale and herring fisheries; (3) its extensive deposits of gold, silver, copper, iron, coal and other minerals; and (4) its vast forests.

The seal-fur fisheries, as is well-known, are leased for twenty years, from 1870, to the Alaska Commercial Company, which pays the Government an annual rental of $55,000 for the islands, and a royalty of $2.62½ each on the 100,000 seal skins allowed to be taken annually. From this one source alone, therefore, the Government receives an annual sum of $317,500, or more than 4½ per cent. per annum on the amount paid to the Russian Government for the Territory.

The salmon, cod and whale fisheries of Alaska are of far greater importance than is generally known, their yield, during 1887, being valued at $3,000,000, exclusive of the various products of the herring fisheries, which are both extensive and valuable. The most important point in the operations of this last-named industry is Killisnoo, on Admiralty Island, where as many as 138,000 barrels of oil have been put up in a single month.

Men are so liable to be carried away by excitement upon finding even the smallest traces of the precious metals, that the outside world, hearing or reading of their discoveries, at a distance, usually pays but little attention to them. While, however, the claims of Alaska to untold wealth in silver and copper must be admitted, if admitted at all, on mere hearsay, except so far as the reports of explorers are borne out by the geological formation of the country, every tourist has an opportunity of visiting, under the most advantageous and pleasurable circumstances, the greatest gold mine in the world, namely, the Treadwell Mine, on Douglas Island, of which more will be said in its proper place.

It will be but a few years before the lumbering operations now going on in the forest belt of the new State of Washington extend to this far northern region. The whole of southeastern Alaska is covered with a dense growth of spruce, hemlock and yellow cedar, frequently containing timber of from thirty to forty feet in diameter at the base, and growing to a height of thirty to forty feet before branching. The yellow cedar is said to be the most valuable timber on the Pacific coast, being highly prized, both by the cabinet-maker and ship-builder.

With regard to agriculture, it will be sufficient to refer to the admirable report of the Governor of Alaska, for 1886, in which he combats the rash statements of various transient visitors, whose prominence obtains for their assertions a credence of which they are not always worthy; and, fortifying his statement with the authority of Mr. W. H. Dall, of the Smithsonian Institution, who has devoted more time and made more thorough researches into the natural resources of Alaska than any other person, declares that there are considerable areas of arable land, with a soil of sufficient depth and fertility to insure the growth of the very best crops, and that the experiments which have been made in the past two or three years have proved most conclusively that all the cereals, as well as the tubers, can be grown to perfection in Alaskan soil and climate. It is impossible in these pages to pursue this interesting and important subject further, but it may be stated that the Governor does not content himself with mere assertion, but that, in addition to giving the results of the various experiments that have been made, he deals at some length with the subject of the native grasses of the Territory, all going to prove that the country is not nearly so worthless for agricultural purposes as interested detractors or careless and superficial observers would have us believe.

Having thus acquainted himself with a few of the more important facts concerning this great Territory, the tourist is now prepared to resume his voyage. Crossing the broad expanse of Dixon Entrance, where, looking westward, we see the open sea, we enter Clarence Strait, over one hundred miles long and nowhere less than four miles in width. We are now within the remarkable geographical area known as Alexander Archipelago, a congeries of straits, inlands, inlets, rocks, and passages extending through nearly five degrees of latitude and seven of longitude. The islands of this archipelago definitely placed on the charts number 1,100, and we have the authority of the United States Coast and Geodetic Survey for the statement that, if all the existing rocks and islands were enumerated, the number stated would have to be very considerably increased.

Throughout the whole of Clarence Strait, we have on our left the great Prince of Wales Island, the home of the Hydahs, with whose marvelous skill in carving, the tourist doubtless became familiar during his brief stay at Victoria. Their miniature totems, cut in dark slate-stone, are greatly sought after by tourists and command a somewhat high price. The artistic skill of this famous tribe has, however, been better exemplified in its spoons, carved out of the horn of the mountain goat; but these have nearly all gone to enrich the collections of eastern visitors during the last two or three seasons, and during his visit to the Territory, in the summer of 1887, the present writer found but a single specimen in many hundreds of carved goat's horn spoons, that sustained the reputation of the Hydahs for that delicacy of workmanship in which they well-nigh rival the ivory workers of Japan.

It may be mentioned in this connection that the recently formed Alaskan Society of Natural History and Ethnology, whose headquarters are at Sitka, has already gathered together an exceedingly interesting and valuable collection of specimens of native handiwork; and visitors are invited to contribute to a fund which is being raised for the purchase and preservation of Alaskan curiosities of every description, especially those made by the natives before the influx of tourists found them the ready market they now possess, and led them, as it unfortunately did, to think more of the quantity than the quality of their work.

The islands on our right as we continue our voyage are the Gravina Group, Revilla Gigedo and, after a promontory of the mainland, Etolin Island, round whose northern coast we steer northeastward to Fort Wrangell, usually the first calling place of the steamer, during the tourist season. The Gravina Islands contain a fine range of mountains, the higher peaks of which have their dark masses relieved by patches of snow. Revilla Gigedo Island likewise is mountainous—its nearer summits clothed with pine, its more distant ones crowned with everlasting snow. On Prince of Wales Island, the mountains rising before us are enveloped, for the most part, in a delicious purple haze. As we approach them, their rocky, precipitous, and deeply fissured sides (the last the result of glacial action, which is plainly visible) afford a striking diversity of outline and color, which, added to the beauties of light and shade lent them by passing clouds, have a very fine effect. Clarence Strait is, indeed, a magnificent sheet of water, well worthy of its place in that remarkable series of devious water-ways through which our voyage lies.

Fort Wrangell, although formerly a place of some importance as the port of the Cassiar mines, away in the interior beyond the international boundary, is, of all the settlements at which the steamer calls, the least attractive in every respect save that it is here that the tourist will find the largest assemblage of totem poles that he will have an opportunity of seeing, as well as several old graves of singularly striking appearance. The village, which occupies a beautiful site, is given up almost entirely to the Stikine tribe of the Thlinket race, and, within a few minutes after the arrival of the steamer at the wharf, the interior of almost every house presents an animated appearance, curio-hunting passengers thronging them to the doors, and bargaining with their inmates for the various objects of interest they see around them.

The ship's officers, Government officials and other persons supposed to be well informed are frequently asked which of the various stopping places is the best for the purchase of curiosities. In anticipation of this inquiry, it may be stated that there is little to choose between Fort Wrangell, Juneau and Sitka, except that in the fine store of Messrs. Koehler & James, at Juneau, the visitor will find a larger collection of the more desirable and costly specimens of native handiwork, as well as of valuable furs, than at either of the other two places. At any one of them, however, and at any moment, he may run across something that could not be duplicated in the entire Territory, although each recurring season renders this less and less probable.

ALASKAN GRAVE AND TOTEM POLES AT FORT WRANGELL.

A strongly marked trait in the character of the Thlinkets is their respect for their ancestors. Independently of their tribal distinctions, which are little more than local, they are divided into four totems or clans, each of which is known by a badge or emblem used much in the same way as is the crest or coat of arms among the old families of Europe. These, according to Mr. W. H. Dall, are the Raven, the Wolf, the Whale and the Eagle; and these emblems are carved on their houses, household utensils, paddles and frequently on amulets of native copper, which they preserve with scrupulous care and consider to be of the greatest value. In front of many of their houses, and also at their burial places, are posts varying from twenty to sixty feet in height and from two to five feet in diameter, carved to represent successive ancestral totems and usually stained black, red and blue. As already stated, several of these totem poles, as they are called, are to be seen at Fort Wrangell, as well as two remarkable graves, one surmounted by a rudely carved whale, and the other by a huge figure of a wolf.

Resuming our voyage, we leave this curious old Stikine town, and after steaming westward to the southern entrance to Wrangell Strait, turn northward and follow that narrow passage into the broader Dry Strait, where we have the magnificent Patterson Glacier on our right and find considerable floating ice. Following the north shore of Kupreanoff Island, we enter Frederick Sound; but quickly resume our almost directly northward course by entering Stephens Passage, where we have Admiralty Island on our left, said, by the way, to be swarming with bear, and the mainland on our right. On Stockade Point, a comparatively low peninsula from which the land rises rapidly to snow-capped mountains, is a ruined blockhouse and stockade, built by the Hudson's Bay Company, and on the other side of a small inlet is Grave Point, a native burial ground. Leaving to the right Taku Inlet, we enter the narrow and picturesque Gastineau Channel, between the mainland and the now famous Douglas Island. Here, on a narrow strip of land, at the foot of a deep ravine between two precipitous mountains, stands Juneau, a cluster of detached white houses, relieved here and there by the unpainted frame-work of others in process of building. The mountain rising behind it, as you approach it from the south, is deeply fissured, and seamed with snow, and the town itself is built mainly upon a huge land-slide. Not a few of the houses have apparently been built by white settlers attracted to the spot by the fabulously rich mineral deposits of the district. These have been followed by general traders, who in addition to supplying the resident population with the necessaries of life, reap a rich harvest, during the tourist season, from the sale of sundry products of native handiwork and the skins of the various fur-bearing animals.

An excellent weekly newspaper, called the *Alaska Free Press*, is published at Juneau. The visitor need not turn to its pages for any later news from the outside world than he is already in possession of, for Alaska has not, as yet, the advantage of telegraphic communication with the rest of the world. He will find, however, much interesting reading relative to the mining resources of the district and the Territory generally; a column or two of spicy local items and, possibly, the report of some recently returned explorer; while the business advertisements of this thriving settlement of the Far North will be by no means devoid of interest.

Juneau itself, however, as a point of interest to the tourist, is soon exhausted, and his thoughts turn to the great Treadwell mine,

The Richest Gold Mine in the World, which lies across the channel on Douglas Island, whither the steamer will proceed after a brief stay at Juneau. It is by no means an easy task to determine which of the many extraordinary statements relative to this valuable property that one hears from time to time are worthy of credence and which are not; and even when the truth has been approximately ascertained, there remains the difficulty of determining how much may properly be made public, and how much should be regarded as only the individual and private concern of the owners of the mine. In view, however, of the fact that the mill has, for some time, had in operation a larger number of stamps than any other mill in the world; that by the time this pamphlet leaves the press, the works will contain more ore-crushing machinery than the five largest mines in Butte City, all combined, and that the Governor of the Territory himself places the output of the mine for 1887 at $100,000 per month, it is surely not incredible that the company should have refused $16,000,000 for its property, or that it pays a dividend of 100 per cent. per month, all the year round; or yet, at least to those who have seen it, that the ore actually in sight is worth about five times the amount paid to the Russian Government for the entire Territory, and that, even at the present enormous rate of production, it can not be exhausted in less than a century.

Although it can not but interfere to some extent with the operations of the mine, visitors are, with great courtesy, shown everything that is likely to prove of interest to them. They see the natives earning $2.50 per day each in the mine, and learn to their surprise that they are better workmen than the whites; they see the ore in every stage from blasting to final separation, and though they may leave with a tinge of regret that it has not been their own luck to have made so valuable a discovery, they will none the less congratulate the owners on their magnificent possession. It will have been inferred, from what has already been said, that it is not a mere vein of gold, of varying richness and uncertain direction, that is here being worked. So far from that, the entire island is nothing less than a mountain of ore, sufficient, according to ex-Governor Stoneman of California, to pay off the whole of the national debt.

Gastineau Channel not having been thoroughly explored, we retrace our course to its southern entrance, where, turning northward, we follow the wider channel that lies to the west of the island. This brings us to that remarkable and never-to-be-forgotten body of water, the Lynn Canal, where not only have we scenery surpassing in wildness and grandeur all that has preceded it, but also many glaciers, while we reach, just under the parallel of 60°, the most northerly point we shall attain on our trip. Soon after entering the canal, and when rounding Point Retreat, we see the great Eagle Glacier to the northeast, coming down from the high mountains that rise in the background. A couple of hours' sail, however, brings us to a point at which we can observe much more closely the still larger Davidson Glacier, on the opposite shore. But even here we do not go ashore, for the far-famed Muir Glacier, which we shall reach within the next twenty-four hours, has the advantage of being as much more easily accessible than its sister glaciers as it exceeds them in magnitude, beauty and general interest.

How unimpressionable soever the tourist may be, a mysterious sense of awe is almost sure to take possession of him when the steamer is exploring the two inlets of Chilkat and Chilkoot, in which the Lynn Canal terminates. Not, perhaps, until vegetation has almost entirely disappeared, will he have noticed its increasing scantiness, but it will not be long before he realizes the fact that in the forbidding mountains, the bare rocks and the nineteen great ice cataracts that here discharge themselves into the sea, he sees a picture more closely resembling the

JUNEAU, ALASKA.

scenes of the now not distant Arctic world than, probably, he will ever again have an opportunity of gazing upon.

The natives of this region are that famous tribe, the Chilkats, whose dexterously woven dancing blankets are so much sought after by all visitors to Alaska who desire to take home with them the finest examples of Alaskan handiwork, regardless of cost. They are made from the wool of the white mountain goat, out of whose black horns are carved the spoons and ladles already referred to. The white wool is hung from an upright frame, and into it nimble fingers weave, by means of ivory shuttles, curious and beautiful patterns from yarn dyed with a variety of brilliant colors.

We have now to retrace our course some sixty-five miles to Point Retreat, where, instead of taking the easterly channel and returning to Juneau, we continue almost directly southward to the point at which the waters of Lynn Canal mingle with those of Icy Strait. Here, our good ship's course is once more directed northward, and after a brief sail, we enter the island-studded Glacier Bay, where innumerable icebergs proclaim our approach to that crowning glory of this veritable Wonderland, the famous Muir Glacier, undoubtedly the

Greatest Glacier in the World, outside of the Polar seas. It is hard to say which has the greater advantage,—the traveler who sees it first from afar; sees it as a vast river of ice flowing down from between the mountains, with many tributaries both on the right and left, and to whom its beauties are gradually unfolded with the nearer approach of the steamer; or he who, awakened from his slumber by the thunderous roar which announces the birth of some huge iceberg, hurries on deck to gaze upon a picture without parallel in the known world—a perpendicular wall of ice, towering to five times the height of the mast-head, and glowing in the sunlight like a mountain of mother-of-pearl. A recent visitor to this indescribable scene—

himself possessing descriptive powers of no mean order—declares that in the narrative of his Alaska trip he would prefer to insert a series of asterisks where his description of the Muir Glacier should come; and certainly we need a new vocabulary to set forth its wondrous beauty with any degree of fidelity. While, as will be inferred from what has already been stated, its dimensions are such as to constitute it one of the physical wonders of the world, its proportions are so admirable that the traveler is less impressed with its immensity than with its utter novelty and incomparable beauty; and it is as much a revelation to those who have seen the glaciers of Switzerland or familiarized themselves with the voyages of Arctic and Antarctic explorers, as it is to those whose ideas of a glacier were of the most indefinite and inadequate character.

The breadth of the glacier at its snout is fully a mile, and when, almost under its shadow, the second officer heaves the lead and sings out: "One hundred and five fathoms, and no bottom, Sir," the wonderment of the traveler is heightened by an immediate realization of the fact that this enormous ice-flow extends at least twice as far below the surface of the water as it rises above it, and that it is accordingly not less than 1,000 feet deep. But its vast dimensions and its marvelous gradations of color, from pure white to deepest indigo, do not alone make up that unapproachable *tout ensemble* which is the wonder and delight of every visitor. To speak of it as a perpendicular wall of ice almost necessarily conveys the idea of comparative regularity, as though it were a suddenly congealed cataract. Instead of that, however, the face of the glacier is composed of crystal blocks of every conceivable size and shape, many of them having angular projections or rising cliff-like from its brink, until, with a roar like that of the distant discharge of heavy ordnance it comes their turn to fall off into the sea.

The disintegration of these immense masses, some of them

weighing thousands of tons, suggests the interesting question: How fast does the glacier move forward? Professor G. Frederick Wright, of Oberlin, Ohio, in an exceedingly interesting article in the *American Journal of Science*, for January, 1887, declares, as the result of careful observation extending over several weeks that its progressive daily movement during the month of August is seventy feet at the centre and ten feet at the margin, or an average of forty feet per day. Its general movement being entirely imperceptible—it is only seven-twelfths of an inch per minute where it is greatest—Professor Wright's assertion has somewhat rashly been disputed by visitors who have not been at the trouble to make observations for themselves. But there is surely nothing incredible in a forward movement averaging, at most, forty feet per day, in view of the continual falling off of such immense masses, especially when it is remembered that Professor J. D. Forbes found the Mer de Glace to move forward at the rate of from 15 to 17.5 inches per day, at a much less angle, with an infinitely smaller volume of ice behind it, and diminishing at its termination, only by the slow process of liquefaction.

The steamer usually remains in front of the glacier an entire day, and passengers are landed on a dry and solid moraine, from which a larger area of the glacier than they will care to explore is within comparatively easy reach. Every one should climb up on to the great ice-field—

> "A crystal pavement by the breath of Heaven
> Cemented firm;"

look down into its profound crevasses, and view also the magnificent panorama of Arctic scenery that it commands, including Mount Crillon, raising its snowy crest against the sky to a height of 15,900 feet.

However indulgent be the Captain, this red-letter day in the experience of the visitor—a veritable epoch in his life—comes to an end at last. The whistle is sounded, and slowly and cautiously the steamer threads her way through the floating ice, and is headed for Sitka. This stage of the trip might be considerably shortened by the steamer putting out to sea through Cross Sound, and it is only to avoid the disagreeable experience to her passengers that would attend the outside passage, that she takes a less direct course.

Proceeding southeastward through Icy Strait, we enter Chatham Strait, one of the most extensive and remarkable of the inland highways of the Alexander Archipelago. From this broad sheet of water we go westward through Peril Straits, a designation that might excite some little apprehension were we not told that it was bestowed upon the channel through which we pass, not because of any difficulty or danger attending its navigation, but on account of the death there, in 1799, of a large number of Aleuts who had partaken of poisonous mussels. For two-thirds of the distance traversed by the steamer, the straits are several miles wide, but they ultimately narrow to a width of less than half a mile, to form, with Neva and Olga Straits, a succession of beautiful channels, studded with charming islands, and presenting a striking contrast to the desolate-looking shores of Glacier Bay.

There is no trip in the world of corresponding duration that is less monotonous than this two weeks' excursion to Alaska. The tourist is continually being greeted by scenes utterly unlike any he has ever before gazed upon, while the contrasts presented by successive days' experiences are, themselves, as delightful as they are surprising. Should the steamer, for example, come to an anchorage in Sitka Sound during the night or in the early morning, the traveler will be almost startled by the novel, picturesque and altogether pleasing appearance of the scene that will greet him when he goes on deck to take his first view of the Capital city. On the one hand are the glistening waters of the bay, studded with innumerable rocky, moss-covered islands, affording a scanty foothold for undersized firs and spruce; with that extraordinary-looking peak, Mount Edgecumbe, rising beyond, an almost perfect cone, save that its apex has been cut off so sharply as to leave it with a perfectly flat top, in which is a crater said to be 2,000 feet in diameter and about 200 feet deep. On the other hand, from a cluster of more or less quaint-looking buildings, rises Baranoff Castle, the former residence of a long succession of stern Muscovite governors, and the emerald green cupola and dome of the Russo-Greek church, with lofty mountains, including the frowning Vostovia, in the background.

It is with an already formed favorable impression of the place that the passenger steps ashore, to visit the two remarkable buildings above mentioned, of which, probably, he has often heard and read; to saunter through the curious streets of the town, and to pick up in its stores and in the houses of the natives additional specimens of Alaskan handiwork and other curiosities; to visit the Training School and Mission, where native boys and girls are being educated, Christianized, and taught useful trades; and, possibly, to pay his respects to some member of that admirable body of United States officials, now administering the affairs of the Territory with so much success.

Baranoff Castle is not a grim, ivy-covered, and decaying stronghold, with turrets, battlements and keep, but a plain, square, substantial, yellow frame building, surmounted by a little look-out tower, upon which might have been seen until recently the revolving anemometer of the United States Signal Service, whose station here has been given up, presumably in view of the fact that observations having been carefully made and recorded for no less than half a century, first by the

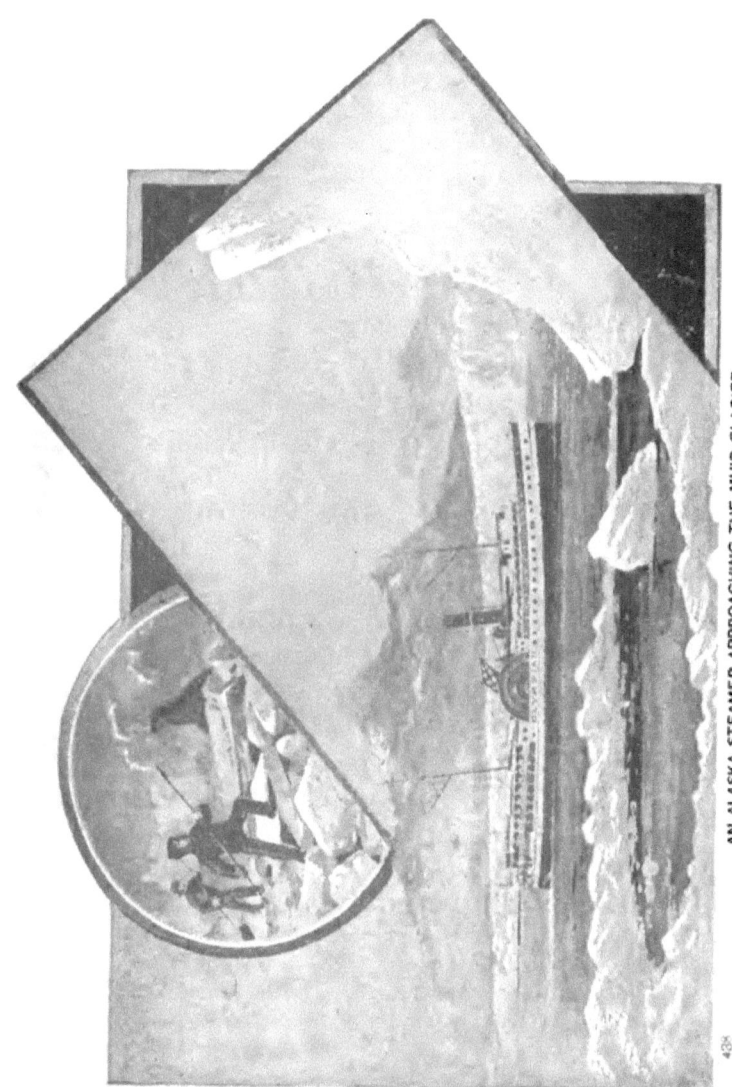

AN ALASKA STEAMER APPROACHING THE MUIR GLACIER.

Russians and afterward by the Americans, there remains no necessity for its further continuance. The interest that attaches to the castle is almost entirely either historical or traditional. Among the memories that haunt its great ballroom is that of the beautiful niece of Baron Romanoff, one of its Muscovite governors, said to have been fatally stabbed on her wedding night by her own lover, in whose enforced absence she had been compelled by her uncle to marry a previously rejected suitor of nobler birth.

The most interesting object in the city, however, is the Russo-Greek church, not so much for what it is in itself, as for the paintings, vestments, and other art treasures it contains. Among these is an exquisite painting of the Madonna and Child, copied from a celebrated picture at Moscow, and so largely covered with gold and silver—after the manner of the Greek Church—that but little of the picture is to be seen except the faces. Another of its treasures is a bishop's crown, supposed to be several hundred years old, and almost covered with emeralds, sapphires and pearls.

Steamer day is a great day at Sitka, and the scanty American population—together with prominent members of the Russo-American community, like Mr. George Kostrometinoff, the Government interpreter—give themselves up almost entirely to showing civilities to the visitors who throng the chief places of interest. They are naturally wishful that tourists should take away a favorable impression of Alaska generally and Sitka in particular, and Dr. Sheldon Jackson, general agent of education in Alaska, under the United States Government, usually affords the visitor an opportunity of judging of the excellence of the work that is being carried on among the natives, not forgetting, at the same time, to urge the utter inadequacy of the miserable pittance annually doled out by Congress for educational purposes in this vast Territory. In this connection it may also be stated that the Russian inhabitants themselves complain bitterly of the faithlessness of our Government to the pledges given to Russia at the time of the purchase, with regard to the provision of educational facilities and other rights of citizenship.

Having visited the Training School, the tourist should continue his walk to Indian River, along the right bank of which a well-marked trail will conduct him to a woodland scene that will form one of the most delightful reminiscences of his visit to Sitka.

Returning to the town, he may have the curiosity to inquire the price of some of the principal articles of food, when he will find that he can buy fresh salmon at from one cent to a cent and a half per pound, halibut and black bass at one-half cent per pound, venison at from six to eight cents per pound, teal ducks at twenty cents per pair, and other varieties of game-food at correspondingly low prices.

When, falling in with some intelligent resident, he learns how many attractive and interesting places there are within easy reach of the town; when he is told of the sublime scenery at the head of Silver Bay, including Sarabinokoff Cataract, with its fall of 500 feet; of the rich mines in its vicinity, with ores assaying from $4,000 to $6,000 per ton; when he hears of the comparative facility with which Mount Edgecumbe can be ascended and—assuming him to be a sportsman—of the abundance of game on the slopes of Mount Vostovia, as well as in other equally accessible localities, the traveler can not help regretting that his visit to so attractive a region must so soon come to an end.

Only a brief reference has thus far been made to the almost nightless day that prevails in this northern latitude at midsummer, and it may therefore be stated that, while, at Sitka, the period between sunrise and sunset at the summer solstice is only two and one-quarter hours longer than it is at New York or Boston, the twilight is of such long duration that it can scarcely be said ever to get dark, the last glow hardly dying out in the northwest before the first flush of dawn appears in the northeast.

It is scarcely too much to say that no tourist ever visited even this southeastern strip of Alaska who did not ever afterward feel a profound interest in whatever concerned the welfare of this distant portion of our great country, and labor to remove the various misconceptions so long current with regard to it. Readers of these pages, therefore, desirous of keeping thoroughly *au courant* with the affairs of the Territory; of knowing, from time to time, how rapidly, and in what new directions, the development of its vast wealth-producing capabilities is proceeding; what scientists are saying with regard to its glaciers and its other remarkable natural features; what success is attending the efforts that are being made, both by educational and religious agencies, to civilize the still half-savage native races of the country, and what light is being thrown on hitherto perplexing questions in ethnology and kindred sciences by the labors of the society recently formed at Sitka for their investigation, will not consider the present writer to have gone needlessly out of his way if he refers them to the interesting columns of *The Alaskan*, a well-conducted weekly journal published at Sitka, in which everything of public interest relating to the Territory finds a place commensurate with its importance.

Sitka is usually the last calling-place of the Alaska excursion, although it occasionally happens that some other point, already dealt with in these pages, is reserved for the steamer's homeward voyage. Should, however, the good ship's return trip be marked by no strikingly novel experiences, and have no break until she is once more moored alongside the wharf at Victoria, the matchless scenery of that long succession of land-locked channels she will traverse, observed from new points of view and under new physical conditions, will, with agreeable companionship and other social pleasures, render the homeward voyage possibly even more truly enjoyable than were those first few days before the barriers of reserve were broken down, and when the rapid succession of one sublime and unlooked-for spectacle after another kept the mind in a state of perpetual tension.

www.ingramcontent.com/pod-product-compliance
Lightning Source LLC
Chambersburg PA
CBHW032138010526
44111CB00035B/612